中文详注剑桥莎士比亚精选

虚惊一场

原版创始主编：[英] 瑞克斯·吉布森（Rex Gibson）
原版主编：[英] 瑞查德·安褚斯（Richard Andrews）
　　　　　[英] 维姬·维南德（Vicki Wienand）
原版编注：[英] 安东尼·帕廷顿（Anthony Partington）
　　　　　[英] 瑞查德·斯班塞（Richard Spencer）
总主编：陈国华
分册主编：程丽霞

MUCH ADO ABOUT NOTHING

社图号 20141

Cambridge School Shakespeare: Much Ado About Nothing [Third edition] [978-1-107-61989-0] was first published by Cambridge University Press in 2014. All rights reserved.

This Simplified Chinese edition for the People's Republic of China is published by arrangement with the Press Syndicate of the University of Cambridge, Cambridge, United Kingdom.

© Cambridge University Press & Beijing Language and Culture University Press 2020.

This book is in copyright. No reproduction of any part may take place without the written permission of Cambridge University Press or Beijing Language and Culture University Press.

本书版权由剑桥大学出版社和北京语言大学出版社共同所有。本书任何部分之文字及图片，如未获得出版者书面同意，不得用任何方式抄袭、节录或翻印。

This edition is for sale in the People's Republic of China (excluding Hong Kong SAR, Macao SAR and Taiwan Province) only.
此版本仅限在中华人民共和国境内销售。

北京市版权局著作权合同登记图字：01-2020-4099 号

图书在版编目（CIP）数据

中文详注剑桥莎士比亚精选. 虚惊一场／陈国华总主编；程丽霞分册主编. -- 北京：北京语言大学出版社，2020.11
书名原文：Cambridge School Shakespeare：Much Ado About Nothing
ISBN 978-7-5619-5747-9

Ⅰ.①中⋯　Ⅱ.①陈⋯　②程⋯　Ⅲ.①多幕剧－剧本－英国－中世纪　Ⅳ.① I561.33

中国版本图书馆 CIP 数据核字（2020）第 169654 号

中文详注剑桥莎士比亚精选：虚惊一场
ZHONGWEN XIANG ZHU JIANQIAO SHASHIBIYA JINGXUAN: XUJING YI CHANG

项目策划：李　亮	责任编辑：孙冠群
封面设计：乔　剑	排版制作：北京创艺涵文化发展有限公司
责任印制：武晓东	

出版发行：北京语言大学出版社
社　　址：北京市海淀区学院路 15 号，100083
网　　址：www.blcup.com
电子信箱：service@blcup.com
电　　话：编辑部　8610-82301019/0178
　　　　　发行部　8610-82303650/3591/3648
　　　　　北语书店　8610-82303653
　　　　　网购咨询　8610-82303908
印　　刷：北京博海升彩色印刷有限公司

版　　次：2020 年 11 月第 1 版　　印　　次：2020 年 11 月第 1 次印刷
开　　本：787 毫米 × 1092 毫米　1/16　印　　张：13.75
字　　数：414 千字
定　　价：69.00 元

PRINTED IN CHINA

序

由于观察角度不同，评判标准不同，关于哪个国家哪位诗人或小说家的成就最大，世人可能难以达成一致；可是说到剧作家，大家的共识是，莎士比亚不仅是英语国家有史以来最伟大的剧作家，也是全世界最伟大的剧作家，在知名度、影响力和传世作品的数量上，没有任何一位剧作家可以与之比肩。正是由于其公认的文学成就和人文精神，在过去400多年里，莎士比亚戏剧的演出在英语国家和许多非英语国家经久不衰，莎剧的阅读和鉴赏已成为这些国家英文教学的必选内容。

莎剧进入中国，已经有100多年历史，莎士比亚全集已经有了四个中文译本。不懂英文的人可以通过译本来欣赏莎士比亚剧作。然而文学作品的语言，尤其是诗歌的语言，具有相当程度的不可译性，而几乎所有莎剧的大部分台词都是素体诗（blank verse）。例如《哈慕雷》（*Hamlet*）里主人翁的名言"To be, or not to be, that is the question"，不论怎样译，都难以完全再现原文的深刻内涵和形式特点。要想真正欣赏莎士比亚的语言和戏剧艺术，还得阅读其英文原作。最早由剑桥大学出版社出版的这套莎剧精选，收录了最受读者和观众喜爱的14部剧目，涵盖莎剧的各个类别，以其独具匠心的设计和编排，成为所有英文原版莎剧中最适合英语学习者阅读、最适合戏剧爱好者排演的莎剧选集。

本选集的创始主编瑞克斯·吉布森（Rex Gibson）在本书引言（Introduction）里指出："不论做什么，都要记住，莎士比亚写下他的剧本是为了演出、观看和享受的。"秉承这一宗旨，这一新版莎剧选集有四个鲜明的区别性特点：

一、书的开本和页面的宽高比例特别适合学校的老师和学生以及剧团的导演和演员在排练莎剧时把书打开，拿在手里，随时参阅，而且左边页面上有许多有关排演活动的建议。

二、书中配有大量世界各国莎剧演出的彩色剧照，为莎剧爱好者和剧团排演莎剧提供了灵感。

三、书的正文部分打开后，右页是未经删减、原汁原味的剧本原文，左页是多种不同栏目，包括导演技巧（Stagecraft）、剧中语言（Language in the play）、人物分析（Characters）、主题分析（Themes）、写作练习（Write about it）及词语注释等。每幕之间（本幕回顾）和最后一幕后（本剧回顾）有与剧情相关的各种思考题。

四、在剧本之后有各种针对全剧的专题论述，以《哈慕雷》为例，包括视角与主题（Perspectives and themes）、人物分析（Characters）、《哈慕雷》的语言（The language of *Hamlet*）、《哈慕雷》的演出（*Hamlet* in performance）、笔论莎士比亚（Writing about Shakespeare）、笔论《哈慕雷》（Writing about *Hamlet*），还有一份莎翁年表（William Shakespeare 1564–1616）。

左页上的栏目对于解读和排演莎剧特别有帮助，剧本后面的专题论述对于撰写有关莎士比亚的文章特别有帮助，而参加莎剧排演，背诵台词，撰写论文，又是提高英语水平的极好途径。

为了方便更多的中国读者阅读、欣赏、排演莎士比亚原作，北京语言大学出版社携手剑桥大学出版社，将这套莎剧精选引入中国。我有幸应邀担任这套书的中文版总主编，组织起一个团队，对原版进行一定程度的改编和汉化，以适应中国读者的需求。我们不仅将原版提供的关键注释基本译成了中文，而且针对中国英语学习者和莎剧爱好者阅读理解上的难点，主要做了以下四件事：

一、参考 The Oxford Dictionary of Original Shakespearean Pronunciation (David Crystal 2016)、Oxford Dictionary of Pronunciation for Current English (Clive Upton 2003) 和 Shakespeare's Names: A Pronouncing Dictionary (Helge Kökeritz 1950)，给每个剧本前面人物表里的人名加上了国际音标。为了便于读者识别，我们将第一本发音词典里一般中国读者不认识的个别音标替换成了大家熟悉的近似音标。

二、为左页顶端的剧情简介添加中文译文。

三、左页中以及剧本后面论文部分里有一些具有挑战性的词和术语（如tableau），我们为其中的大部分添加了相应的中文释义。

四、适当增加了原版里没有的词语注释。

给剧中人物的名字加了国际音标之后，我们发现，现有莎剧中文译本里一些人名的中文译名与原文的读音差别较大且互不相同。根据定名不咎、译音循本、音义兼顾、音系对应的原则，我们给出了新译名。根据前两个原则，我们将剧本 Julius Caesar /ˈdʒuːliəs ˈsiːzə(r)/ 译成《儒略·恺撒》，而没有采用《尤利/力乌斯·恺撒》《裘利/力斯·凯撒》《居里厄斯·恺撒》等现成译名中的任何一个，因为从公元前1世纪到公元16世纪西方使用的儒略历（Julian calendar）就是以这位 Julius Caesar（拉丁文读音是 /ˈjuːlɪʊs ˈkaɛsər/）命名的。根据音义兼顾的原则，我们将剧本 Hamlet /ˈ(h)amlət/ 译成《哈慕雷》而不是《哈姆莱特》或《哈姆雷特》，因为"慕雷"比"姆莱"或"姆雷"更适合用来给男子起名，结尾的辅音 /t/ 在实际说话中往往不发音。根据音系对应的原则，我们借鉴了曹禺的译法，将剧本 Romeo and Juliet 译成《柔密欧与茱丽叶》，没有将 Romeo 译成更常见的"罗密欧"，因为"柔 /rou/"比"罗 /luo/"更接近原名 Romeo /ˈroːmɪoː/ 的读音；同时我们将 Juliet /ˈdʒuːlɪət/ 译成"茱丽叶"而不是"朱丽叶"，因为这样做不容易让人误以为这个女孩姓"朱"。

这套经过改编并且带中文注释的《中文详注剑桥莎士比亚精选》不仅可以用作中国高中和大学的英文教材，而且适合中国所有具有较高英语能力的莎剧爱好者阅读和欣赏，将戏剧从书中提升到自己心中，将剧本从课堂搬演到戏台。

相信《中文详注剑桥莎士比亚精选》会带给中国广大英语爱好者一个惊喜。

陈国华

2020年5月于英国剑桥家中

Contents 目录

Introduction 引言	iv
Photo gallery 剧照精选	v

Much Ado About Nothing 《虚惊一场》

List of characters 人物表	1
Act 1 第1幕	3
Act 2 第2幕	27
Act 3 第3幕	65
Act 4 第4幕	101
Act 5 第5幕	129
Perspectives and themes 视角与主题	164
Fashion and appearance 时尚与外貌	171
Characters 人物分析	174
The language of *Much Ado About Nothing* 《虚惊一场》的语言	182
Much Ado About Nothing in performance 《虚惊一场》的演出	190
Writing about Shakespeare 笔论莎士比亚	198
Writing about *Much Ado About Nothing* 笔论《虚惊一场》	200
William Shakespeare 1564–1616 莎翁年表	202
Acknowledgements 鸣谢	203

Introduction 引言

This *Much Ado About Nothing* is part of the **Cambridge School Shakespeare** series. Like every other play in the series, it has been specially prepared to help all students in schools and colleges.

The **Cambridge School Shakespeare** *Much Ado About Nothing* aims to be different. It invites you to lift the words from the page and to bring the play to life in your classroom, hall or drama studio. Through enjoyable and focused activities, you will increase your understanding of the play. Actors have created their different interpretations of the play over the centuries. Similarly, you are invited to make up your own mind about *Much Ado About Nothing*, rather than having someone else's interpretation handed down to you.

Cambridge School Shakespeare does not offer you a cut-down or simplified version of the play. This is Shakespeare's language, filled with imaginative possibilities. You will find on every left-hand page: a summary of the action, an explanation of unfamiliar words, and a choice of activities on Shakespeare's stagecraft, characters, themes and language.

Between each act and in the pages at the end of the play, you will find notes, illustrations and activities. These will help to encourage reflection after every act and give you insights into the background and context of the play as a whole.

This edition will be of value to you whether you are studying for an examination, reading for pleasure or thinking of putting on the play to entertain others. You can work on the activities on your own or in groups. Many of the activities suggest a particular group size, but don't be afraid to make up larger or smaller groups to suit your own purposes. Please don't think you have to do every activity: choose those that will help you most.

Although you are invited to treat *Much Ado About Nothing* as a play, you don't need special dramatic or theatrical skills to do the activities. By choosing your activities, and by exploring and experimenting, you can make your own interpretations of Shakespeare's language, characters and stories.

Whatever you do, remember that Shakespeare wrote his plays to be acted, watched and enjoyed.

Rex Gibson
Founding editor

This new edition contains more photographs, more diversity and more supporting material than previous editions, whilst remaining true to Rex's original vision. Specifically, it contains more activities and commentary on stagecraft and writing about Shakespeare, to reflect contemporary interest. The glossary has been enlarged too. Finally, this edition aims to reflect the best teaching and learning possible, and to represent not only Shakespeare through the ages, but also the relevance and excitement of Shakespeare today.

Richard Andrews and Vicki Wienand
Series editors

This edition of *Much Ado About Nothing* uses the text of the play established by F. H. Mares in **The New Cambridge Shakespeare**.

Much Ado About Nothing is particularly admired for the wit and intelligence of Beatrice and Benedick, the warring couple comically tricked into falling in love.

'I wonder that you will still be talking, Signor Benedick, nobody marks you.'

The story begins with the return of Don Pedro's army from the wars. In this 1993 Kenneth Branagh film, the young women of Governor Leonato's household in Messina, led by Beatrice (left) and Leonato's daughter Hero (centre), scamper (奔跑) excitedly down the hill to greet the men.

Don Pedro's company enters Governor Leonato's courtyard. The prince (centre) has his trusted friends Count Claudio and Signor Benedick on his right. On the prince's left is his brother, the villainous Don John, defeated leader of a recent rebellion against him.

Count Claudio, highly praised for his bravery in the recent war, wishes to marry Hero, Leonato's only child. The wealthy governor of Messina is only too delighted to have his daughter make such a magnificent alliance.

Don Pedro plans to help Claudio win Hero's heart. At the masked ball he poses as his young friend, woos Hero and gains her consent to marry.

'She told me, not thinking I had been myself, that I was the prince's jester (俳优).' At the masked ball, Benedick also pretends to be someone else. Beatrice, however, sees through his disguise and uses the opportunity to make wittily insulting comments about the 'absent Benedick'.

▲ Don Pedro arranges a second deception. Benedick and Beatrice are both tricked into believing the other is secretly in love with them. Benedick's overhearing of his friends' 'secret' conversation is often played for laughs, as in the production above, set in twentieth-century Sicily.

▶ The 'gulling' (tricking) of Beatrice is usually played more seriously. The mirror she hides behind here is made of semi-transparent glass, so the audience can see both the hoaxers (骗子) and Beatrice's shocked yet delighted reaction.

◀ Don John maliciously (蓄意) tricks Claudio and Don Pedro into believing they have seen Hero entertaining another man in her bedroom. At the wedding ceremony, Claudio publicly and savagely rejects Hero as a common whore.

▼ Faced with such accusations, Hero faints with shock. Beatrice believes her cousin to be innocent. She urges Benedick to challenge Claudio to single combat. On the Friar's (修士) advice, Leonato orders that Hero be hidden and reported dead until her innocence is proved.

Fortunately, Don John's plot is accidentally uncovered by the town's incompetent Watchmen, led by Dogberry, their even more inept (无能) Master Constable. Still believing Hero is dead, a penitent (懊悔) Claudio agrees to marry Leonato's niece, said to be the 'image' of Hero. She is, of course, Hero herself.

When love sonnets in their own handwriting are produced, Beatrice and Benedick reluctantly admit their love for each other and also agree to marry.

▶ A delighted Benedick kisses his bride-to-be, then leads the whole company in a celebratory dance. Not even news that Don John has been captured can spoil his happiness.

▼ 'Prince, thou art sad, get thee a wife, get thee a wife'. Productions often show Don Pedro (seated) alone at the end of the play, while couples dance happily around him.

List of characters 人物表

Leonato's Household 列纳托家

SIGNOR /ˈsiːnjɔː(r)/ LEONATO /lɪəˈnɑːtoː/ (列纳托) governor of Messina /məˈsiːnə/ (墨西拿总督)
SIGNOR ANTONIO /anˈtoːnɪoː/ (安托纽) Leonato's brother
HERO /ˈhiːroː/ (希柔) Leonato's only daughter
BEATRICE /ˈbiːətrɪs/ (碧翠) an orphan, Leonato's niece
MARGARET /ˈmɑː(r)grɪt/ (玛格蕊) ⎫
URSULA /ˈɑː(r)sjələ/ (阿秀菈) ⎭ gentlewomen attending on Hero (服侍希柔的贵妇)
FRIAR FRANCIS /ˈfransɪs/ (福冉希修士)
Musicians, Attendants, Maskers (戴假面的人) and Wedding Guests

The Military 军方

DON PEDRO /dɒn ˈpeɪdroː/ (唐佩卓) Prince of Arragon /ˈarəgɒn/ (阿若岗亲王)
DON JOHN /dɒn ˈdʒɒn/ (唐约翰) Don Pedro's bastard brother
COUNT CLAUDIO /ˈklɔːdɪoː/ (克劳丢伯爵) ⎫
 of Florence /ˈflɒrəns/ (佛罗伦萨) ⎬ companions of Don Pedro
SIGNOR BENEDICK /ˈbenɪdɪk/ (本尼迪) ⎪
 of Padua /ˈpadjʊə/ (帕多瓦) ⎭
BORACHIO /bɒˈratʃɪoː/ (鲍拉丘) ⎫
CONRADE /ˈkɒnrad/ (康拉) ⎭ followers of Don John
MESSENGER (信使)
BALTHASAR /ˈbaltəˌzɑː(r)/ (巴尔特扎) a singer
BOY (侍童) servant to Benedick

The Town 镇民

DOGBERRY /ˈdɒgbərəɪ/ (道博瑞) Constable (治安官) of Messina
VERGES /ˈvɑː(r)dʒɪz/ (瓦吉) Deputy Constable (治安副官) (or Headborough /ˈhedbrə/ [镇长])
SEXTON /ˈsekstən/ (教堂司事)
GEORGE SEACOLE /dʒɑː(r)dʒ ˈsiːkoːl/ (乔治·希寇尔) Senior Watchman (巡夜队长)
WATCHMAN 1 (巡夜甲)
WATCHMAN 2 (巡夜乙)
Other Watchmen (其他巡夜)

The play is set in Messina, Sicily /ˈsɪsɪləɪ/ (西西里).

A Messenger brings a letter informing Governor Leonato that Don Pedro and his victorious army will shortly arrive in Messina. The Messenger reports that young Count Claudio has performed great deeds of bravery in the war.

 剧情简介：信使送信给列纳托总督，报告唐佩卓亲王率领他的部队凯旋，很快就会到达墨西拿。信使还报告说克劳丢伯爵年轻勇猛，战功卓著。

1 Messina: a man's world? (in groups of four to six)

Stand in a circle and read through lines 1–118 with as much energy and enthusiasm as possible. Discuss clues in the characters' speech and behaviour that suggest this play will focus on the position and role of women in a male-dominated world. Identify the words Leonato uses to describe Beatrice and Benedick's 'battle of the sexes', and take turns to read them out.

Stagecraft 导演技巧
Sending the audience a 'message'

Stagecraft is the technical side of performance, such as the way stage designers approach a scene.

In the 2002 Royal Shakespeare Company production (pictured below), the director and designer made the decision to begin the play with Beatrice entering the stage on a real Second World War-era motorbike. What sort of a 'statement' would this impressive theatrical moment have made about the character of Beatrice and the setting of that particular production? Suggest other ways in which the director and designer might use the technical opportunities of a modern theatre to create an impressive opening 'spectacle' for the audience.

1 **by this** 到现在
2 **leagues** 里格（航海计程单位，1里格约等于3英里）
3 **gentlemen** 贵族
4 **action** 战斗
5 **sort** 地位高
6 **none of name** 无一有名望
7 **achiever** 胜者
8 **bestowed much honour** 非常器重
9 **Florentine** 佛罗伦萨人
10 **equally remembered** 适当嘉奖
11 **borne himself** 战场上表现
12 **figure** 外表
13 **feats** 英勇
14 **bettered expectation** 超过了期望
15 **badge** 迹象
16 **kind** 自然
17 **weep at joy** 喜极而泣

Much Ado About Nothing

Act 1 Scene 1
Messina Leonato's house

Enter LEONATO, *governor of Messina,* HERO *his daughter and* BEATRICE *his niece, with a* MESSENGER

LEONATO I learn in this letter, that Don Pedro of Arragon comes this night to Messina.

MESSENGER He is very near by this[1], he was not three leagues[2] off when I left him.

LEONATO How many gentlemen[3] have you lost in this action[4]?

MESSENGER But few of any sort[5], and none of name[6].

LEONATO A victory is twice itself, when the achiever[7] brings home full numbers. I find here, that Don Pedro hath bestowed much honour[8] on a young Florentine[9] called Claudio.

MESSENGER Much deserved on his part, and equally remembered[10] by Don Pedro. He hath borne himself[11] beyond the promise of his age, doing in the figure[12] of a lamb the feats[13] of a lion. He hath indeed better bettered expectation[14] than you must expect of me to tell you how.

LEONATO He hath an uncle here in Messina will be very much glad of it.

MESSENGER I have already delivered him letters, and there appears much joy in him, even so much that joy could not show itself modest enough without a badge[15] of bitterness.

LEONATO Did he break out into tears?

MESSENGER In great measure.

LEONATO A kind[16] overflow of kindness: there are no faces truer than those that are so washed. How much better is it to weep at joy[17], than to joy at weeping!

Beatrice questions the Messenger about Benedick, sarcastically calling him Signor Mountanto. Faced with a barrage of mocking comments about a fellow soldier, the Messenger politely attempts to defend Benedick's reputation.

剧情简介：碧翠向信使打听本尼迪的情况，讽刺他是"上刺先生"。面对这场对战友一连串冷嘲热讽的人身攻击，信使试图有礼貌地维护本尼迪的名誉。

Characters 人物分析
First impressions

Beatrice's lines in this scene mark her out as an intelligent and witty woman – quite a match for the Messenger, whom she teases and torments until Don Pedro arrives. Note how Beatrice's insults and accusations shape the audience's opinion of Benedick before he enters the scene. Why do you think that Shakespeare has done this? What does it add to Benedick's eventual arrival?

1. Signor 先生（意大利语）
2. Mountanto 向上刺（剑术）；趴在……身上（此处有性暗示；参见本页Activity 2）
3. set up his bills 贴告示
4. Cupid 丘比特（罗马神话中佩戴弓箭的爱神）
5. at the flight 射箭比赛
6. subscribed 签字
7. birdbolt 钝头箭
8. tax 批判；挑剔
9. be meet 报复，算账
10. musty victual 发霉的食物
11. holp = helped
12. trencherman 大肚汉
13. stomach 胃口；胆量
14. betwixt = between
15. skirmish 小冲突
16. five wits 五种才智（指常识、想象、奇想、本能、记忆）
17. went halting off 一瘸一拐地走没了
18. sworn brother 结拜兄弟
19. next block 下一个制帽模子，最新潮的帽形（参见第171页；block指帽子制作工艺中用来定帽形的木头模子）

1 On guard! (in fours)

One of your group reads Beatrice's part (lines 23–56), in which she mocks the Messenger and sets out to deliberately 'mistake' his meaning. The other three take the parts of the Messenger, Leonato and Hero. Beatrice should say the lines quickly and with great energy, perhaps even moving around the stage. Think about how the other characters could say their lines, and what physical and facial gestures they might use to defend themselves from her verbal blows.

2 What does Beatrice think of 'Signor Mountanto'?

'Mountanto' (line 23) was a fencing term, which Beatrice uses here to imply that Benedick is a flashy (炫耀技艺，浮夸招摇) swordsman. But is she talking about his skills in battle or about his ability to 'conquer' ladies? This is an early example of the **double entendre** (双关语)(double meaning) that Beatrice uses for comic effect.

Read through lines 23–70. Make a list of Benedick's 'failings' (缺点，短处), as identified by Beatrice. Suggest why you think she might dislike him so much.

◀ This Beatrice was as sharp with a sword as she was with her tongue.

BEATRICE I pray you, is Signor[1] Mountanto[2] returned from the wars or no?
MESSENGER I know none of that name, lady, there was none such in the army of any sort.
LEONATO What is he that you ask for, niece?
HERO My cousin means Signor Benedick of Padua.
MESSENGER O he's returned, and as pleasant as ever he was.
BEATRICE He set up his bills[3] here in Messina, and challenged Cupid[4] at the flight[5]: and my uncle's fool, reading the challenge, subscribed[6] for Cupid, and challenged him at the birdbolt[7]. I pray you, how many hath he killed and eaten in these wars? But how many hath he killed? – for indeed I promised to eat all of his killing.
LEONATO Faith, niece, you tax[8] Signor Benedick too much, but he'll be meet[9] with you, I doubt it not.
MESSENGER He hath done good service, lady, in these wars.
BEATRICE You had musty victual[10], and he hath holp[11] to eat it: he is a very valiant trencherman[12], he hath an excellent stomach[13].
MESSENGER And a good soldier too, lady.
BEATRICE And a good soldier to a lady, but what is he to a lord?
MESSENGER A lord to a lord, a man to a man, stuffed with all honourable virtues.
BEATRICE It is so indeed, he is no less than a stuffed man, but for the stuffing – well, we are all mortal.
LEONATO You must not, sir, mistake my niece: there is a kind of merry war betwixt[14] Signor Benedick and her: they never meet but there's a skirmish[15] of wit between them.
BEATRICE Alas, he gets nothing by that. In our last conflict, four of his five wits[16] went halting off[17], and now is the whole man governed with one: so that if he have wit enough to keep himself warm, let him bear it for a difference between himself and his horse, for it is all the wealth that he hath left to be known a reasonable creature. Who is his companion now? He hath every month a new sworn brother[18].
MESSENGER Is't possible?
BEATRICE Very easily possible: he wears his faith but as the fashion of his hat, it ever changes with the next block[19].

As Beatrice continues to speak mockingly of Benedick to the Messenger, the prince, Don Pedro, and his followers arrive. Leonato eloquently welcomes his royal guest and Beatrice begins her taunting of Benedick.

剧情简介：碧翠继续向信使挖苦本尼迪，这时唐佩卓亲王一行驾到。列纳托热情洋溢地欢迎王室贵宾大驾光临，碧翠开始奚落本尼迪。

1 The warriors return (in large groups)

Stage your own performance of lines 70–88, where Leonato welcomes the prince and his comrades in arms. Act out the scene in two different ways:

- A highly organised, hierarchical and formal greeting, as shown in the image below. The characters (except for the hiding Beatrice!) line up neatly and according to rank.
- A relaxed and good-humoured greeting, where the characters behave warmly towards each other. Some directors make the staging less formal by, for example, having Don Pedro hug Leonato ('You embrace your charge too willingly', line 76).

a Why did you position the different characters where you did in each performance? To what extent do you think the dialogue encourages physical interaction between the actors? Discuss these points in your group.

b Decide which of the two interpretations above you think is the most appropriate and dramatically interesting, and write a paragraph outlining how you would like to stage this scene.

▼ Benedick is centre left, in the black coat with white collar. Beatrice stands entirely hidden, except for part of her face, behind the characters on the other side of the stage. Why has the director placed her there?

1	**not in your books** 不是您好书中的人物；不在您好人的名册上
2	**and he were** = if he were
3	**study** 书房
4	**squarer** 街头混混，流氓
5	**pestilence** 瘟疫
6	**taker** 被传染的人
7	**presently** 立刻
8	**noble** 可敬
9	**caught the Benedict** 染上本尼迪式疯病
10	**ere** = before
11	**a** = he
12	**a hot January** 炎热的一月（一月通常很冷，意指不可能）
13	**JOHN** *the bastard* 野种约翰
14	**sorrow abides** 忧愁永驻
15	**charge** 负担，花费
16	**have it full** 被很好地回敬
17	**fathers herself** 很像她父亲
18	**marks** 听，关注
19	**Lady Disdain** 高傲小姐

MESSENGER I see, lady, the gentleman is not in your books[1].
BEATRICE No, and he were[2], I would burn my study[3]. But I pray you, who is his companion? Is there no young squarer[4] now, that will make a voyage with him to the devil?
MESSENGER He is most in the company of the right noble Claudio.
BEATRICE O Lord, he will hang upon him like a disease: he is sooner caught than the pestilence[5], and the taker[6] runs presently[7] mad. God help the noble[8] Claudio, if he hath caught the Benedict[9]. It will cost him a thousand pound ere[10] a[11] be cured.
MESSENGER I will hold friends with you, lady.
BEATRICE Do, good friend.
LEONATO You will never run mad, niece.
BEATRICE No, not till a hot January[12].
MESSENGER Don Pedro is approached.

Enter DON PEDRO, CLAUDIO, BENEDICK, BALTHASAR *and* JOHN *the bastard*[13]

DON PEDRO Good Signor Leonato, are you come to meet your trouble? The fashion of the world is to avoid cost, and you encounter it.
LEONATO Never came trouble to my house in the likeness of your grace: for trouble being gone, comfort should remain: but when you depart from me, sorrow abides[14], and happiness takes his leave.
DON PEDRO You embrace your charge[15] too willingly. I think this is your daughter?
LEONATO Her mother hath many times told me so.
BENEDICK Were you in doubt, sir, that you asked her?
LEONATO Signor Benedick, no, for then were you a child.
DON PEDRO You have it full[16], Benedick: we may guess by this, what you are, being a man. Truly, the lady fathers herself[17]: be happy, lady, for you are like an honourable father.
BENEDICK If Signor Leonato be her father, she would not have his head on her shoulders for all Messina, as like him as she is.
BEATRICE I wonder that you will still be talking, Signor Benedick, nobody marks[18] you.
BENEDICK What, my dear Lady Disdain[19]! Are you yet living?

Beatrice and Benedick renew their 'merry war', each trying to score points off the other, each attempting to have the last word. Leonato invites Don Pedro and his followers to stay as guests at his house.

 剧情简介：碧翠和本尼迪又开始打嘴仗，二人都想贬损对方，压对方一头。列纳托邀请唐佩卓亲王一行在自己府上住下。

1 'Courtesy itself must convert to Disdain' (in pairs)

Beatrice once again interrupts the men's conversation. But this time she faces Benedick, a much more formidable opponent.

a Decide in your pair who will act the part of Beatrice and who will be Benedick. Face your partner and read lines 86–107 a few times, until you are comfortable with speaking the words. Select the most insulting or amusing phrases your character uses and compile a shortened script using just these phrases (with perhaps a few extra words of your own to help it all make sense). Then use your revised script to hurl the best insults back and forth.

b Show your version to the rest of the class. Debate and decide which character is forced to break off hostilities first, and whether there is a clear winner to this particular battle in Beatrice and Benedick's 'merry war'.

Stagecraft 导演技巧

Exposition (背景交代)

This section of the play introduces us to new characters. It gives us a glimpse into their backgrounds and suggests what has shaped them. This is technically referred to as **exposition**. A character's first words are often very revealing. It was Don John who led the recent rebellion against his brother, Don Pedro, although the two are now friends again ('reconciled').

Imagine you are a director, and write notes for the actors playing Don John and Don Pedro, advising them on how to make lines 113–18 an uneasy moment in an otherwise happy reunion. How do you think the two royal brothers should behave towards each other?

2 Beatrice and Benedick do battle! (in pairs)

Lines 86–107 are a very well-known sequence in the play. The interplay between Beatrice and Benedick is often compared to fencing or a boxing match. Try performing the scene in the following ways (as well as any others you can come up with) and decide which physical approach is the most impactful and effective:

- slowly circling one another at a distance
- in close proximity, almost head to head, whispering
- moving from one end of the stage to the other, almost shouting across the space
- standing completely still, with all emphasis on facial expressions and tone of voice.

---

1 Courtesy … presence 只要有您在场，礼貌本身也会变成傲慢
2 turn-coat 叛徒
3 excepted 不包括
4 dear happiness 极好的运气
5 pernicious 邪恶
6 humour 性情
7 scape … face 逃脱脸被挠伤的厄运（scape = escape）
8 and 'twere = if it were
9 parrot-teacher 鹦鹉教师；话匣子
10 so good a continuer 一样不知疲倦
11 jade 不听话的劣马
12 prays 希望
13 occasion 事情
14 hypocrite 伪君子，言行不一的人
15 be forsworn 发假誓
16 reconciled to 与……言归于好
17 Exeunt （剧本中的说明，两个以上演员）退场，下场

8

Much Ado About Nothing Act 1 Scene 1

虚惊一场

BEATRICE Is it possible Disdain should die, while she hath such meet food to feed it, as Signor Benedick? Courtesy itself must convert to Disdain, if you come in her presence[1].

BENEDICK Then is Courtesy a turn-coat[2]: but it is certain I am loved of all ladies, only you excepted[3]: and I would I could find in my heart that I had not a hard heart, for truly I love none.

BEATRICE A dear happiness[4] to women, they would else have been troubled with a pernicious[5] suitor. I thank God and my cold blood, I am of your humour[6] for that: I had rather hear my dog bark at a crow than a man swear he loves me.

BENEDICK God keep your ladyship still in that mind, so some gentleman or other shall scape a predestinate scratched face[7].

BEATRICE Scratching could not make it worse, and 'twere[8] such a face as yours were.

BENEDICK Well, you are a rare parrot-teacher[9].

BEATRICE A bird of my tongue is better than a beast of yours.

BENEDICK I would my horse had the speed of your tongue, and so good a continuer[10]: but keep your way a God's name. I have done.

BEATRICE You always end with a jade's[11] trick: I know you of old.

DON PEDRO That is the sum of all: Leonato, Signor Claudio and Signor Benedick, my dear friend Leonato, hath invited you all. I tell him we shall stay here at the least a month, and he heartily prays[12] some occasion[13] may detain us longer: I dare swear he is no hypocrite[14], but prays from his heart.

LEONATO If you swear, my lord, you shall not be forsworn[15]. [*To Don John*] Let me bid you welcome, my lord, being reconciled to[16] the prince your brother: I owe you all duty.

DON JOHN I thank you, I am not of many words, but I thank you.

LEONATO Please it your grace lead on?

DON PEDRO Your hand, Leonato, we will go together.

Exeunt[17] *all except Benedick and Claudio*

Claudio tells Benedick of his love for Hero and asks Benedick what he thinks of her. Benedick is unimpressed by Hero's charms and quite dismayed that his young friend Claudio should be considering marriage.

剧情简介：克劳丢向本尼迪倾诉自己对希柔的爱慕，并问他对希柔的看法。本尼迪没觉得希柔有动人之处，对克劳丢年纪轻轻竟考虑婚姻感到惊讶和失落。

Characters 人物分析

Benedick the play-actor

In lines 136–7, Benedick pretends to think that Claudio is mocking him by making impossible remarks (Cupid, the god of love, was blind; Vulcan, the god of fire, was a blacksmith).

a Find other examples of Benedick's agility (敏捷) of mind and love of play-acting (演戏) in the script opposite. Has he made any genuinely serious remarks since he appeared?

b 'Shall I never see a bachelor of three score again?' asks Benedick, the apparently cynical (看破红尘) woman-hater (lines 147–8). Find quotations that suggest he might be more interested in women – and Beatrice in particular – than he would care to admit. Add to these notes as you progress through the play.

Benedick is often played as a slightly older character than Claudio. Does Benedick sound older than Claudio to you?

Write about it 写作练习

Noting or nothing?

This play's title has a number of meanings. 'Noting' and 'nothing' were pronounced very similarly in Shakespeare's time. Both Claudio and Benedick talk of 'noting' (observing) Leonato's daughter.

a Look out for other 'notings' – list anything else significant that has been 'noted' by other characters so far.

b Write two paragraphs exploring whether you think Benedick genuinely feels 'nothing' for Beatrice. Use quotations to support your points.

1 noted her not　没有刻意端详她
2 modest　贤惠
3 after my custom　以我平时习惯
4 professed tyrant　公开的冤家对头，众人皆知的克星
5 low　个子矮
6 commendation　称赞，赞美之词
7 in sport　开玩笑
8 with a sad brow　一脸严肃
9 play the flouting Jack　扮演胡说八道的无赖
10 Cupid is a good hare-finder　丘比特是抓兔子的能手（传说中丘比特是盲人）
11 Vulcan a rare carpenter　瓦尔肯是绝世的木匠（传说中瓦尔肯是铁匠）
12 go in the song　合您的拍，顺您的意
13 and she … fury　要不是她那股凶劲儿（and = if）
14 as the first … December　就像五月初的天气要胜过十二月底一样
15 I would scarce trust myself　我会觉得自己配不上
16 wear his cap　戴绿帽子（为了遮掩头上长出的角；参见第12页）
17 bachelor of three score　60岁的单身汉
18 and thou wilt needs　如果你一定要
19 yoke　牛轭（驾车时套在两头牛脖子上的木梁）
20 sigh away Sundays　星期天困在家里唉声叹气

CLAUDIO   Benedick, didst thou note the daughter of Signor Leonato?
BENEDICK I noted her not[1], but I looked on her.
CLAUDIO   Is she not a modest[2] young lady?
BENEDICK Do you question me as an honest man should do, for my simple true judgement? Or would you have me speak after my custom[3], as being a professed tyrant[4] to their sex?
CLAUDIO   No, I pray thee speak in sober judgement.
BENEDICK Why i'faith, methinks she's too low[5] for a high praise, too brown for a fair praise, and too little for a great praise. Only this commendation[6] I can afford her, that were she other than she is, she were unhandsome, and being no other, but as she is – I do not like her.
CLAUDIO   Thou thinkest I am in sport[7]. I pray thee, tell me truly how thou lik'st her?
BENEDICK Would you buy her, that you enquire after her?
CLAUDIO   Can the world buy such a jewel?
BENEDICK Yea, and a case to put it into. But speak you this with a sad brow[8]? Or do you play the flouting Jack[9], to tell us Cupid is a good hare-finder[10], and Vulcan a rare carpenter[11]? Come, in what key shall a man take you, to go in the song[12]?
CLAUDIO   In mine eye, she is the sweetest lady that ever I looked on.
BENEDICK I can see yet without spectacles, and I see no such matter. There's her cousin, and she were not possessed with a fury[13], exceeds her as much in beauty as the first of May doth the last of December[14]. But I hope you have no intent to turn husband, have you?
CLAUDIO   I would scarce trust myself[15], though I had sworn the contrary, if Hero would be my wife.
BENEDICK Is't come to this? In faith, hath not the world one man, but he will wear his cap[16] with suspicion? Shall I never see a bachelor of three score[17] again? Go to, i'faith, and thou wilt needs[18] thrust thy neck into a yoke[19], wear the print of it, and sigh away Sundays[20]. Look, Don Pedro is returned to seek you.

Don Pedro returns to find out why his friends have stayed behind. Benedick reveals that Claudio is secretly in love with Hero and vows that he himself will never be so foolish as to be tempted into marriage.

 剧情简介：唐佩卓回来问两位好友为何没有跟上。本尼迪透露说克劳丢暗恋希柔，他发誓自己永远不会蠢到被引诱到婚姻里。

Language in the play 剧中语言
Serious about joking (in small groups)

Wordplay is a significant feature in this play. Elizabethan drama focused on the power of the word (see 'the Language of *Much Ado About Nothing*', pp. 182–9). Ability with language was also a sign of high status, with many aristocrats in Shakespeare's time taking up poetry writing.

In the same way, the friends in this play show off their education and skill with words. They often make jokes, even about matters deeply important to Elizabethans, such as love, religion, allegiance and troth (honour).

a Find examples from lines 151–215 of the three men playing lightheartedly with these concerns.

b Can you identify individual words that have a comic impact? Try performing sections of this scene and over-emphasising these words to maximise their impact.

1 Horns and cuckolds (被戴绿帽子的人)

A favourite object of ridicule in Shakespeare's time was the cuckold – a man whose wife was unfaithful to him. The cuckold was supposed to grow horns on his forehead, invisible to himself but obvious to everyone else. This explains Benedick's remark about the married man needing to wear a cap (line 147).

a Write a paragraph explaining how Benedick elaborates on this idea in lines 178–82. Remember that bugles (号角) or hunting horns were originally made from actual animal horns; a 'recheat' is a hunting call; 'winded' means blown or played; and a 'baldrick' is a belt.

b The cuckold may have been a male figure of fun, but what does this conversation suggest to you about Elizabethan attitudes towards women? Write an Elizabethan definition (use contemporary language) of what it means to be a cuckold.

1 constrain 强迫
2 allegiance 效忠
3 your grace's part 这是亲王您应该问的问题
4 fetch me in 让我上套
5 By my troth 以我的信誉担保
6 worthy 尊贵
7 I will … stake 为了我的信念，我宁愿被烧死在火刑柱上
8 obstinate 顽固不化
9 heretic 异端分子
10 the despite of 鄙视……的
11 never … part 绝不可能继续扮演他那个角色
12 but … will 除非靠他意志的力量
13 recheat 呜哩哇（狩猎用语，指召唤猎犬回来的号角声；have a recheat winded 的意思是"吹呜哩哇"）
14 baldrick 腰带
15 fine 结论

Enter DON PEDRO

DON PEDRO What secret hath held you here, that you followed not to Leonato's?

BENEDICK I would your grace would constrain[1] me to tell.

DON PEDRO I charge thee on thy allegiance[2].

BENEDICK You hear, Count Claudio, I can be secret as a dumb man – I would have you think so. But on my allegiance (mark you this, on my allegiance) he is in love. With who? Now that is your grace's part[3]: mark how short his answer is. With Hero, Leonato's short daughter.

CLAUDIO If this were so, so were it uttered.

BENEDICK Like the old tale, my lord: 'It is not so, nor 'twas not so, but indeed, God forbid it should be so.'

CLAUDIO If my passion change not shortly, God forbid it should be otherwise.

DON PEDRO Amen, if you love her, for the lady is very well worthy.

CLAUDIO You speak this to fetch me in[4], my lord.

DON PEDRO By my troth[5], I speak my thought.

CLAUDIO And in faith, my lord, I spoke mine.

BENEDICK And by my two faiths and troths, my lord, I spoke mine.

CLAUDIO That I love her, I feel.

DON PEDRO That she is worthy[6], I know.

BENEDICK That I neither feel how she should be loved, nor know how she should be worthy, is the opinion that fire cannot melt out of me: I will die in it at the stake[7].

DON PEDRO Thou wast ever an obstinate[8] heretic[9] in the despite of[10] beauty.

CLAUDIO And never could maintain his part[11], but in the force of his will[12].

BENEDICK That a woman conceived me, I thank her: that she brought me up, I likewise give her most humble thanks: but that I will have a recheat[13] winded in my forehead, or hang my bugle in an invisible baldrick[14], all women shall pardon me. Because I will not do them the wrong to mistrust any, I will do myself the right to trust none: and the fine[15] is (for the which I may go the finer) I will live a bachelor.

Don Pedro predicts that Benedick will also one day fall in love. Supremely confident, Benedick lays down a challenge: his friends can do all manner of things to ridicule him if he ever does fall for a woman's charms.

剧情简介：唐佩卓预言本尼迪有一天也会坠入爱河。本尼迪信心十足，提出挑战：如果他受到女人的吸引而爱上她，可以任由朋友们嘲笑他。

1 Benedick the married man (in pairs or small groups)

a Draw pictures of the three things that Benedick promises Claudio and Don Pedro can do to him if he falls in love (lines 184–99). You can include text captions in your pictures. Talk together about how and why you have drawn the image the way you have.

b Many people joke about things that disturb or worry them. Discuss the following questions and prepare a short summary of your thoughts to share with the class:

- Is Benedick genuinely antagonistic (敌对的，有敌意的) to women, or is he masking his fear of commitment (承诺，义务)?
- Benedick refers to animals when describing the effect of love on a man. Why do you think he uses the **metaphors** (隐喻) of a cat, a bull and a horse?

Language in the play 剧中语言
Letter writing and fashionable metaphors

The closeness of the relationship between Benedick, Claudio and Don Pedro is shown in the way that they tease one another and mock the formality shown by the likes of Leonato. When Don Pedro addresses Benedick as 'good Signor Benedick' (line 205) and Benedick says 'so I commit you' (line 209), they are both jokingly adopting the language of formal letter writing.

a Find two other examples of the language of letter writing (epistolary [书信体] language) being used in a jokey fashion on this page. How does the use of such language add to the humour in this scene and how could it be brought to life using gestures, facial expressions and stage action?

b Benedick uses an extended metaphor in lines 212–15 to compare the way Claudio and Don Pedro talk (their 'discourse') to a fancy garment (item of clothing). Use the glossary (词汇表) to help you explain what you think Benedick's metaphor suggests or implies. Try to summarise it in no more than fifty words, using at least two pieces of evidence (quotations) from the script opposite to support your explanation.

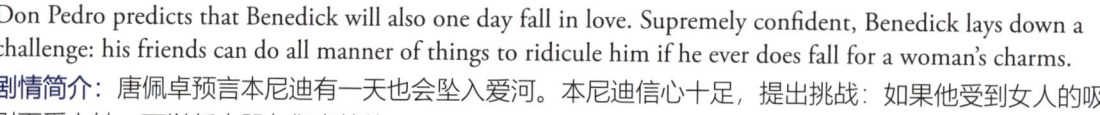

1 lose … drinking 为爱消耗气血过多，靠饮酒补不回来
2 ballad-maker 写（爱情）民谣的人
3 brothel 妓院
4 sign of blind Cupid 瞎眼丘比特的招牌（当时妓院的招牌上常画着丘比特）
5 fall from this faith 改变这一信念
6 notable argument 绝妙话题
7 bottle 柳条篮子
8 Adam 神箭手亚当（当时有一个名叫Adam Bell的射箭高手）
9 as time shall try 时间会证明
10 In … yoke 总有一天野牛也会俯首帖耳
11 vilely painted 浑身涂得乌七八糟
12 horn-mad 气得发狂
13 quiver 箭囊
14 Venice 威尼斯（当时以风气败坏闻名）
15 temporise with the hours 随着时间而改变
16 repair 回到，去
17 embassage 差事
18 commit 托付
19 To … house （这句话是信封上写的收信人和发信地址，意思是"上帝台鉴：寄自鄙人宅邸"）
20 The … Benedick （这句话是写信时间和写信人）
21 body of your discourse 主体
22 guarded with fragments 用碎布装饰
23 slightly basted 缝得不密实
24 old ends 旧布头（此处可理解为"陈词滥调"）

Much Ado About Nothing Act 1 Scene 1
虚惊一场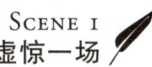

DON PEDRO   I shall see thee, ere I die, look pale with love.
BENEDICK   With anger, with sickness, or with hunger, my lord, not with love: prove that ever I lose more blood with love than I will get again with drinking[1], pick out mine eyes with a ballad-maker's[2] pen, and hang me up at the door of a brothel[3] house for the sign of blind Cupid[4].   185
DON PEDRO   Well, if ever thou dost fall from this faith[5], thou wilt prove a notable argument[6].   190
BENEDICK   If I do, hang me in a bottle[7] like a cat, and shoot at me, and he that hits me, let him be clapped on the shoulder, and called Adam[8].
DON PEDRO   Well, as time shall try[9]: 'In time the savage bull doth bear the yoke[10].'
BENEDICK   The savage bull may, but if ever the sensible Benedick bear it, pluck off the bull's horns, and set them in my forehead, and let me be vilely painted[11], and in such great letters as they write, 'Here is good horse to hire', let them signify under my sign, 'Here you may see Benedick the married man.'   195
CLAUDIO   If this should ever happen, thou wouldst be horn-mad[12].   200
DON PEDRO   Nay, if Cupid have not spent all his quiver[13] in Venice[14], thou wilt quake for this shortly.
BENEDICK   I look for an earthquake too then.
DON PEDRO   Well, you will temporise with the hours[15]. In the mean time, good Signor Benedick, repair[16] to Leonato's, commend me to him, and tell him I will not fail him at supper, for indeed he hath made great preparation.   205
BENEDICK   I have almost matter enough in me for such an embassage[17], and so I commit[18] you –
CLAUDIO   To the tuition of God: from my house[19] if I had it –   210
DON PEDRO   The sixth of July: your loving friend Benedick[20].
BENEDICK   Nay, mock not, mock not: the body of your discourse[21] is sometime guarded with fragments[22], and the guards are but slightly basted[23] on, neither: ere you flout old ends[24] any further, examine your conscience: and so I leave you.   *Exit*   215

Claudio confesses how much his love for Hero has grown since his return from the war. The prince offers to help him win her. That night at the masked ball he will pretend to be Claudio and woo Hero on his behalf.

  剧情简介：克劳丢坦白从战场上回来后他对希柔的爱慕更加强烈，唐佩卓亲王提出要帮他赢得她的芳心。当晚他要在假面舞会上假扮克劳丢，代他追求希柔。

Write about it 写作练习

The soldier becomes the lover

In lines 223–31, Claudio tells Don Pedro that he saw and liked Hero before they set off on their campaign (战役), but thoughts of war were too pressing to allow thoughts of love to grow. Now the war is over, Hero's charms cannot be denied.

a Find out how words about love and war echo through the characters' language. Read through the dialogue between Claudio and Don Pedro in lines 223–54. Draw a table with two columns. Label one 'soft/love' and the other 'rough/war'. Write quotations from the passage appropriately under the headings. What do you notice? Is there any crossover (转变)? You may wish to continue to update this list to show similar examples of such language and imagery as you continue to read the play.

b Use these quotations to help you write one or two paragraphs explaining what this tells you about male notions of how to woo a woman in Elizabethan times, and whether this is still relevant today.

1 apt 急切，迅速
2 heir 继承人（暗示希柔不仅美貌还富有）
3 affect 喜欢
4 drive 促使
5 thronging 聚集
6 break 提这件事，透露
7 his complexion 爱的相貌
8 salved it 和缓地表达
9 treatise 描述，解释
10 What … flood? 桥比河水宽太多又有何用？
11 The … necessity 最好的礼物是雪中送炭
12 Look what 无论什么
13 'tis once 一句话
14 fit thee 提供给你
15 revelling 狂欢
16 unclasp 解开
17 amorous tale 情话

1 Romantic verse (韵文；韵体) (in pairs)

Up to the departure of Benedick (line 215), the characters have talked in elegant and witty prose (散文；散体). Now Claudio and Don Pedro begin to speak in **blank verse** (无韵诗；素体诗) (unrhymed verse, see pp. 186–9) to highlight the romantic mood and the sophistication (微妙) of the subject matter: love.

Take a part each, sit face to face and read aloud lines 216–54. Is there a difference in the way the verse lines sound or are spoken compared to prose? How might the audience respond to the change in tone or rhythm (节奏)?

16

CLAUDIO	My liege, your highness now may do me good.
DON PEDRO	My love is thine to teach, teach it but how,
	And thou shalt see how apt[1] it is to learn
	Any hard lesson that may do thee good.
CLAUDIO	Hath Leonato any son, my lord?
DON PEDRO	No child but Hero, she's his only heir[2]:
	Dost thou affect[3] her, Claudio?
CLAUDIO	O my lord,
	When you went onward on this ended action,
	I looked upon her with a soldier's eye,
	That liked, but had a rougher task in hand,
	Than to drive[4] liking to the name of love;
	But now I am returned, and that war-thoughts
	Have left their places vacant, in their rooms
	Come thronging[5] soft and delicate desires,
	All prompting me how fair young Hero is,
	Saying I liked her ere I went to wars.
DON PEDRO	Thou wilt be like a lover presently,
	And tire the hearer with a book of words:
	If thou dost love fair Hero, cherish it,
	And I will break[6] with her, and with her father,
	And thou shalt have her. Wast not to this end,
	That thou began'st to twist so fine a story?
CLAUDIO	How sweetly you do minister to love,
	That know love's grief by his complexion[7]!
	But lest my liking might too sudden seem,
	I would have salved it[8] with a longer treatise[9].
DON PEDRO	What need the bridge much broader than the flood?[10]
	The fairest grant is the necessity[11].
	Look what[12] will serve is fit: 'tis once[13], thou lovest,
	And I will fit thee[14] with the remedy.
	I know we shall have revelling[15] tonight,
	I will assume thy part in some disguise,
	And tell fair Hero I am Claudio,
	And in her bosom I'll unclasp[16] my heart,
	And take her hearing prisoner with the force
	And strong encounter of my amorous tale[17]:
	Then after, to her father will I break,
	And the conclusion is, she shall be thine:
	In practice let us put it presently.

Exeunt

Antonio tells Leonato that Don Pedro's conversation with Claudio has been overheard. Apparently, the prince is in love with Hero and plans that very evening at the masked ball to ask for her hand in marriage.

 剧情简介：安托纽告诉列纳托有人无意听到了唐佩卓和克劳丢的对话。唐佩卓亲王看来是爱上了希柔，要在当晚的假面舞会上向希柔求婚。

Stagecraft 导演技巧
Excited preparations

Act 1 Scene 2 is a short scene designed to show the excited preparations ahead of the banquet and dancing at Leonato's house. The hustle and bustle (热闹，忙乱) on stage should make it all the more believable that mistaken conclusions, mishearings and misunderstandings could occur. Some productions present Antonio and Leonato as bumbling (笨手笨脚，跌跌撞撞) and out of control (sometimes emphasising their old age) in the middle of all the frenzied (慌乱) activity.

a As a designer, how would you use music, lights and props (道具) to show the preparations and perhaps add to the humour of this scene? Make notes on a copy of the script or write a set of instructions.

b Imagine you are directing the play. Write notes for this scene, instructing the actors, especially the non-speaking ones, how to create an atmosphere of domestic activity and excited preparations.

1	How now	哎；怎么样
2	cousin	亲戚
3	As the events stamps them	那要看事态的发展
4	cover	外表
5	show well outward	看起来是好事
6	thick-pleached	树篱茂密
7	a man of mine	我的一个手下
8	discovered	透露
9	accordant	同意，一致
10	take … top	抓住这个机会（英国有俗语：Take time by the forelock, for she is bald behind.）
11	break with you of it	跟您商量此事
12	Hath … this?	= Does the fellow that told you this have any wit?
13	appear itself	真的发生了
14	acquaint my daughter	告诉我女儿
15	withal	= with this, with it
16	peradventure	也许
17	cry you mercy	求您发慈悲

1 How easily are we deceived by appearances?
(in pairs)

Leonato's brother, Antonio, seems convinced by his servant's report that it is Don Pedro who loves Hero and wants to marry her! This is just the first of many eavesdroppings (偷听), mistaken conclusions and misreportings in the play.

a Read the scene through several times, taking a part each. Speak to your brother as though you were both discussing an exciting rumour that you don't want others to know you know. Is Leonato as easily convinced by the servant's story as Antonio seems to be?

b Find two phrases that specifically refer to outward appearances. How many similar phrases can you find in the opening lines of the play (Act 1 Scene 1, lines 1–22)?

2 Does Antonio have a son?

In line 1 of this scene, Leonato refers to Antonio's son preparing the music. In one version of the play, the son appears on stage with the musician. However, this son is never mentioned again, and in Act 5 Scene 1 we are told that Hero is the sole heir of both Antonio and Leonato.

Why do you think this single reference to Antonio's son is included? Suggest why we never hear from Antonio's son, or research suggestions given by critics.

Act 1 Scene 2
Leonato's house

Enter LEONATO *and an old man* ANTONIO, *brother to Leonato*

LEONATO How now¹, brother, where is my cousin² your son? Hath he provided this music?

ANTONIO He is very busy about it: but, brother, I can tell you strange news that you yet dreamed not of.

LEONATO Are they good?

ANTONIO As the events stamps them³, but they have a good cover⁴: they show well outward⁵. The prince and Count Claudio walking in a thick-pleached⁶ alley in mine orchard, were thus much overheard by a man of mine⁷: the prince discovered⁸ to Claudio that he loved my niece your daughter, and meant to acknowledge it this night in a dance, and if he found her accordant⁹, he meant to take the present time by the top¹⁰, and instantly break with you of it¹¹.

LEONATO Hath the fellow any wit that told you this?¹²

ANTONIO A good sharp fellow, I will send for him, and question him yourself.

LEONATO No, no, we will hold it as a dream till it appear itself¹³: but I will acquaint my daughter¹⁴ withal¹⁵, that she may be the better prepared for an answer, if peradventure¹⁶ this be true: go you, and tell her of it.

[*Several persons cross the stage*]

Cousins, you know what you have to do. O I cry you mercy¹⁷, friend, go you with me and I will use your skill: good cousin, have a care this busy time.

Exeunt

Full of malice and ill-humour, Don John has chosen not to attend the supper. Conrade urges him to avoid causing further offence now that he has so few friends left, but Don John's bitter anger will not be softened.

剧情简介：唐约翰心怀怨恨，郁郁寡欢，决定不参加晚宴。康拉力劝他既然没剩几个朋友，就不要惹更多人不高兴了，但是唐约翰的怨恨并没有纾解。

Stagecraft 导演技巧

Happiness turns to menace (in fours)

On Shakespeare's stage, the action probably flowed quickly from scene to scene. Indeed, the earliest published versions of his plays did not divide the script into separate acts or scenes at all. The conversations between Leonato and Antonio in Scene 2, and Don John and Conrade in Scene 3, could take place on different parts of the stage.

Think how you might show this and keep the action going. How would you use different furniture, levels or areas of the stage to emphasise the change of atmosphere? Write notes to direct the actors, and then try staging the scene according to these instructions.

Characters 人物分析

The 'plain-dealing (坦诚) villain' (in threes)

The opening stage direction in Scene 3 describes Don John as 'the bastard', meaning he was born to parents who were not married. In Shakespeare's day, an illegitimate child (私生子) was expected to be jealous, scheming (狡诈) and bad-tempered.

a Read the scene out loud in your groups, paying close attention to the lines. What part has 'the bastard' played in the recent war? Why is he so resentful of his brother and of Claudio?

b Don John says that Conrade, born under the planet Saturn, should be sour (阴郁) and gloomy like himself (lines 8–10). Does Conrade say anything to suggest this might be true?

c Speak Don John's 'thought-lists'. Read aloud lines 8–13 and 20–7, handing over to the next person at the end of each thought (generally marked by a full stop or colon). Emphasise the patterns in Don John's words.

1 What the good year 究竟怎么回事
2 out of measure 过度
3 measure 节制
4 breeds 增加，蔓延
5 present 立刻
6 born under Saturn 生在土星当空时（当时人们认为土星不吉利，在土星当空时出生的孩子性格阴郁）
7 a moral medicine 道德说教
8 mortifying mischief 致命的病
9 claw 讨好，奉承
10 without controlment 没有约束
11 stood out 违抗，反抗
12 ta'en = taken
13 take true root 真的扎根，真的站稳脚跟
14 frame 造出
15 canker 野蔷薇
16 fashion a carriage 装模作样
17 plain-dealing 正大光明
18 trusted with muzzle 上了笼嘴
19 enfranchised 释放
20 clog 重木块（拖住动物防止逃跑）
21 decreed 下定决心

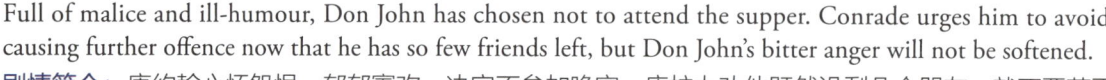

Act 1 Scene 3
Outside Leonato's house

Enter DON JOHN *the bastard and* CONRADE *his companion*

CONRADE What the good year[1], my lord, why are you thus out of measure[2] sad?

DON JOHN There is no measure[3] in the occasion that breeds[4], therefore the sadness is without limit.

CONRADE You should hear reason.

DON JOHN And when I have heard it, what blessing brings it?

CONRADE If not a present[5] remedy, at least a patient sufferance.

DON JOHN I wonder that thou (being as thou sayest thou art, born under Saturn[6]) goest about to apply a moral medicine[7] to a mortifying mischief[8]. I cannot hide what I am: I must be sad when I have cause, and smile at no man's jests: eat when I have stomach, and wait for no man's leisure: sleep when I am drowsy, and tend on no man's business: laugh when I am merry, and claw[9] no man in his humour.

CONRADE Yea, but you must not make the full show of this till you may do it without controlment[10]. You have of late stood out[11] against your brother, and he hath ta'en[12] you newly into his grace, where it is impossible you should take true root[13], but by the fair weather that you make yourself: it is needful that you frame[14] the season for your own harvest.

DON JOHN I had rather be a canker[15] in a hedge, than a rose in his grace, and it better fits my blood to be disdained of all, than to fashion a carriage[16] to rob love from any. In this (though I cannot be said to be a flattering honest man) it must not be denied but I am a plain-dealing[17] villain. I am trusted with a muzzle[18], and enfranchised[19] with a clog[20], therefore I have decreed[21] not to sing in my cage. If I had my mouth, I would bite: if I had my liberty, I would do my liking. In the mean time, let me be that I am, and seek not to alter me.

CONRADE Can you make no use of your discontent?

DON JOHN I make all use of it, for I use it only. Who comes here?

Borachio comes from the great supper and tells of Don Pedro's plan to woo Hero on Claudio's behalf. Don John decides to use this information to get his revenge on Claudio, whom he particularly hates.

剧情简介：鲍拉丘赴宴回来，讲了唐佩卓要替克劳丢向希柔求婚的打算。唐约翰决定借此机会报复克劳丢，一个他恨之入骨的人。

Themes 主题分析

Misogyny (厌女症)

Don Pedro's disaffected (不满的) brother is clearly a woman-hater. 'What is he for a fool that betroths himself to unquietness?' says Don John (lines 34–5). This means 'What kind of fool wishes to get married and give himself nothing but worry and noise?'

Look back at page 11. Which other man has expressed similarly misogynistic (women-hating) attitudes? Does there appear to be any difference in the tone the two men adopt in their comments about women? As the play continues, look out for and make notes on other examples of hostile male attitudes to women.

1 yonder 从那边
2 intelligence 消息
3 for any model 作为一个计划
4 build mischief on 捣乱
5 betroths himself 给自己订婚
6 Marry 马利亚啊（圣母马利亚 [Virgin Mary] 的简称，功能与今天的 Jesus 相似，表示对事实的感叹或惊奇、义愤等情感）
7 right hand 左膀右臂
8 proper squire 英俊绅士
9 forward March-chick 早熟的三月小鸡（三月孵出的小鸡出世早，成熟也早）
10 Being entertained for a perfumer 被派去给房间熏香
11 smoking 用烟熏
12 sad conference 严肃的谈话
13 whipped me behind the arras 迅速藏在挂毯后面
14 let us thither 咱们去那儿吧
15 start-up 暴发户
16 Would … mind 但愿厨子和我想的一样
17 go prove 去弄清楚
18 wait upon 听从……的吩咐

1 Show Don John's darkest thoughts! (in large groups)

'Would the cook were a my mind', says Don John as he leaves for the banquet (line 53). This suggests that he'd like to see everyone poisoned!

Devise a mime (哑剧) version of what Don John wishes to happen at the banquet. Be as over-the-top (过火) as you like to emphasise the villainy of Don John. The best mimes use facial expressions cleverly to show the relationships between the different characters. Can your audience guess who is playing which character?

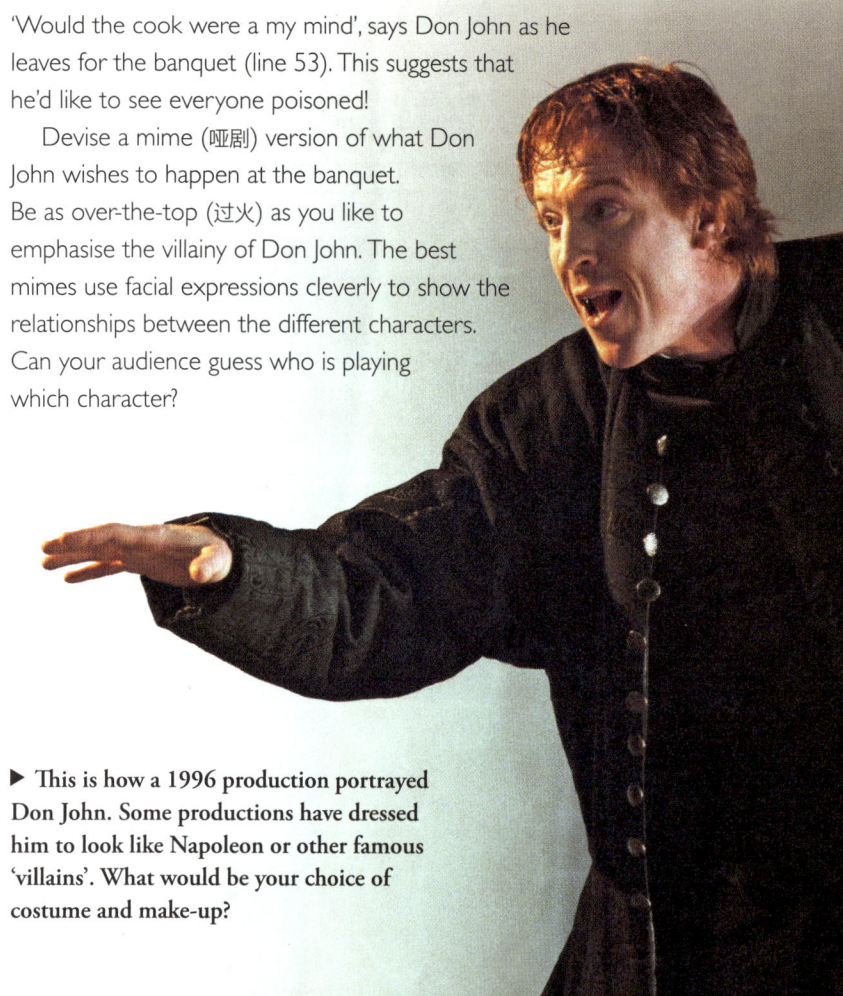

▶ This is how a 1996 production portrayed Don John. Some productions have dressed him to look like Napoleon or other famous 'villains'. What would be your choice of costume and make-up?

Much Ado About Nothing Act 1 Scene 3
虚惊一场

Enter BORACHIO

What news, Borachio? 30

BORACHIO I came yonder¹ from a great supper, the prince your brother is royally entertained by Leonato, and I can give you intelligence² of an intended marriage.

DON JOHN Will it serve for any model³ to build mischief on⁴? What is he for a fool that betroths himself⁵ to unquietness? 35

BORACHIO Marry⁶, it is your brother's right hand⁷.

DON JOHN Who, the most exquisite Claudio?

BORACHIO Even he.

DON JOHN A proper squire⁸! And who, and who, which way looks he?

BORACHIO Marry, on Hero, the daughter and heir of Leonato. 40

DON JOHN A very forward March-chick⁹. How came you to this?

BORACHIO Being entertained for a perfumer¹⁰, as I was smoking¹¹ a musty room, comes me the prince and Claudio, hand in hand, in sad conference¹²: I whipped me behind the arras¹³, and there heard it agreed upon, that the prince should woo Hero for himself, and having 45 obtained her, give her to Count Claudio.

DON JOHN Come, come, let us thither¹⁴, this may prove food to my displeasure, that young start-up¹⁵ hath all the glory of my overthrow: if I can cross him any way, I bless myself every way. You are both sure, and will assist me? 50

CONRADE To the death, my lord.

DON JOHN Let us to the great supper, their cheer is the greater that I am subdued. Would the cook were a my mind¹⁶: shall we go prove¹⁷ what's to be done?

BORACHIO We'll wait upon¹⁸ your lordship. 55

Exeunt

MUCH ADO ABOUT NOTHING
虚惊一场

Looking back at Act 1 第1幕回顾
Activities for groups or individuals

1 Improvising scenes

a The gossip columnist (八卦专栏作家) and the local news station

Improvise (即兴创作) a scene in which one of your group plays a gossip columnist. The other group members should prepare a list of different pieces of news from Act 1. They will play the locals, who are desperate to tell the columnist of the latest news and scandal in Messina society. The gossip columnist should cross-examine each of the informants to make sure the details are correct. You could also improvise a television news feature using the same information, with a reporter instead of a gossip columnist.

b The Messenger

Improvise the Messenger returning to his regiment (军团) and telling his friends about the news he carried to Leonato. The Messenger should give them his impressions of Leonato, Hero and Beatrice. As he relates his story, his friends question him about the characters, the events and the household he describes.

2 Three comrades in arms (in threes)

Benedick, Don Pedro and Claudio seem to be good friends. They have, after all, just fought together against Don John.

a In threes, each person chooses a character. Make a large outline drawing of your character and inside it write:
- your status in relation to your two friends
- what you have in common with your friends
- how you are different from your friends
- what binds you together.

b Show your drawing to the other members of your group. Ask them to add their ideas about your character. As you continue to read the play and find out more details, you can add information and track the development of your thoughts about the character.

3 A web of love and hate

Act 1 is concerned with people falling in love (Hero and Claudio) and falling out (争吵) (Beatrice and Benedick).

a Make notes on the relationships between these four characters. How does the 'love' pair, Claudio and Hero, compare with the 'love-hate' pair, Beatrice and Benedick? How does Beatrice contrast with her cousin Hero, and how much alike are Benedick and his friend Claudio? What makes them similar and how are they different?

b Draw these four characters on a large sheet of paper, one in each quarter of the page. Think how they link, what they have in common and what sets them apart. Show the relationships between them by drawing lines and annotating (注释，加注) them with brief comments.

4 Creative writing

a The villain masked and unmasked

When his brother is present, Don John has to mask his ill-feeling. However, Shakespeare often gives his villains opportunities to confess their secret thoughts to the audience.

Write a monologue for Don John, which he might deliver to the audience at the end of Act 1 Scene 3 after Borachio and Conrade have left. Write it in the same prose style that Don John uses earlier in the scene.

b What does Benedick think of Beatrice?

The returning soldier Benedick is apparently carefree and immune to love. But is he? Or is Beatrice getting to him already? What does he really think of Beatrice and what are his thoughts after their latest 'skirmish of wit'?

Write two extracts from Benedick's diary or blog: one written that evening, and one written after an earlier meeting with Beatrice before he went away to war.

Beatrice describes her ideal man, remarking how poorly Don John and Benedick match up to her requirements. Leonato warns her that such talk will not get her a husband, but Beatrice says she is happy to stay single.

剧情简介：碧翠描述她心目中的白马王子，说唐约翰和本尼迪离她的标准差得如何远。列纳托提醒她，说这种话会让她找不到丈夫，碧翠说自己乐得独身。

Themes 主题分析

Appearance and reality: Family matters (in fours)

This scene opens with a glimpse into Leonato's family life. Although this appears to be a brutally honest conversation, there is a difference between what the characters say and what their deepest feelings are. How complex are this family's relationships?

a **Conversation or battle?** Read lines 1–60 in two ways: first as a relaxed and leisurely family conversation, and then more forcefully, as though you were engaged in a battle of wits and opinions. Perform both readings for another group, and afterwards discuss with them which way seems to work better and why this might be.

b **What are they really thinking?** Perform the scene again. This time, the actor who is playing Hero should stop the action by tapping the other actors on the shoulder at the points listed below. The actors who have been interrupted should then speak their characters' inner thoughts aloud.

- Antonio after line 16. What does he mean here?
- Leonato after line 25. Does he believe she'll find a husband?
- Beatrice after line 31. Is Beatrice truly happy to stay single for the rest of her days?

1 **tartly** 尖酸刻薄
2 **I ... but** 我每次见到他必定
3 **heart-burned** 烧心，胃灼热
4 **melancholy disposition** 郁郁寡欢的性情
5 **image** 雕像
6 **my lady's eldest son** 娇生惯养的大少爷
7 **tattling** 喋喋不休
8 **foot / purse / will / horns** （均隐含有性暗示；见第28页）
9 **if a could** = if he could
10 **shrewd** 尖刻泼辣
11 **curst** = cursed （该死；心眼坏，脾气糟）
12 **lessen God's sending** 减少上帝的赐予
13 **Just** 就这样（这正是我想要的）
14 **for the which blessing** 为了这份福气
15 **at him** 向上帝祈祷
16 **the woollen** 让人感觉扎的粗羊毛毯
17 **light on** 找到，遇到
18 **apparel** 穿戴
19 **gentlewoman** 身份高贵的侍女
20 **in earnest of the bearward** 从耍狗熊的那里预先得到的赏钱（旧时耍熊的人也养猴子，老处女的下场据说是牵着猴子下地狱）

▼ An animated (活泼) Beatrice shares a drink and a joke with Leonato and Antonio in this 2007 National Theatre production.

Act 2 Scene 1
The great chamber of Leonato's house

Enter LEONATO, *his brother* ANTONIO, HERO *his daughter and* BEATRICE *his niece*

LEONATO	Was not Count John here at supper?
ANTONIO	I saw him not.
BEATRICE	How tartly[1] that gentleman looks, I never can see him but[2] I am heart-burned[3] an hour after.
HERO	He is of a very melancholy disposition[4].
BEATRICE	He were an excellent man that were made just in the mid-way between him and Benedick: the one is too like an image[5] and says nothing, and the other too like my lady's eldest son[6], evermore tattling[7].
LEONATO	Then half Signor Benedick's tongue in Count John's mouth, and half Count John's melancholy in Signor Benedick's face –
BEATRICE	With a good leg and a good foot[8], uncle, and money enough in his purse[8], such a man would win any woman in the world if a could[9] get her good will[8].
LEONATO	By my troth, niece, thou wilt never get thee a husband, if thou be so shrewd[10] of thy tongue.
ANTONIO	In faith, she's too curst[11].
BEATRICE	Too curst is more than curst, I shall lessen God's sending[12] that way: for it is said, God sends a curst cow short horns[8], but to a cow too curst, he sends none.
LEONATO	So, by being too curst, God will send you no horns.
BEATRICE	Just[13], if he send me no husband, for the which blessing[14] I am at him[15] upon my knees every morning and evening: Lord, I could not endure a husband with a beard on his face, I had rather lie in the woollen[16]!
LEONATO	You may light on[17] a husband that hath no beard.
BEATRICE	What should I do with him – dress him in my apparel[18] and make him my waiting gentlewoman[19]? He that hath a beard is more than a youth: and he that hath no beard is less than a man: and he that is more than a youth, is not for me, and he that is less than a man, I am not for him: therefore I will even take sixpence in earnest of the bearward[20], and lead his apes into hell.

Beatrice mockingly advises Hero on when and when not to obey her father in the matter of marriage. She then gives her own views of courtship, weddings and the regrets of life after a hasty marriage.

 剧情简介：碧翠以嘲讽的口吻指点希柔何时遵从、何时反对父亲安排她的婚姻。她还对求婚、婚礼、草率结婚导致终身遗憾等发表自己的看法。

Language in the play 剧中语言

Beatrice's 'foul language' (in pairs)

Elizabethans would have enjoyed the game of sexual innuendo (暗指) that Beatrice and Leonato play in lines 11–47. 'Will' (line 13) could mean lust or the sexual organs, and 'foot' (line 11) was a biblical euphemism (委婉说法) for the penis. 'Purse' (line 12), 'horns' (line 18) and 'fitted' (line 42) also possessed sexual overtones (言外之意).

a Read through the lines together, and try to emphasise the bawdy (下流) comedy through gestures, actions, cheeky (厚脸皮)/funny line delivery and strong emphasis on suggestive words. Afterwards, discuss what was most effective and rehearse the scene again with these points in mind.

b Perform your interpretation for another pair, and see if you can make them laugh! Watch the other pair's version and decide on the funniest parts of both your performances.

1 Beatrice the 'ladette' (假小子) and Hero the 'lady' (in fours)

Hero listens to all the raucous (刺耳的) wordplay of her cousin and father in near silence, but what is she thinking? Hero has been told that the prince will propose marriage to her this very evening. Will she accept? Why might she not dare to refuse?

Prepare a performance of lines 38–57 in which Hero breaks her silence. After each line, Hero should add her own comment to the audience, agreeing or disagreeing with what has been said and explaining the reasons for her opinion each time.

▶ Beatrice and Hero provide extreme examples of female personalities, whilst remaining great friends. What do you think they have in common? Try to find examples in the script of how they enjoy each other's company.

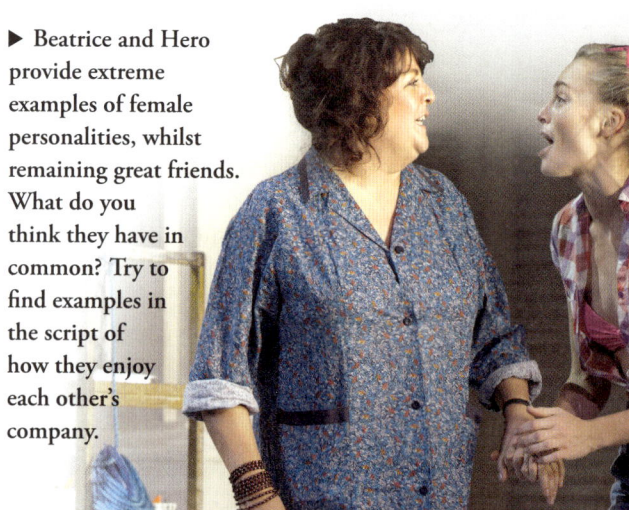

1 Saint Peter 圣彼得（天堂的门卫）
2 ruled 被管束
3 make curtsy 行屈膝礼
4 fitted 相配（有性暗示）
5 metal 材料，材质
6 earth / dust / clod / marl 土壤、尘土、土块、泥灰（指《圣经》里上帝用泥土造的第一个人亚当）
7 overmastered 受制于，被征服
8 Adam's sons （指所有男人）
9 brethren 兄弟（复数）
10 match in my kindred 与我的近亲结婚
11 solicit you in that kind 向您求婚
12 important 急不可耐
13 measure 适度，节制
14 Scotch jig 苏格兰快步舞
15 a measure 一种缓慢庄重的舞蹈
16 cinquepace 五步舞（读作 sink-apace，一种步速欢快的舞蹈）
17 the first suit 第一步（即求婚）
18 mannerly modest (as a measure) 姿态庄重（作为一种舞步）
19 state and ancientry 正式礼节和风俗习惯
20 passing shrewdly 极其犀利
21 revellers 赴宴者
22 make good room 让路

MUCH ADO ABOUT NOTHING ACT 2 SCENE 1
虚惊一场

LEONATO Well then, go you into hell.
BEATRICE No, but to the gate, and there will the devil meet me like an old cuckold with horns on his head, and say, get you to heaven, Beatrice, get you to heaven, here's no place for you maids. So deliver I up my apes, and away to Saint Peter[1]: for the heavens, he shows me where the bachelors sit, and there live we, as merry as the day is long.
ANTONIO Well, niece, I trust you will be ruled[2] by your father.
BEATRICE Yes faith, it is my cousin's duty to make curtsy[3], and say, father, as it please you: but yet for all that, cousin, let him be a handsome fellow, or else make another curtsy, and say, father, as it please me.
LEONATO Well, niece, I hope to see you one day fitted[4] with a husband.
BEATRICE Not till God make men of some other metal[5] than earth[6]: would it not grieve a woman to be overmastered[7] with a piece of valiant dust[6]? to make an account of her life to a clod[6] of wayward marl[6]? No, uncle, I'll none: Adam's sons[8] are my brethren[9], and truly I hold it a sin to match in my kindred[10].
LEONATO Daughter, remember what I told you: if the prince do solicit you in that kind[11], you know your answer.
BEATRICE The fault will be in the music, cousin, if you be not wooed in good time: if the prince be too important[12], tell him there is measure[13] in everything, and so dance out the answer. For hear me, Hero, wooing, wedding, and repenting, is as a Scotch jig[14], a measure[15] and a cinquepace[16]: the first suit[17] is hot and hasty like a Scotch jig (and full as fantastical), the wedding mannerly modest (as a measure)[18] full of state and ancientry[19], and then comes Repentance, and with his bad legs falls into the cinquepace faster and faster, till he sink into his grave.
LEONATO Cousin, you apprehend passing shrewdly[20].
BEATRICE I have a good eye, uncle, I can see a church by daylight.
LEONATO The revellers[21] are entering, brother, make good room[22].

[*Exit Antonio*]

Don Pedro, his friends and attendants enter wearing masks. The room fills with people and the masked dancing begins. As they dance, each woman uses the opportunity to mock her masked partner.

 剧情简介：唐佩卓和他的好友及随从戴着面具上场。房间里满是人，假面舞会正式开始。每位女士一边跳舞一边借机嘲笑戴着面具的舞伴。

Stagecraft 导演技巧
Masking (in small groups)

Masking was a favourite entertainment in great Elizabethan households. A group of masked male dancers would enter the chamber (hall) and take partners from the assembled guests. Shakespeare has filled his masked dance with ill-matched couples, and rotates (轮流) the dialogue between various couples as they dance.

This presents the director with some stagecraft challenges. In groups, discuss the following problems and feed back some creative solutions. Imagine you have all the technical opportunities a modern theatre provides. Your aim is to write director's notes for a funny, vibrant (热闹，有活力) and easily understandable mask sequence.

- How will the audience know which character is behind each mask? Will you have the actor lift their mask to the audience?
- There is clearly music playing. What type of music will you use, and how will you allow the audience to hear the dialogue over it?
- The action focuses on one pair at a time, but lots of couples are dancing. How will you draw the audience's attention to just one couple?

Write about it 写作练习
Hero speaks at last

So far, Hero has barely spoken to anyone, yet here (lines 61–70) she more than holds her own with Don Pedro, even daring, perhaps, to mock his bald head! Why is Hero so talkative with the prince, when she has until now been virtually silent in male company?

Expand upon the following points with your own ideas, supporting and explaining what you write by using quotations from lines 61–70.

- Hero is suddenly very talkative with the prince because …
- Hero mocks Don Pedro by …
- Hero's personality is shown to be …
- Line 65 suggests that Hero is …

1 **walk a bout** 跳一支舞
2 **So you** 只要您
3 **walk away** 挪步到一边
4 **in your company** 在您身旁
5 **favour** 脸，面孔
6 **God … case** 上帝不会让鲁特琴和琴盒一样不好看（意思是"我希望您本人比面具好看"）
7 **visor** 面具
8 **Philemon's roof** 费莱蒙的屋顶（费莱蒙和鲍西丝 [Baucis] 是古罗马诗人奥维德所著《变形记》里的一对老夫妇。一天，主神朱庇特与其子墨丘利伪装成乞丐出游，来到弗里吉亚 [Phrygia]，眼看天色已晚，便向当地居民借宿，不料到处都吃了闭门羹。最后他们来到一个房顶缺了不少茅草的茅屋跟前。主人费莱蒙夫妇虽然穷，却款待了他们，最后得到好报。）
9 **Jove** 乔武（即朱庇特，罗马诸神之王）
10 **thatched** 在屋顶加些茅草（可能暗指对方秃顶）
11 **ill qualities** 坏习惯，缺点
12 **clerk** 教堂执事（其职责是引领祈祷者附和祷告词）
13 **waggling** 摇摆
14 **counterfeit** 装扮成
15 **do him so ill-well** 把他的毛病学得这么像
16 **dry hand** 干瘪的手（上了年纪的标志）
17 **up and down** 到处，从上到下
18 **Go to, mum** 算了，别说了

Enter DON PEDRO, CLAUDIO, BENEDICK *and* BALTHASAR, *Maskers with a drum;* [*re-enter* ANTONIO, *masked, followed by*] DON JOHN [*and* BORACHIO *and others including* MARGARET *and* URSULA. *The dance begins*]

DON PEDRO Lady, will you walk a bout[1] with your friend?

HERO So you[2] walk softly, and look sweetly, and say nothing, I am yours for the walk, and especially when I walk away[3].

DON PEDRO With me in your company[4].

HERO I may say so when I please.

DON PEDRO And when please you to say so?

HERO When I like your favour[5], for God defend the lute should be like the case[6].

DON PEDRO My visor[7] is Philemon's roof[8], within the house is Jove[9].

HERO Why then your visor should be thatched[10].

DON PEDRO Speak low if you speak love.

[*They move on in the dance*]

[BALTHASAR] Well, I would you did like me.

MARGARET So would not I for your own sake, for I have many ill qualities[11].

[BALTHASAR] Which is one?

MARGARET I say my prayers aloud.

[BALTHASAR] I love you the better, the hearers may cry amen.

MARGARET God match me with a good dancer.

BALTHASAR Amen.

MARGARET And God keep him out of my sight when the dance is done: answer, clerk[12].

BALTHASAR No more words, the clerk is answered.

[*They move on in the dance*]

URSULA I know you well enough, you are Signor Antonio.

ANTONIO At a word, I am not.

URSULA I know you by the waggling[13] of your head.

ANTONIO To tell you true, I counterfeit[14] him.

URSULA You could never do him so ill-well[15], unless you were the very man: here's his dry hand[16] up and down[17], you are he, you are he.

ANTONIO At a word, I am not.

URSULA Come, come, do you think I do not know you by your excellent wit? Can virtue hide itself? Go to, mum[18], you are he, graces will appear, and there's an end.

[*They move on in the dance*]

Benedick, believing his true identity to be hidden behind his mask, teases Beatrice, who promptly turns the tables on him. Don John and Borachio tell Claudio that Don Pedro loves Hero and intends to marry her.

剧情简介：本尼迪相信其面具掩护着其真实身份，戏弄起碧翠来，碧翠迅速扭转局面。唐约翰和鲍拉丘告诉克劳丢，唐佩卓爱上了希柔，要娶她。

▼ Benedick reveals his true face – stung by Beatrice's words. Can you find the lines in the script opposite that may have provoked this response?

1 had = got
2 *The Hundred Merry Tales* 《笑话百则》（当时一本知名的笑话书）
3 What's he? = Who's he?
4 only his gift 他唯一的才能
5 devising 编造
6 impossible 难以置信
7 libertines 浪荡公子
8 villainy 无赖行为
9 angers them 惹怒他们（即拿他们开玩笑）
10 fleet 舰队（这里喻指人群）
11 boarded me 登我这艘船（有性暗指）
12 but … me 说两句俏皮话贬损我一通
13 peradventure = perhaps
14 marked 注意
15 partridge wing 山鹑翅膀（几乎没有肉）
16 amorous on 爱上
17 visor 戴面具的人
18 his bearing 他走路的姿态
19 dissuade him from 劝阻他
20 no equal for his birth 配不上他的出身

Stagecraft 导演技巧
What was that? (in large groups)

In movies and TV shows, we often see the plot quickly developing as the action jumps between conversations among groups of characters. Here, we see Shakespeare doing the same thing, as one conversation blurs into the next. We also see him attempting to recreate the feeling of a party – in this case, a masked dance. The start of the music and the end of the dancing help move characters around and off the stage.

Stage the party (lines 61–114) where we hear snippets (片段) of conversations. Use the director's notes you created in the Stagecraft activity on page 30. You might need actors to play more than one character, as there are a lot of people in this scene! Keep the actors moving, and think about the drama and the audience experience. Experiment with placing the various groups around the stage. Highlight certain conversations by 'turning the volume up and down', by freezing groups who are not speaking or by bringing groups to the front.

BEATRICE	Will you not tell me who told you so?	
BENEDICK	No, you shall pardon me.	
BEATRICE	Nor will you not tell me who you are?	
BENEDICK	Not now.	95
BEATRICE	That I was disdainful, and that I had[1] my good wit out of *The Hundred Merry Tales*[2]: well, this was Signor Benedick that said so.	
BENEDICK	What's he?[3]	
BEATRICE	I am sure you know him well enough.	
BENEDICK	Not I, believe me.	100
BEATRICE	Did he never make you laugh?	
BENEDICK	I pray you, what is he?	
BEATRICE	Why he is the prince's jester, a very dull fool, only his gift[4] is, in devising[5] impossible[6] slanders: none but libertines[7] delight in him, and the commendation is not in his wit, but in his villainy[8], for he both pleases men and angers them[9], and then they laugh at him, and beat him: I am sure he is in the fleet[10], I would he had boarded me[11].	105
BENEDICK	When I know the gentleman, I'll tell him what you say.	
BEATRICE	Do, do, he'll but break a comparison or two on me[12], which peradventure[13] (not marked[14], or not laughed at) strikes him into melancholy, and then there's a partridge wing[15] saved, for the fool will eat no supper that night. We must follow the leaders.	110
BENEDICK	In every good thing.	
BEATRICE	Nay, if they lead to any ill, I will leave them at the next turning.	

Music for the Dance. [*They Dance.*] *Exeunt* [*all but Don John, Borachio and Claudio*]

DON JOHN	Sure my brother is amorous on[16] Hero, and hath withdrawn her father to break with him about it: the ladies follow her, and but one visor[17] remains.	115
BORACHIO	And that is Claudio, I know him by his bearing[18].	
DON JOHN	Are not you Signor Benedick?	
CLAUDIO	You know me well, I am he.	120
DON JOHN	Signor, you are very near my brother in his love, he is enamoured on Hero, I pray you dissuade him from[19] her, she is no equal for his birth[20]: you may do the part of an honest man in it.	
CLAUDIO	How know you he loves her?	
DON JOHN	I heard him swear his affection.	125
BORACHIO	So did I too, and he swore he would marry her tonight.	
DON JOHN	Come, let us to the banquet.	

Exeunt Don John and Borachio

Claudio believes Don John's lie. Benedick also tells him that Don Pedro has won the heart of Hero. The unhappy Claudio creeps away, leaving Benedick smarting at the memory of Beatrice's taunting words.

 剧情简介：克劳丢信了唐约翰的谎言。本尼迪也说唐佩卓已赢得希柔的芳心。克劳丢黯然离去，留下本尼迪因为碧翠的奚落心酸不已。

1 Claudio feels sorry in verse (in fours)

Alone for a moment, Claudio reveals his thoughts in blank verse (see pp. 186–9). A character speaking alone on stage, seemingly to themselves, is a dramatic device known as **soliloquy** (独白).

a Read Claudio's soliloquy (lines 128–38) aloud in your group, handing over to the next person at a colon or full stop. Try reading through the lines a few times, in different ways: quickly and angrily, slowly and resignedly (无奈，勉强), full of anguish and despair.

b Afterwards, discuss which reading works best. Where do you think Claudio places the blame – on Don Pedro or on Hero?

2 Benedick feels sorry in prose (in fours)

In contrast, when Benedick is alone, he reveals his thoughts about Beatrice's words in ordinary prose. Shakespeare uses interesting punctuation in lines 154–9, breaking up the speech with colons.

a Read the speech aloud in your group, with a new speaker starting at each colon. To show how Benedick's mood seems to swing wildly through the speech, decide on the tone you will adopt for reading your section – this could be mocking, bitter, hurt, angry or something different. After your contribution, pause the performance and explain your interpretation to the rest of the group.

b Discuss the way this speech shifts in tone, and what that might be attempting to convey. How is punctuation used to shape the audience's impression of Benedick? What impact does it have on the potential comic effect of this speech?

Write about it 写作练习

Comparing Claudio and Benedick's soliloquies

Why do you think Shakespeare decided to use similar, but different, ways for these two characters to share their innermost thoughts? Write a short speech in which you explain your opinion. Consider in your writing:
- what thoughts Claudio and Benedick share with the audience
- why one character speaks in verse and one in prose
- why Shakespeare has set up this comparison.

Read your speech aloud to a small group, and compare responses and ideas.

---

1 **ill news** 坏消息
2 **office and affairs** 职务和事务
3 **agent** 中间人
4 **faith** 忠诚（对朋友）
5 **blood** 激情，情欲
6 **accident of hourly proof** 被反复证实的事情
7 **mistrusted not** 毫不怀疑
8 **the same** 正是
9 **Whither** = To which place; To whatever place
10 **willow** 垂柳（失恋的象征）
11 **county** = count（伯爵的昵称）
12 **garland** 花环（失恋者的标志）
13 **usurer's chain** 高利贷者的大粗金链子
14 **lieutenant's scarf** 军官的斜披带
15 **drovier** 牛贩子
16 **served** 对待
17 **fowl** 禽鸟
18 **sedges** 芦苇丛
19 **base (though bitter)** 卑鄙（不过令人痛心）
20 **puts … person** 她自认为代表全世界的人
21 **so gives me out** 把我说成这样

MUCH ADO ABOUT NOTHING ACT 2 SCENE 1
虚惊一场

CLAUDIO   Thus answer I in name of Benedick,
             But hear these ill news[1] with the ears of Claudio:
             'Tis certain so, the prince woos for himself,   130
             Friendship is constant in all other things,
             Save in the office and affairs[2] of love:
             Therefore all hearts in love use their own tongues.
             Let every eye negotiate for itself,
             And trust no agent[3]: for beauty is a witch,   135
             Against whose charms faith[4] melteth into blood[5]:
             This is an accident of hourly proof[6],
             Which I mistrusted not[7]: farewell therefore, Hero.

Enter BENEDICK

BENEDICK   Count Claudio.
CLAUDIO   Yea, the same[8].   140
BENEDICK   Come, will you go with me?
CLAUDIO   Whither[9]?
BENEDICK   Even to the next willow[10], about your own business, county[11]:
             what fashion will you wear the garland[12] of? About your neck, like an
             usurer's chain[13]? Or under your arm, like a lieutenant's scarf[14]? You   145
             must wear it one way, for the prince hath got your Hero.
CLAUDIO   I wish him joy of her.
BENEDICK   Why that's spoken like an honest drovier[15], so they sell bull-
             ocks: but did you think the prince would have served[16] you thus?
CLAUDIO   I pray you leave me.   150
BENEDICK   Ho now you strike like the blind man, 'twas the boy that stole
             your meat, and you'll beat the post.
CLAUDIO   If it will not be, I'll leave you.   *Exit*
BENEDICK   Alas poor hurt fowl[17], now will he creep into sedges[18]: but that my
             Lady Beatrice should know me, and not know me: the prince's fool!   155
             Hah, it may be I go under that title because I am merry: yea but so I
             am apt to do myself wrong: I am not so reputed, it is the base (though
             bitter)[19] disposition of Beatrice, that puts the world into her person[20],
             and so gives me out[21]: well, I'll be revenged as I may.

Benedick accuses Don Pedro of stealing Hero for himself, but the prince assures him that he has kept his promise to Claudio. Benedick angrily relates how cruelly Beatrice insulted him during the dance.

 剧情简介：本尼迪指责唐佩卓将希柔占为己有，但亲王向他保证自己遵守了对克劳丢的许诺。本尼迪愤愤地诉说碧翠在舞会上如何羞辱了他。

▲ Benedick genuinely believes that Don Pedro has taken Hero for himself. How happy is he with the prince's explanation (lines 177–8)? Use quotations from the script to support your answer.

Language in the play 剧中语言
Clash of the Classics

We are close to the climax of the feud (矛盾) between Benedick and Beatrice. Shakespeare uses references to Greek and Roman mythology (the Classics), with which his audience members would have been familiar, to add vivid imagery to Benedick's descriptions of his opponent (lines 190–7).

- Beatrice renders men powerless, just as the queen of Lydia enslaved the mighty Hercules (see pp. 183–4). In Beatrice's company, Benedick feels like a man used as target practice ('at a mark') by an army of archers.
- Beatrice is Ate, the goddess of discord (不和，纷争), who lived by the gates of hell. Benedick wants her 'conjured' back there. Men now sin deliberately ('upon purpose') just to be sent to hell and get out of Beatrice's way.

Use a library or the Internet to research these figures from mythology. Create a display or present your ideas to the class, so that others can learn about these ancient stories.

1. Troth 说实话
2. Lady Fame 长舌妇；谣言（文艺复兴时期戏剧中Lady Fame的服饰上画满舌头）
3. lodge in a warren 猎场中的小屋
4. willow 垂柳（枝条柔软，可以用来编筐、扎花环、绑东西、做藤鞭）
5. bind him up a rod 给他绑成一根藤鞭
6. flat transgression 明明白白的过错
7. amiss 白费，无用
8. bestowed on 献给，授予
9. past … block 超过了一个木头人的容忍度；即便是块木头也无法忍受
10. my very visor 甚至我的面具
11. duller than a great thaw 比雨后的稀泥还糊涂
12. impossible conveyance 难以置信的花言巧语
13. poniards 匕首
14. her terminations 她的用词
15. Adam … transgressed 在亚当犯错之前（《圣经》中亚当吃禁果而被逐出伊甸园）
16. turned spit 转动烤肉叉
17. cleft his club 把他的木棒劈了
18. infernal Ate 邪恶的阿苔（希腊神话中的邪恶和谬误女神，是天父宙斯[Zeus]和纷争女神厄蕊丝[Eris]的长女，平时穿得破破烂烂，能使神和人一时失去理智而铸成大错）
19. conjure 降服
20. sanctuary 提供庇护的圣所（原指教堂内供避难者藏身的最神圣的处所）
21. perturbation 动荡不安

Much Ado About Nothing Act 2 Scene 1
虚惊一场

Enter DON PEDRO

DON PEDRO Now, signor, where's the count, did you see him?

BENEDICK Troth[1], my lord, I have played the part of Lady Fame[2], I found him here as melancholy as a lodge in a warren[3]; I told him, and I think I told him true, that your grace had got the good will of this young lady, and I offered him my company to a willow[4] tree, either to make him a garland, as being forsaken, or to bind him up a rod[5], as being worthy to be whipped.

DON PEDRO To be whipped: what's his fault?

BENEDICK The flat transgression[6] of a schoolboy, who being overjoyed with finding a bird's nest, shows it his companion, and he steals it.

DON PEDRO Wilt thou make a trust a transgression? The transgression is in the stealer.

BENEDICK Yet it had not been amiss[7] the rod had been made, and the garland too, for the garland he might have worn himself, and the rod he might have bestowed on[8] you, who (as I take it) have stolen his bird's nest.

DON PEDRO I will but teach them to sing, and restore them to the owner.

BENEDICK If their singing answer your saying, by my faith, you say honestly.

DON PEDRO The Lady Beatrice hath a quarrel to you, the gentleman that danced with her told her she is much wronged by you.

BENEDICK Oh she misused me past the endurance of a block[9]: an oak but with one green leaf on it, would have answered her: my very visor[10] began to assume life, and scold with her: she told me, not thinking I had been myself, that I was the prince's jester, that I was duller than a great thaw[11], huddling jest upon jest, with such impossible conveyance[12] upon me, that I stood like a man at a mark, with a whole army shooting at me: she speaks poniards[13], and every word stabs: if her breath were as terrible as her terminations[14], there were no living near her, she would infect to the north star: I would not marry her, though she were endowed with all that Adam had left him before he transgressed[15]: she would have made Hercules have turned spit[16], yea, and have cleft his club[17] to make the fire too: come, talk not of her, you shall find her the infernal Ate[18] in good apparel. I would to God some scholar would conjure[19] her, for certainly, while she is here, a man may live as quiet in hell, as in a sanctuary[20], and people sin upon purpose, because they would go thither, so indeed all disquiet, horror and perturbation[21] follows her.

Benedick, in hugely extravagant fashion, leaves to avoid meeting Beatrice. She hints that they may have loved each other once. Don Pedro informs Claudio that he has won Hero's hand on Claudio's behalf.

 剧情简介：为躲避碧翠，本尼迪极其夸张地离去。碧翠透露他俩也许曾互有好感。唐佩卓告诉克劳丢，他已经成功地替他向希柔求了婚。

1 A 'merry war' no longer?

Some productions have made this a comic, yet painful, moment by showing Beatrice overhearing Benedick's long list of things he would rather do than meet with her (lines 199–208). The missions he asks Don Pedro to send him on are ridiculous, impossible and pointless. Is Benedick's use of **hyperbole** (exaggeration) funny or just hurtful? Does he go too far and protest too much?

a Try performing lines 199–217 in different ways, to bring out the comedy, or the pain, or both.

b What do you imagine is going through the minds of Beatrice and Benedick? Devise a short monologue for each character, exploring their thoughts at this point in the play.

2 How did the 'merry war' first start?

Sometimes an actor will prepare for a role by imagining their character's life history before the play. Shakespeare offers a tantalising (吊人胃口) glimpse of Beatrice and Benedick's 'pre-history' in lines 209–16.

a Make a list of what clues you think there are in these lines, and then discuss or create a mind map of an imagined 'back-story' for Beatrice and Benedick.

b Improvise or script a short scene showing this imagined 'back-story'.

1	command ... end 把我派到世界尽头做任何事
2	Antipodes 地球的另一边
3	tooth-picker 牙签
4	Prester John 祭司王约翰（中世纪传说中的一个统治者，信基督教，常被认定为阿比西尼亚 [今埃塞俄比亚] 国王）
5	Great Cham 大汗，蒙古王
6	embassage 差事
7	Pygmies 侏儒国
8	conference 谈话
9	Harpy 哈庇（希腊神话中的鹫身人面女怪，常用来比喻美丽但暗藏危险的人）
10	with false dice 做了手脚的骰子（指作弊）
11	put him down 把他压服（也有"交配"的意思）
12	wherefore = why
13	civil as an orange (civil与Seville谐音，Seville orange 是一种苦橙，橙色象征嫉妒)
14	blazon 描述，形容
15	conceit 想法
16	broke with her father 向她父亲提亲

▼ The feud between Beatrice and Benedick obviously causes them pain. Why are they so sensitive to each other's jibes (嘲笑)?

MUCH ADO ABOUT NOTHING ACT 2 SCENE 1
虚惊一场

Enter CLAUDIO *and* BEATRICE, LEONATO [*and*] HERO

DON PEDRO Look, here she comes.

BENEDICK Will your grace command me any service to the world's end[1]? I will go on the slightest errand now to the Antipodes[2] that you can devise to send me on: I will fetch you a tooth-picker[3] now from the furthest inch of Asia: bring you the length of Prester John's[4] foot: fetch you a hair off the Great Cham's[5] beard: do you any embassage[6] to the Pygmies[7], rather than hold three words conference[8] with this Harpy[9]: you have no employment for me? 200

205

DON PEDRO None, but to desire your good company.

BENEDICK Oh God, sir, here's a dish I love not, I cannot endure my Lady Tongue.   *Exit*

DON PEDRO Come, lady, come, you have lost the heart of Signor Benedick. 210

BEATRICE Indeed, my lord, he lent it me a while, and I gave him use for it, a double heart for his single one: marry once before he won it of me, with false dice[10], therefore your grace may well say I have lost it.

DON PEDRO You have put him down[11], lady, you have put him down.

BEATRICE So I would not he should do me, my lord, lest I should prove the mother of fools: I have brought Count Claudio, whom you sent me to seek. 215

DON PEDRO Why how now, count, wherefore[12] are you sad?

CLAUDIO Not sad, my lord.

DON PEDRO How then? Sick? 220

CLAUDIO Neither, my lord.

BEATRICE The count is neither sad, nor sick, nor merry, nor well: but civil, count, civil as an orange[13], and something of that jealous complexion.

DON PEDRO I'faith, lady, I think your blazon[14] to be true, though I'll be sworn, if he be so, his conceit[15] is false: here, Claudio, I have wooed in thy name, and fair Hero is won: I have broke with her father[16], and his good will obtained: name the day of marriage, and God give thee joy. 225

39

Claudio and Hero are formally betrothed. When Beatrice jokingly complains that she is the only one left without a husband, Don Pedro offers himself as a candidate for Beatrice's hand in marriage, but she refuses.

剧情简介：克劳丢与希柔正式订婚，碧翠戏称自己是唯一没有丈夫的女人，唐佩卓毛遂自荐，向碧翠求婚，但被她拒绝。

▲ Is this engagement a happy moment? Or does it feel more like a business transaction? Track the personal pronouns ('my', 'he', 'his' etc.) and the titles ('Count', 'Lady', 'cousin') to judge who is keen to impress whom.

1 his grace　殿下（对亲王的尊称）
2 all grace　上帝
3 'tis your cue　该您了（cue指演出时的提示）
4 dote upon　疯狂地爱
5 on the windy side of　远离（让船处在上风口以免遭袭击）
6 alliance　亲戚
7 goes … world　每人都有了归宿（结为夫妇）
8 sunburnt　晒伤；不招人喜欢
9 Heigh ho for a husband　哎哟喂，没有丈夫啊
10 getting　子嗣
11 beseech　乞求，恳求
12 mirth　说笑
13 no matter　没正经话
14 out a question　毫无疑问
15 star … born　当时有颗星星在跳舞，在那个星光下我出生了（即那颗跳舞的星星影响了她的性格）
16 I cry you mercy　对不起

Characters　人物分析

Beatrice, Princess of Arragon? (in pairs)

What happens between Beatrice and Don Pedro in lines 241–55? Depending on how these lines are played, and who is cast in the parts, the audience may interpret the lines in one of several different ways:

- As Beatrice flirts with Don Pedro, he makes a light-hearted proposal, which she gently turns down.
- Don Pedro makes a serious proposal, which Beatrice politely rejects.
- Don Pedro makes a serious proposal, which Beatrice bluntly, almost cruelly, turns down.
- Beatrice's boldness in inviting a prince to propose to her offends Don Pedro and she quickly has to apologise.

Decide which version you want to perform (as a class), making sure that at least one pair has chosen each version. Rehearse your scene, and then perform it in front of the other pairs. Watch the other performances, and afterwards discuss the positive and negative points of each interpretation.

LEONATO	Count, take of me my daughter, and with her my fortunes: his grace[1] hath made the match, and all grace[2] say amen to it.	230
BEATRICE	Speak, count, 'tis your cue[3].	
CLAUDIO	Silence is the perfectest herald of joy, I were but little happy if I could say, how much! Lady, as you are mine, I am yours: I give away myself for you, and dote upon[4] the exchange.	
BEATRICE	Speak, cousin, or (if you cannot) stop his mouth with a kiss, and let not him speak neither.	235
DON PEDRO	In faith, lady, you have a merry heart.	
BEATRICE	Yea, my lord, I thank it, poor fool it keeps on the windy side of[5] care: my cousin tells him in his ear that he is in her heart.	
CLAUDIO	And so she doth, cousin.	240
BEATRICE	Good Lord for alliance[6]: thus goes every one to the world[7] but I, and I am sunburnt[8], I may sit in a corner and cry, 'Heigh ho for a husband[9].'	
DON PEDRO	Lady Beatrice, I will get you one.	
BEATRICE	I would rather have one of your father's getting[10]: hath your grace ne'er a brother like you? Your father got excellent husbands, if a maid could come by them.	245
DON PEDRO	Will you have me, lady?	
BEATRICE	No, my lord, unless I might have another for working-days, your grace is too costly to wear every day: but I beseech[11] your grace pardon me, I was born to speak all mirth[12], and no matter[13].	250
DON PEDRO	Your silence most offends me, and to be merry, best becomes you, for out a question[14], you were born in a merry hour.	
BEATRICE	No sure, my lord, my mother cried, but then there was a star danced, and under that was I born[15]: cousins, God give you joy.	255
LEONATO	Niece, will you look to those things I told you of?	
BEATRICE	I cry you mercy[16], uncle: by your grace's pardon. *Exit*	

The marriage of Hero and Claudio is set for a week ahead. In the meantime, Don Pedro proposes some entertainment for them all. He has a plan to trick Beatrice and Benedick into falling in love with each other.

剧情简介：克劳丢与希柔的婚礼定在一周之后。唐佩卓建议大家消遣一下，他要设计使碧翠和本尼迪爱上对方。

1 'There's little of the melancholy element in her'
(in pairs)

Many Elizabethans still held to the ancient belief that there were four **humours** (体液), fluids that controlled temperaments, in the human body. They defined four types of personality, depending on the predominant humour:

Melancholy (黑胆汁) (cold and dry): cold, gloomy, depressed (melancholic [抑郁质])

Choler (黄胆汁) (hot and dry): angry, quarrelsome, violent (choleric [胆汁质])

Phlegm (黏液) (cool and moist): cool, sluggish (迟缓), apathetic (phlegmatic [黏液质])

Blood (warm and moist): warm, hopeful, confident (sanguine [多血质])

Do Shakespeare's characters suggest combinations of certain humours? Write an 'ingredients list' (for example, one part choler/four parts blood) for some of the characters, and find lines in the play to support your claims as to how much of each humour you need to add.

▶ In this image, how does Don Pedro convey that he is a man of great power and passion? Why do you think he inspires loyalty in others?

Characters 人物分析

Don Pedro's power and charisma (个人魅力) (in small groups)

Don Pedro dominates this section of the play. His powers of persuasion have succeeded in bringing Hero and Claudio together, and in lines 274–92 he vows to do the same for Beatrice and Benedick. He seems to be a man who inspires people's affections and loyalty.

a Identify at least three words in lines 258–92 that highlight Don Pedro's power and status. Compare your choices with others in the group.

b Perform lines 258–92 as a group. Use body language, facial expressions and tone of voice to emphasise Don Pedro's charm and the other characters' devoted admiration. Stress the 'power words' that you identified in part **a** of this activity.

---

1 **melancholy element** 忧郁的性格倾向
2 **out of suit** 不敢追求她
3 **time goes on crutches** 时间拄着拐杖走（走得慢）
4 **rites** 结婚的所有仪式（rites与rights "[丈夫的] 权利"谐音）
5 **a just seven-night** 刚好一周
6 **answer my mind** 像我想的那样安排好
7 **breathing** 歇口气
8 **Hercules' labours** 派给大神赫丘力的任务
9 **fain** 高兴
10 **fashion it** 促成，使之成为可能
11 **minister such assistance** 提供这种帮助
12 **ten nights' watchings** 十个晚上不睡觉
13 **office** 任务
14 **noble strain** 出身高贵
15 **approved valour** 有目共睹的勇猛
16 **humour** 顺着……行事
17 **practise on** 在……身上设计
18 **queasy stomach** 羸弱的脾胃
19 **my drift** 我的计策

Much Ado About Nothing Act 2 Scene 1
虚惊一场

DON PEDRO By my troth a pleasant spirited lady.

LEONATO There's little of the melancholy element[1] in her, my lord, she is never sad, but when she sleeps, and not ever sad then: for I have heard my daughter say, she hath often dreamed of unhappiness, and waked herself with laughing.

DON PEDRO She cannot endure to hear tell of a husband.

LEONATO Oh by no means, she mocks all her wooers out of suit[2].

DON PEDRO She were an excellent wife for Benedick.

LEONATO Oh Lord, my lord, if they were but a week married, they would talk themselves mad.

DON PEDRO County Claudio, when mean you to go to church?

CLAUDIO Tomorrow, my lord: time goes on crutches[3], till love have all his rites[4].

LEONATO Not till Monday, my dear son, which is hence a just seven-night[5], and a time too brief too, to have all things answer my mind[6].

DON PEDRO Come, you shake the head at so long a breathing[7], but I warrant thee, Claudio, the time shall not go dully by us. I will in the interim undertake one of Hercules' labours[8], which is, to bring Signor Benedick and the Lady Beatrice into a mountain of affection, th'one with th'other: I would fain[9] have it a match, and I doubt not but to fashion it[10], if you three will but minister such assistance[11] as I shall give you direction.

LEONATO My lord, I am for you, though it cost me ten nights' watchings[12].

CLAUDIO And I, my lord.

DON PEDRO And you too, gentle Hero?

HERO I will do any modest office[13], my lord, to help my cousin to a good husband.

DON PEDRO And Benedick is not the unhopefullest husband that I know: thus far can I praise him, he is of a noble strain[14], of approved valour[15], and confirmed honesty. I will teach you how to humour[16] your cousin, that she shall fall in love with Benedick, and I, with your two helps, will so practise on[17] Benedick, that in despite of his quick wit, and his queasy stomach[18], he shall fall in love with Beatrice: if we can do this, Cupid is no longer an archer, his glory shall be ours, for we are the only love-gods. Go in with me, and I will tell you my drift[19].

Exeunt

Don John's first plot against Claudio has failed. Borachio now proposes a much more dishonest scheme that will convince Claudio and Don Pedro that Hero is having an affair with another man.

剧情简介：唐约翰针对克劳丢的第一个计策失败。鲍拉丘提出更阴损的计谋：让克劳丢和唐佩卓相信希柔与他人有染。

Language in the play 剧中语言
Dark tones

Whilst Beatrice and Benedick's friends are planning some innocent amusement at their expense, Don John and Borachio have a more unpleasant aim – to ruin Hero's honour. This darker purpose is reflected in the language that Shakespeare uses in this scene.

a Write down all the 'evil' or 'villainous' words used in the script opposite. Decide which of the two men is the greater villain, and why.

b Find words relating to sickness or death that Don John and Borachio use as they discuss their plan.

Stagecraft 导演技巧
Villainy here, but where and when?

It seems that Shakespeare provided few or no stage directions for his plays; if he did, many of them have not survived. Ever since the first appearance of his plays in print, in the Folios (对开本) and Quarto (四开本) editions, editors have been helping readers and performers by adding suggestions about settings. Some argue that the lack of strict, 'official' guidance from Shakespeare is one of the reasons that his plays have proved so versatile (灵活) to adaptation. It allows each director and his or her company to stamp their own interpretation on the performance.

Neither the time nor the setting for this scene was made clear in early editions of the play. It is suggested in this script that it takes place in and around Leonato's residence, but it could be inside Leonato's house, in his garden, or outside in the street. Nor is it clear whether the action follows on immediately from the end of Scene 1, or whether some time has elapsed.

a Read the final lines of the previous scene (lines 287–92) together with the opening lines of this scene (lines 1–10). Does it matter where the new scene is set? Why do you think this? Decide where and when this scene should take place, and write down the reasons behind your decision.

b Sketch what you imagine as the setting for this scene. Support your ideas with references to the script. When you have finished, compare your sketches in a small group.

1 **cross it** 阻止它
2 **be medicinable to me** 对我有疗效，让我感到舒服
3 **sick in displeasure** 极其厌恶
4 **comes athwart his affection** 阻挠他愿望的实现
5 **ranges evenly with mine** 令我满意
6 **covertly** 隐秘
7 **since** = ago
8 **unseasonable** 不合适
9 **temper** 混合，调配
10 **whose … up** 他的美德您大加颂扬（大大抬高他的身价）
11 **contaminated stale** 染病的雏儿（娼妇）
12 **misuse** 欺瞒
13 **vex** 令……懊恼
14 **issue** 后果
15 **despite** 恶意伤害

Act 2 Scene 2
Leonato's house

Enter DON JOHN *and* BORACHIO

DON JOHN It is so, the Count Claudio shall marry the daughter of Leonato.

BORACHIO Yea, my lord, but I can cross it[1].

DON JOHN Any bar, any cross, any impediment, will be medicinable to me[2], I am sick in displeasure[3] to him, and whatsoever comes athwart his affection[4], ranges evenly with mine[5]. How canst thou cross this marriage?

BORACHIO Not honestly, my lord, but so covertly[6], that no dishonesty shall appear in me.

DON JOHN Show me briefly how.

BORACHIO I think I told your lordship a year since[7], how much I am in the favour of Margaret, the waiting gentlewoman to Hero.

DON JOHN I remember.

BORACHIO I can at any unseasonable[8] instant of the night, appoint her to look out at her lady's chamber window.

DON JOHN What life is in that to be the death of this marriage?

BORACHIO The poison of that lies in you to temper[9]; go you to the prince your brother, spare not to tell him, that he hath wronged his honour in marrying the renowned Claudio, whose estimation do you mightily hold up[10], to a contaminated stale[11], such a one as Hero.

DON JOHN What proof shall I make of that?

BORACHIO Proof enough, to misuse[12] the prince, to vex[13] Claudio, to undo Hero, and kill Leonato; look you for any other issue[14]?

DON JOHN Only to despite[15] them I will endeavour anything.

Borachio's plan is that he and Margaret will appear on the night before the wedding at Hero's bedroom window. They will call each other Hero and Claudio, so deceiving the watching Don Pedro and Claudio.

剧情简介：鲍拉丘的计策是婚礼前夜他和玛格蕊在希柔卧室的窗前相会，互称对方希柔和克劳丢，骗过暗中观察的唐佩卓和克劳丢。

Themes 主题分析

Deception: a complex plan (in pairs)

In lines 25–37, Borachio outlines a detailed plan. Don John will fool Don Pedro and Claudio into believing Hero is unfaithful, and not a virgin. The plan, like the speech, is quite complex. In order for it to work in practice, Borachio has to give very precise instructions to Don John. This conversation can sound odd, as it appears that Don John is being given orders by his own follower. In order for the speech to work dramatically, the plan has to be clear to the audience.

a Identify the command words (imperatives) that Borachio uses with Don John here. How confident do you think Borachio should appear when delivering these? Should he convey caution or confidence? Experiment by speaking them in different ways.

b In your pair, try performing this scene in two different ways: firstly, excitedly and full of passionate energy; then more slowly and conspiratorially. Discuss which approach seems the most effective and conveys the planned deception most clearly to the audience.

1 meet 合适
2 intend 假装您有
3 zeal 热诚
4 as in love of 好像您很关心
5 made this match 做这个媒
6 like to be 将要
7 cozened with 被骗
8 the semblance of a maid 假冒的黄花闺女
9 trial 证据，证明
10 instances 证据
11 likelihood 合乎情理
12 term me Claudio 叫我克劳丢（造成希柔和另一男人取笑克劳丢的假象）
13 fashion the matter 布这个局
14 jealousy shall be called assurance 怀疑就会变成确定不疑
15 preparation overthrown 婚礼的准备就会落空
16 ducats 达克（一种曾在欧洲通用的金币）
17 constant 一口咬定，坚定不移

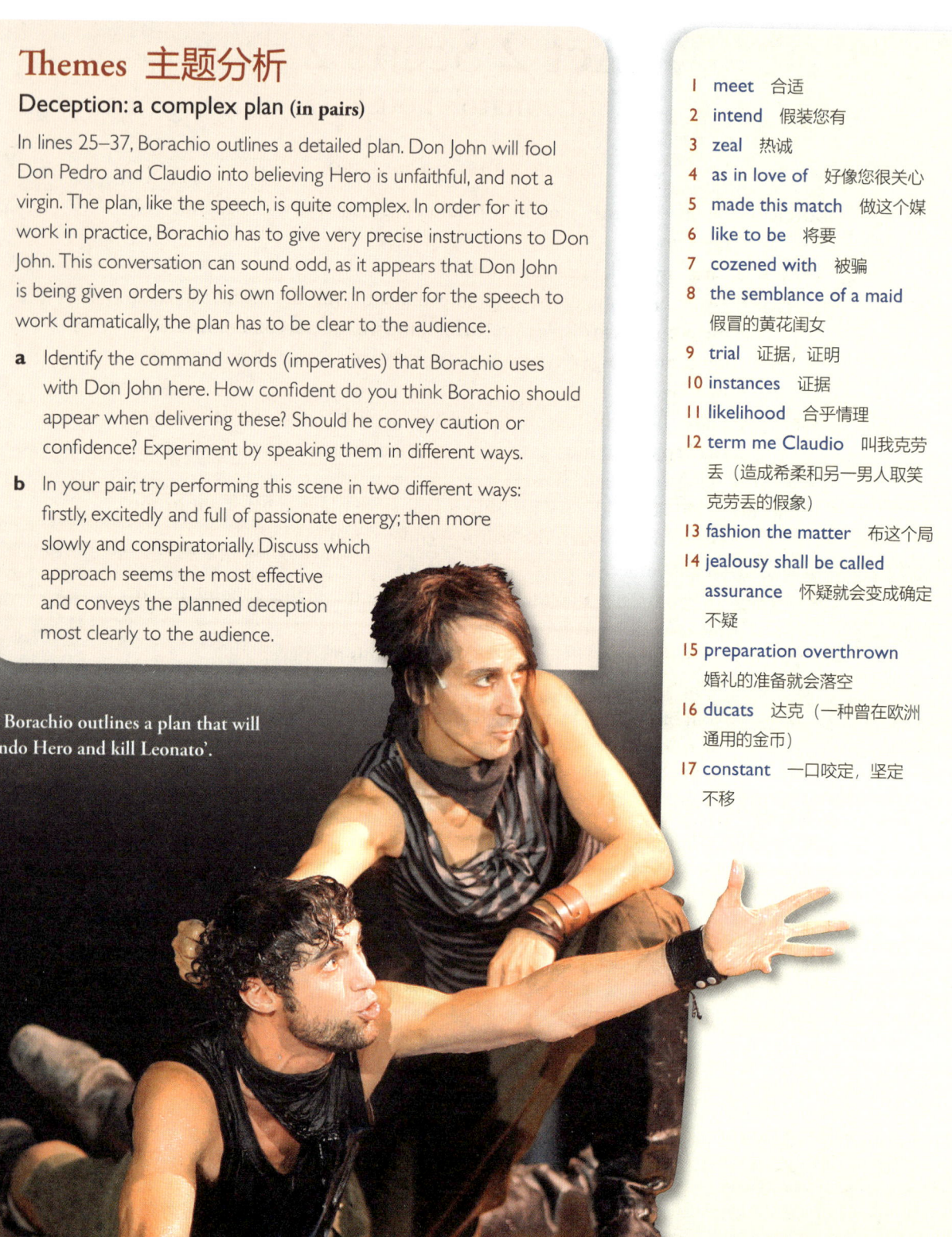

▶ Borachio outlines a plan that will 'undo Hero and kill Leonato'.

MUCH ADO ABOUT NOTHING ACT 2 SCENE 2
虚惊一场

BORACHIO Go then, find me a meet¹ hour to draw Don Pedro and the Count Claudio alone, tell them that you know that Hero loves me, intend² a kind of zeal³ both to the prince and Claudio (as in love of⁴ your brother's honour who hath made this match⁵, and his friend's reputation, who is thus like to be⁶ cozened with⁷ the semblance of a maid⁸) that you have discovered thus: they will scarcely believe this without trial⁹: offer them instances¹⁰ which shall bear no less likelihood¹¹, than to see me at her chamber window, hear me call Margaret Hero, hear Margaret term me Claudio¹², and bring them to see this the very night before the intended wedding, for in the mean time, I will so fashion the matter¹³, that Hero shall be absent, and there shall appear such seeming truth of Hero's disloyalty, that jealousy shall be called assurance¹⁴, and all the preparation overthrown¹⁵.

DON JOHN Grow this to what adverse issue it can, I will put it in practice: be cunning in the working this, and thy fee is a thousand ducats¹⁶.

BORACHIO Be you constant¹⁷ in the accusation, and my cunning shall not shame me.

DON JOHN I will presently go learn their day of marriage.

Exeunt

Benedick muses on men like Claudio who say they will not fall in love and then do so. He lists the many virtues he would require in a future wife. When the prince, Claudio and Leonato approach, Benedick hides.

剧情简介：本尼迪揣摩着克劳丢那种男人，嘴上说不会坠入爱情，却说一套做一套。他罗列一大堆未来妻子应有的美德。唐佩卓、克劳丢、列纳托走近，本尼迪藏了起来。

Stagecraft 导演技巧

When does the Boy return? (in small groups)

The script does not tell us when the Boy returns from his errand. Some productions have set up a running joke as the Boy chases through scene after scene vainly attempting to deliver Benedick's book.

a After reading through this whole scene, decide as a group where the Boy might most amusingly attempt to give Benedick his book.

b Stage mime scenes or tableaux (定格；活人画) showing various versions of the Boy's interruptions.

▼ Benedick is confident that he is immune to the power of love. In lines 18–21, he wonders if one day he too might fall in love, then quickly dismisses the idea. Do you think that his smugness (自命清高) provokes his friends' trickery?

1 hither = to this place
2 am here already 马上去办（下一句中本尼迪按字面义理解）
3 behaviours 情绪和行为
4 argument 对象
5 the drum and the fife 战鼓和军笛（指军乐）
6 the tabor and the pipe 泰伯鼓（军队行进或节日庆典活动中用的小鼓）和管乐（指平和音乐）
7 armour 盔甲
8 carving 设计
9 doublet 小双衣（流行于伊丽莎白时代的男士紧身上衣，有的带短裙）
10 wont 习惯
11 turned orthography 变得咬文嚼字，拿腔捏调
12 fantastical 梦幻般
13 oyster 牡蛎（关进牡蛎壳里郁郁寡欢、沉默不语）
14 well 不为所动
15 come in my grace 赢得我的好感
16 cheapen 出价买
17 noble 诺贝尔（英国旧币名称，值三分之一镑金质君主币，双关语，也有"高贵"的意思）
18 angel 安吉尔（英国旧币名称，值二分之一镑金质君主币，双关语，也有"天使"的意思）
19 discourse 言谈
20 Monsieur Love 恋爱先生（本尼迪故意用具有浪漫之称的法语嘲讽恋爱中的克劳丢）

Act 2 Scene 3
Leonato's orchard

Enter BENEDICK *alone*

BENEDICK Boy.

BOY [*within*] Signor.

[*Enter* BOY]

BENEDICK In my chamber window lies a book, bring it hither[1] to me in the orchard.

BOY I am here already[2], sir.

BENEDICK I know that, but I would have thee hence and here again.

Exit [*Boy*]

I do much wonder, that one man seeing how much another man is a fool, when he dedicates his behaviours[3] to love, will after he hath laughed at such shallow follies in others, become the argument[4] of his own scorn, by falling in love: and such a man is Claudio. I have known when there was no music with him but the drum and the fife[5], and now had he rather hear the tabor and the pipe[6]: I have known when he would have walked ten mile afoot, to see a good armour[7], and now will he lie ten nights awake carving[8] the fashion of a new doublet[9]: he was wont[10] to speak plain and to the purpose (like an honest man and a soldier) and now is he turned orthography[11], his words are a very fantastical[12] banquet, just so many strange dishes: may I be so converted and see with these eyes? I cannot tell, I think not: I will not be sworn but love may transform me to an oyster[13], but I'll take my oath on it, till he have made an oyster of me, he shall never make me such a fool: one woman is fair, yet I am well[14]: another is wise, yet I am well: another virtuous, yet I am well: but till all graces be in one woman, one woman shall not come in my grace[15]: rich she shall be, that's certain: wise, or I'll none: virtuous, or I'll never cheapen[16] her: fair, or I'll never look on her: mild, or come not near me: noble[17], or not I for an angel[18]: of good discourse[19], an excellent musician – and her hair shall be of what colour it please God. Hah! the prince and Monsieur Love[20], I will hide me in the arbour.

Don Pedro, Claudio and Leonato pretend not to notice the hidden Benedick. They prepare to listen to Balthasar's singing. Benedick is not impressed by the romantic music.

剧情简介：唐佩卓、克劳丢和列纳托假装没看见藏起来的本尼迪，他们开始听巴尔特扎唱歌。本尼迪并不欣赏这浪漫音乐。

▲ How might the hidden Benedick respond to the romantic chatter and musical sentimentality (see Balthasar holding a lute) he hears from his friends?

1 hushed 安静
2 grace harmony 喜爱的音乐
3 the music ended 音乐结束
4 pennyworth 小便宜
5 tax not 不要责备
6 slander 侮辱，糟蹋
7 the witness still 总是证明
8 put a strange face on 假装不承认
9 suit 求婚
10 in notes = in musical notes （用乐谱）
11 Note 注意
12 notes 乐谱，曲调
13 a note of mine 我的一个乐符
14 noting 注意
15 crotchets 音符
16 Note notes 注意乐谱或曲调
17 forsooth 确实，实在
18 ravished 被夺走，忘乎所以
19 sheep's guts 羊肠（鲁特琴的弦是用羊肠制作的）
20 hale 拖拽，用力拉
21 horn 狩猎号

Language in the play 剧中语言

Benedick's poetic friends (in pairs)

Knowing Benedick is hidden nearby, the prince and his friends speak poetic blank verse as befits the love-obsessed characters they are pretending to be (lines 30–49).

a Write down your favourite romantic line/phrase from the script opposite, plus a line that you think is decidedly unromantic. Give reasons for your choices. Compare these with your partner.

b The unromantic Benedick interrupts in prose when Balthasar is about to sing (line 50), saying 'now is his soul ravished [overcome with pleasure]'. In your pair, decide to whom he might be referring and what that character could have done to prompt Benedick's sardonic (讥讽的) outburst. Share your conclusions with another pair, and discuss any differences in opinion.

Much Ado About Nothing Act 2 Scene 3
虚惊一场

Enter DON PEDRO, LEONATO, CLAUDIO [*and* BALTHASAR *with*] *music*

DON PEDRO	Come, shall we hear this music?	
CLAUDIO	Yea, my good lord: how still the evening is,	30
	As hushed[1] on purpose to grace harmony[2]!	
DON PEDRO	See you where Benedick hath hid himself?	
CLAUDIO	Oh very well, my lord: the music ended[3],	
	We'll fit the kid-fox with a pennyworth[4].	
DON PEDRO	Come, Balthasar, we'll hear that song again.	35
BALTHASAR	Oh, good my lord, tax not[5] so bad a voice,	
	To slander[6] music any more than once.	
DON PEDRO	It is the witness still[7] of excellency,	
	To put a strange face on[8] his own perfection:	
	I pray thee sing, and let me woo no more.	40
BALTHASAR	Because you talk of wooing I will sing,	
	Since many a wooer doth commence his suit[9],	
	To her he thinks not worthy, yet he woos,	
	Yet will he swear he loves.	
DON PEDRO	Nay, pray thee come,	
	Or if thou wilt hold longer argument,	45
	Do it in notes[10].	
BALTHASAR	Note[11] this before my notes[12],	
	There's not a note of mine[13] that's worth the noting[14].	
DON PEDRO	Why these are very crotchets[15] that he speaks,	
	Note notes[16] forsooth[17], and nothing.	
	[*Music*]	
BENEDICK	Now divine air, now is his soul ravished[18]: is it not strange that sheep's guts[19] should hale[20] souls out of men's bodies? Well, a horn[21] for my money when all's done.	50

Balthasar sings his song about the fickleness of men. He is sent by Don Pedro to prepare the music that will be used to serenade Hero at her chamber window the next night.

 剧情简介：巴尔特扎歌唱男人的变化无常。他被唐佩卓派去准备小夜曲，第二天晚上到希柔的闺房窗下歌唱。

1 'Sigh no more, ladies, sigh no more'
(in small groups)

Shakespeare often uses music and song in his plays, always with the purpose of intensifying dramatic effect. But why should he put a song here just when the audience wants to see how Benedick will be fooled? Try some or all of the following activities:

a **Men are faithless and deceitful** Deception is a major preoccupation of the play. Speak the song, taking a line each.

- Which lines echo this theme, and how will Benedick, Claudio, Don Pedro and Leonato all be deceived?
- List the many examples of deception practised so far in the play. Have they all been perpetrated (犯下) by men?

b **Sing the song!** Compose an appropriate tune for this song. One of you sings the first verse, while the others listen in role as one of the characters. Then all of you sing the second verse together. Talk about the emotions your song evokes.

c **Is the song sung well?** Decide how impressed Don Pedro and Benedick are with Balthasar's singing (lines 69–75). If you were producing the play, would you have the song sung well or badly? Talk about:

- the effect of a movingly beautiful song heard at this moment
- the comic effect that bad singing would create.

d Pool your ideas and devise a presentation to provide at least four reasons why Shakespeare included lines 29–80. Use the script carefully to support your points. You might even perform the song to prove your point!

---

1 **blithe and bonny** 欢声笑语
2 **hey nonny nonny** （这是为了押韵而编的无意义语句）
3 **ditties** 快活的歌曲
4 **no mo** = no more
5 **dumps** 难过、伤心的曲子
6 **fraud** 背信弃义，不忠诚
7 **leavy** = leafy （枝繁叶茂）
8 **for a shift** 还算凑合
9 **And he** = If he
10 **bode** 预示
11 **had as lief** 宁愿
12 **night-raven** 半夜叫的乌鸦（叫声刺耳，预示疾病或死亡）

MUCH ADO ABOUT NOTHING ACT 2 SCENE 3
虚惊一场

The Song

[BALTHASAR]   Sigh no more, ladies, sigh no more,
    Men were deceivers ever,
One foot in sea, and one on shore,   55
    To one thing constant never.
Then sigh not so, but let them go,
    And be you blithe and bonny[1],
Converting all your sounds of woe,
    Into hey nonny nonny[2].   60

Sing no more ditties[3], sing no mo[4],
    Of dumps[5] so dull and heavy,
The fraud[6] of men was ever so,
    Since summer first was leavy[7].
Then sigh not so, but let them go,   65
    And be you blithe and bonny,
Converting all your sounds of woe,
    Into hey nonny nonny.

DON PEDRO By my troth a good song.
BALTHASAR And an ill singer, my lord.   70
DON PEDRO Ha, no no faith, thou sing'st well enough for a shift[8].
BENEDICK And he[9] had been a dog that should have howled thus, they would have hanged him: and I pray God his bad voice bode[10] no mischief, I had as lief[11] have heard the night-raven[12], come what plague could have come after it.   75
DON PEDRO Yea marry, dost thou hear, Balthasar? I pray thee get us some excellent music: for tomorrow night we would have it at the Lady Hero's chamber window.
BALTHASAR The best I can, my lord.
DON PEDRO Do so, farewell.   80
                      Exit Balthasar

Don Pedro and the others begin their deception of Benedick. They talk about how Beatrice is madly in love with Benedick, but is too frightened to tell him of her secret passion.

 剧情简介：唐佩卓他们开始捉弄本尼迪，说碧翠如何疯狂地爱着本尼迪，却不敢向他表露内心隐藏的激情。

Stagecraft 导演技巧

The fooling of Benedick (in small groups)

The trick ('gull') Benedick's friends play on him makes marvellous theatre. To get a first impression, and to see if their plot works, read through lines 81–213. Then explore Benedick's reactions.

a Various productions of the play have different, inventive ways of hiding Benedick on the stage. In one version, Benedick pretended to be a gardener clipping a hedge. In another production, he hid in a tree and peered through the foliage (枝叶). He puffed smoke from his cigar, coughed, choked, and at one point fell out of the tree! Decide how you would 'hide' Benedick so that your audience can still see his reactions (surprise, anger, pleasure, curiosity, hurt). Sketch a rough stage design to show how this would work.

b Suggest ways that modern lighting or sound effects could be used to enhance this scene. Could Benedick's reactions be amplified or filmed in such a way to add impact?

c When preparing your version of lines 81–213, show the enjoyment of Benedick's friends as they set about their plan. Make a note of which lines the plotters whisper to themselves, and which they say deliberately loudly for Benedick's benefit.

d Choose a location in your school or college that would be suitable for an open-air performance of this scene. If you can get permission, have a go at performing the scene there. Where could you most originally and amusingly hide Benedick? Remember, the audience needs to both see and hear him.

1 aye = yes
2 stalk … sits 悄悄往前走，鸟已经停落
3 dote on 爱慕，爱恋
4 ever to abhor 一直讨厌
5 Sits … corner? 真有这回事吗？
6 enraged affection 炽热的爱情
7 it … thought 令人难以置信但的确是真的
8 counterfeit 假装
9 near the life of passion 近似真情实感
10 discovers 展示，揭示
11 gull 计谋，骗局
12 knavery 诡计
13 reverence 尊贵
14 ta'en th'infection 中计
15 hold it up 继续
16 oft = often
17 scorn 轻视，藐视
18 smock 衬裙，内衣

Much Ado About Nothing Act 2 Scene 3

虚惊一场

Come hither, Leonato, what was it you told me of today, that your niece Beatrice was in love with Signor Benedick?

CLAUDIO Oh aye[1], stalk on, stalk on, the fowl sits[2]. I did never think that lady would have loved any man.

LEONATO No nor I neither, but most wonderful, that she should so dote on[3] Signor Benedick, whom she hath in all outward behaviours seemed ever to abhor[4].

BENEDICK Is't possible? Sits the wind in that corner?[5]

LEONATO By my troth, my lord, I cannot tell what to think of it, but that she loves him with an enraged affection[6], it is past the infinite of thought[7].

DON PEDRO May be she doth but counterfeit[8].

CLAUDIO Faith like enough.

LEONATO Oh God! Counterfeit? There was never counterfeit of passion, came so near the life of passion[9] as she discovers[10] it.

DON PEDRO Why what effects of passion shows she?

CLAUDIO Bait the hook well, this fish will bite.

LEONATO What effects, my lord? She will sit you – you heard my daughter tell you how.

CLAUDIO She did indeed.

DON PEDRO How, how, I pray you! You amaze me, I would have thought her spirit had been invincible against all assaults of affection.

LEONATO I would have sworn it had, my lord, especially against Benedick.

BENEDICK I should think this a gull[11], but that the white-bearded fellow speaks it: knavery[12] cannot sure hide himself in such reverence[13].

CLAUDIO He hath ta'en th'infection[14], hold it up[15].

DON PEDRO Hath she made her affection known to Benedick?

LEONATO No, and swears she never will, that's her torment.

CLAUDIO 'Tis true indeed, so your daughter says: shall I, says she, that have so oft[16] encountered him with scorn[17], write to him that I love him?

LEONATO This says she now when she is beginning to write to him, for she'll be up twenty times a night, and there will she sit in her smock[18], till she have writ a sheet of paper: my daughter tells us all.

85

90

95

100

105

110

115

55

Don Pedro and the others talk about Beatrice's many fine qualities. They express their fear that Benedick will mock her if he learns of her great love for him.

剧情简介：唐佩卓和其他人说起碧翠的种种美好品德。他们担心本尼迪一旦得知碧翠对他的热恋，会对她大加嘲讽。

Language in the play 剧中语言

Lay it on with a trowel (镘子，抹泥刀)

The list is one of Shakespeare's favourite language techniques. In lines 126–8, he has Claudio go comically over the top describing Beatrice's lovesick misery.

Read these lines aloud, stressing the details that the lists add to Claudio's speech.

Characters 人物分析

Does Don Pedro love Beatrice? (in fours)

Don Pedro seems to have it all, but he does not have a wife. He has already asked Beatrice to marry him (Act 2 Scene 1, lines 241–8). Was he serious then? And is he again in lines 144–5 opposite, when he says that he wishes Beatrice were in love with him? If so, why does he go to such great lengths to trick Benedick? If the prince were played as genuinely being in love with Beatrice, how would that affect your perception of his character and hers?

a In your groups, improvise conversations between Don Pedro and a confidant (密友，知己), and Beatrice and a friend.

b Improvise these scenes again, but with each character revealing their motives and feelings in **asides** (旁白) to the imagined audience. The other characters do not hear these, and so should not react to them – perhaps they could freeze during the asides.

1 sheet 纸张；床单
2 halfpence 半便士；碎片
3 railed 大喊大叫
4 flout 嘲笑
5 ecstasy 狂热
6 overborn her 控制了她，压倒了她
7 by some other 从别人那里
8 make … it 只会拿它开玩笑
9 And he should 如果他竟然
10 alms 善事，善行
11 out of all suspicion 毫无疑问
12 blood 血气，激情
13 dotage 痴情
14 daffed all other respects 不再考虑其他任何可能
15 bate 放弃，减少
16 tender 提出，拿出
17 contemptible 心怀蔑视

◀ Benedick hangs around in amazement as his 'friends' criticise him. Which comment in particular do you think provoked this response?

Much Ado About Nothing Act 2 Scene 3
虚惊一场

CLAUDIO   Now you talk of a sheet[1] of paper, I remember a pretty jest your daughter told us of.

LEONATO   Oh when she had writ it, and was reading it over, she found Benedick and Beatrice between the sheet. 120

CLAUDIO   That.

LEONATO   Oh she tore the letter into a thousand halfpence[2], railed[3] at herself, that she should be so immodest to write to one that she knew would flout[4] her: I measure him, says she, by my own spirit, for I should flout him, if he writ to me, yea, though I love him I should. 125

CLAUDIO   Then down upon her knees she falls, weeps, sobs, beats her heart, tears her hair, prays, curses, Oh sweet Benedick, God give me patience.

LEONATO   She doth indeed, my daughter says so, and the ecstasy[5] hath so much overborn her[6], that my daughter is sometime afeared she will do a desperate outrage to herself, it is very true. 130

DON PEDRO   It were good that Benedick knew of it by some other[7], if she will not discover it.

CLAUDIO   To what end? He would make but a sport of it[8], and torment the poor lady worse. 135

DON PEDRO   And he should[9], it were an alms[10] to hang him: she's an excellent sweet lady, and (out of all suspicion[11]) she is virtuous.

CLAUDIO   And she is exceeding wise.

DON PEDRO   In everything but in loving Benedick.

LEONATO   Oh my lord, wisdom and blood[12] combating in so tender a body, we have ten proofs to one, that blood hath the victory: I am sorry for her, as I have just cause, being her uncle, and her guardian. 140

DON PEDRO   I would she had bestowed this dotage[13] on me, I would have daffed all other respects[14], and made her half myself: I pray you tell Benedick of it, and hear what a will say. 145

LEONATO   Were it good, think you?

CLAUDIO   Hero thinks surely she will die, for she says she will die, if he love her not, and she will die ere she make her love known, and she will die if he woo her, rather than she will bate[15] one breath of her accustomed crossness. 150

DON PEDRO   She doth well: if she should make tender[16] of her love, 'tis very possible he'll scorn it, for the man (as you know all) hath a contemptible[17] spirit.

Don Pedro, Claudio and Leonato leave, hoping they have completed their deception of Benedick. Don Pedro orders a similar trick to be played on Beatrice by Hero and her attendant gentlewomen.

✒ **剧情简介**：唐佩卓、克劳丢、列纳托离开，寄希望于他们已经让本尼迪上当。唐佩卓令希柔和服侍她的贵妇给碧翠也设一个类似的骗局。

▲ This is how one actor showed Benedick's reaction to what he overheard. He is shocked, but completely convinced! Think of four reasons why he might believe what his friends have 'revealed'.

1 proper 英俊
2 outward happiness 让人喜爱的外表
3 valiant 勇敢
4 Hector 赫克托（特洛伊英雄）
5 a must = he must
6 howsoever 尽管，无论
7 by … make 从他那些粗俗的笑话看
8 wear it out 把心中的爱情磨掉
9 with good counsel 好言相劝
10 wear her heart out first 先把她的心磨尽
11 dote on her 向她示爱
12 never trust my expectation 不再相信我的预见力
13 same net spread 撒下同样的网（狩猎术语）
14 another's dotage 另一方的痴情
15 no such matter 实际上没这回事
16 merely a dumb show 只是一场哑剧（双方都不说话）

Themes 主题分析

Insults and anger (in pairs)

This scene is a good example of the difference between how things *appear* to a character and how they really are. Don Pedro is having great fun pretending to insult Benedick. All the while, Benedick is both fuming with anger and astonished at what he is hearing about Beatrice. In some productions, Benedick is shown to be barely able to stop himself leaping out and punching Don Pedro!

a List all the ways that Don Pedro insults Benedick in lines 155–72. Perform a short sequence with your partner, in which one of you speaks Don Pedro's insults and the other uses facial expressions to show Benedick's angry reactions.

b Write a short imagined letter of response from Benedick. It should outline the ways in which Don Pedro's words have insulted Benedick's 'Elizabethan-age' understanding of the masculine ideal.

MUCH ADO ABOUT NOTHING ACT 2 SCENE 3
虚惊一场

CLAUDIO   He is a very proper¹ man.   155
DON PEDRO   He hath indeed a good outward happiness².
CLAUDIO   Before God, and in my mind, very wise.
DON PEDRO   He doth indeed show some sparks that are like wit.
LEONATO   And I take him to be valiant³.
DON PEDRO   As Hector⁴, I assure you, and in the managing of quarrels   160
            you may say he is wise, for either he avoids them with great discre-
            tion, or undertakes them with a most christianlike fear.
LEONATO   If he do fear God, a must⁵ necessarily keep peace: if he break
            the peace, he ought to enter into a quarrel with fear and trembling.
DON PEDRO   And so will he do, for the man doth fear God, howsoever⁶ it   165
            seems not in him, by some large jests he will make⁷: well, I am sorry
            for your niece: shall we go seek Benedick, and tell him of her love?
CLAUDIO   Never tell him, my lord, let her wear it out⁸ with good counsel⁹.
LEONATO   Nay that's impossible, she may wear her heart out first¹⁰.
DON PEDRO   Well, we will hear further of it by your daughter, let it cool   170
            the while: I love Benedick well, and I could wish he would modestly
            examine himself, to see how much he is unworthy so good a lady.
LEONATO   My lord, will you walk? Dinner is ready.
CLAUDIO   If he do not dote on her¹¹ upon this, I will never trust my
            expectation¹².   175
DON PEDRO   Let there be the same net spread¹³ for her, and that must
            your daughter and her gentlewomen carry: the sport will be, when
            they hold one an opinion of another's dotage¹⁴, and no such matter¹⁵:
            that's the scene that I would see, which will be merely a dumb show¹⁶:
            let us send her to call him in to dinner.   180

                                      [*Exeunt all but Benedick*]

Benedick is convinced that Beatrice loves him and resolves to return her affection. When she reluctantly appears to call him to dinner, he looks for some sign of love in her and, amazingly, finds one!

剧情简介：本尼迪确信碧翠爱他，决定回报她这份情。当碧翠极不情愿地出现在他面前请他赴宴时，他察言观色，看能否发现碧翠暗恋他的蛛丝马迹，令人惊奇的是他竟然发现了！

Characters 人物分析

Benedick swallows the bait (in small groups)

Some actors speak Benedick's soliloquy (lines 181–200) as if trying to rationalise their sudden commitment to Beatrice. Others seem bewildered, or react with barely concealed delight. Some of the many possibilities are:

- **'This can be no trick'** Benedick's opening five words can be said in several different ways (e.g. with delight, smug self-satisfaction, horror or solemn certainty), depending on the actor's interpretation of the character's mood at this time.
- **'I hear how I am censured'** When saying lines 184–8 (to 'mending'), actors play with how mature and honest Benedick is in response to his friends' criticisms.
- **'they say the lady is fair'** Beatrice suddenly seems a most desirable woman, and so lines 188–92 (to 'horribly in love with her') are delivered with utter conviction (信心十足).
- **'I may chance have … '** Benedick realises he will now be the butt of many jokes and so rehearses his defences in lines 192–8.

Discuss which of Benedick's remarks you think the audience will find the funniest, and why. Share your ideas with another group.

1. the conference was sadly borne 谈话很严肃
2. have their full bent （像拉弓一样）被拉到最大程度
3. requited 回报
4. censured 评判
5. detractions 错误
6. put them to mending 改正这些错误
7. reprove 不赞同
8. odd quirks 老掉牙的笑话
9. remnants 剩余部分
10. meat 食物
11. quips 讽刺打趣的俏皮话
12. sentences 名句，格言
13. paper bullets of the brain 纸质子弹（指闲言碎语）
14. awe 威吓，震慑
15. career 路线，道路
16. humour 倾向，爱好
17. choke a daw 堵寒鸦的嘴（寒鸦就像八哥，会模仿人说话）
18. stomach （打架的）欲望
19. Jew 犹太佬（当时犹太人常被认为冷酷无情、不可信任，含有种族歧视的意味；参见第184页）

▶ The last time they met, Benedick called Beatrice a 'Harpy' (Act 2 Scene 1, line 204). Use this photo to describe to a partner what sort of mood Beatrice is in when she is sent to collect him. In what ways does Benedick seem like a changed man?

Much Ado About Nothing Act 2 Scene 3
虚惊一场

BENEDICK This can be no trick, the conference was sadly borne[1], they have the truth of this from Hero, they seem to pity the lady: it seems her affections have their full bent[2]: love me? Why, it must be requited[3]: I hear how I am censured[4], they say I will bear myself proudly, if I perceive the love come from her: they say too, that she will rather die than give any sign of affection: I did never think to marry, I must not seem proud, happy are they that hear their detractions[5], and can put them to mending[6]: they say the lady is fair, 'tis a truth, I can bear them witness: and virtuous, 'tis so, I cannot reprove[7] it: and wise, but for loving me: by my troth it is no addition to her wit, nor no great argument of her folly, for I will be horribly in love with her: I may chance have some odd quirks[8] and remnants[9] of wit broken on me, because I have railed so long against marriage: but doth not the appetite alter? A man loves the meat[10] in his youth, that he cannot endure in his age. Shall quips[11] and sentences[12], and these paper bullets of the brain[13] awe[14] a man from the career[15] of his humour[16]? No, the world must be peopled. When I said I would die a bachelor, I did not think I should live till I were married – here comes Beatrice: by this day, she's a fair lady, I do spy some marks of love in her.

Enter BEATRICE

BEATRICE Against my will I am sent to bid you come in to dinner.

BENEDICK Fair Beatrice, I thank you for your pains.

BEATRICE I took no more pains for those thanks, than you took pains to thank me, if it had been painful I would not have come.

BENEDICK You take pleasure then in the message.

BEATRICE Yea, just so much as you may take upon a knife's point, and choke a daw[17] withal: you have no stomach[18], signor, fare you well. *Exit*

BENEDICK Ha, against my will I am sent to bid you come in to dinner: there's a double meaning in that: I took no more pains for those thanks than you took pains to thank me: that's as much as to say, any pains that I take for you is as easy as thanks: if I do not take pity of her I am a villain, if I do not love her I am a Jew[19], I will go get her picture. *Exit*

Much Ado About Nothing
虚惊一场

Looking back at Act 2 第2幕回顾
Activities for groups or individuals

1 'Act 2 in two' – breaking down the plot

Act 2 is when the plot really begins to thicken and the various deceptions and tricks are established. It is important at this point that we make sense of all the different layers of the plot.

a Select ten lines (or words) and events that you think are key to the development of the plot in Act 2.

b Use these chosen lines and events to develop a two-minute sequence – 'Act 2 in two' – that provides an overview of the act. You can use improvised tableaux, mimes and other creative staging techniques.

2 Your thoughts on Beatrice and Benedick

Beatrice seems victorious in the battle of wits (Act 2 Scene 1, lines 103–7) when she calls Benedick 'the prince's jester'. She may feel less happy when Benedick later retaliates (反击), branding her a 'Harpy' (Act 2 Scene 1, lines 199–208).

a In pairs, devise two different mimes of these moments. Show the feelings of Beatrice and Benedick, using body language and facial expressions.

b Look back at Benedick's reaction on overhearing that Beatrice is secretly in love with him (Act 2 Scene 3, lines 181–214). Write a short paragraph about Benedick, listing the admirable husband-like qualities he reveals. Suggest why he was so easily duped (愚弄) by his friends.

3 Plots, patterns and connections

Two pairs of lovers, two pairs of brothers, two conventional lovers, two unconventional lovers, two male friends, two female friends, two benevolent (善意) plots, two malevolent (恶意) plots … and so much more! Oppositions, pairings and patterns in the play are becoming clearer.

a Develop a sequence of profile cards for the main characters in Act 2, containing basic information about them. You might base these cards upon the type of 'profiles' people give themselves on social networking websites.

b In groups, place these cards on a board or upon a wall and use string, or draw lines, to 'connect' them to each other. Who are close 'friends', who are 'pairs', who are 'enemies'? Explore creative ways of using these profile cards to show the patterns and connections between the different characters.

4 Make 'em laugh!

Act 2 Scene 3 is often considered to be the funniest scene in the play. There are many ways of staging the scene to make it inventive and humorous.

a Find as many types of verbal and visual humour as you can in Act 2. Look for witty or bitter wordplay, comic insults, sexual innuendoes and embarrassing situations, as well as further slapstick (滑稽) comedy possibilities (in one production, when Beatrice stormed off the dance floor, Benedick was reduced to grabbing a small child for a partner).

b Choose and list your five favourite funny moments, lines or jokes from Act 2.

c In writing, describe how comedic value may be added by different directors and actors. Refer to actions or intonations that they could add to the lines to emphasise the comedy in Shakespeare's language.

LOOKING BACK AT ACT 2

This image sums up much of the playfulness in Beatrice and Benedick's relationship. The director of this production, set in India, has placed them on a swing in order to emphasise the childish nature of their feud. Which line from Act 2 do you think Beatrice might be delivering here?

Hero begins her plan to trick Beatrice. Margaret is sent to tell Beatrice that Hero and Ursula are in the orchard talking about her. Beatrice steals in to eavesdrop on their conversation.

剧情简介：希柔开始实施蒙骗碧翠的计策。玛格蕊被派去告诉碧翠，希柔和阿秀拉正在果园里谈论她。碧翠悄悄溜进果园偷听她们的谈话。

Characters 人物分析
A new Hero

Up to this point, Hero has been rather overshadowed by her cousin Beatrice. Shakespeare uses this scene to allow the quiet, dutiful Hero to suddenly blossom. Playwrights often use different settings and scenes to allow characters to show different sides to their personality. These developments of the character maintain the interest of the audience.

Identify and list three new things that we discover about Hero from her two speeches in the script opposite.

Stagecraft 导演技巧
Giving notes

The transformation of Hero presents challenges for the director and actor. What is the motivation for this change? How can it be acted so that it seems believable for the character? How can the development be signalled in the preceding and following scenes?

Write notes for the actor playing Hero in this scene. As well as using the questions above as sub-headings, give the actor some guidance on her possible thoughts, actions and tone of delivery.

1. Proposing 交谈，聊天
2. Ursley = Ursula
3. steal into 轻手轻脚溜进
4. pleachèd bower 两旁树枝交织在一起的林荫道
5. honeysuckles 金银花，忍冬
6. favourites 宠臣
7. that power 君权
8. propose 谈话
9. trace 走，散步
10. let it be thy part 你的任务就是
11. crafty 精巧，巧妙
12. by hearsay 用听来的话
13. lapwing 田凫（又称凤头麦鸡，觅食时紧贴地面引颈向前寻找昆虫；这里比喻碧翠蹑手蹑脚地打算藏身于隐蔽处；此类比喻用法见第66页）

* blocking 戏台调度，指导演对演员在戏台上的动作进行的设计和安排，包括演员与演员、演员与戏台景物之间的相对位置及其变化。

1 'Blocking'* the scene (in threes)

'Blocking' is the technical term for deciding where the actors will stand at particular points. The director should move the actors around the stage ('block' their movement) to accentuate (突出，强调) their words and make the scene exciting.

Two of you take the parts of Hero and Margaret in the orchard, and one of you directs the scene. In the distance is the house where Beatrice and the men are. As Hero slowly reads lines 1–25, she must point clearly to every place and person mentioned. For example:

> Good Margaret (*point to Margaret*), run thee (*point again to Margaret*) to the parlour (*point to door*), / There shalt thou (*point to Margaret*) find my (*point to self*) cousin Beatrice.

Act out the scene in front of an audience, and ask them how effective this 'blocking' was in adding clarity and drama to the performance.

Much Ado About Nothing Act 3 Scene 1
虚惊一场

Act 3 Scene 1
The orchard

Enter HERO *and two gentlewomen,* MARGARET *and* URSULA

HERO   Good Margaret, run thee to the parlour,
There shalt thou find my cousin Beatrice,
Proposing[1] with the prince and Claudio,
Whisper her ear and tell her I and Ursley[2]
Walk in the orchard, and our whole discourse   5
Is all of her, say that thou overheard'st us,
And bid her steal into[3] the pleachèd bower[4],
Where honeysuckles[5] ripened by the sun,
Forbid the sun to enter: like favourites[6],
Made proud by princes, that advance their pride,   10
Against that power[7] that bred it: there will she hide her,
To listen our propose[8]: this is thy office,
Bear thee well in it, and leave us alone.

MARGARET   I'll make her come I warrant you, presently.   *Exit*

HERO   Now, Ursula, when Beatrice doth come,   15
As we do trace[9] this alley up and down,
Our talk must only be of Benedick:
When I do name him, let it be thy part[10],
To praise him more than ever man did merit:
My talk to thee must be how Benedick   20
Is sick in love with Beatrice: of this matter
Is little Cupid's crafty[11] arrow made,
That only wounds by hearsay[12]: now begin,

Enter BEATRICE

For look where Beatrice like a lapwing[13] runs
Close by the ground, to hear our conference.   25

65

Beatrice, thinking herself unobserved, listens in on Hero and Ursula's conversation. They talk of Benedick's 'love' for Beatrice, and Hero expresses concern about Beatrice's proud and scornful nature.

剧情简介：碧翠以为自己没有被发现，偷听希柔和阿秀菈说话。她们说起本尼迪对碧翠的"爱"，希柔表示她为碧翠傲慢自大的个性担忧。

Language in the play 剧中语言
Bird imagery

When tricking Benedick, the men spoke largely in lively prose, a more natural medium for a comic 'gulling'. These women, however, speak entirely in imagery-rich verse, as if love were too serious a matter for riotous (狂欢的) comedy. In lines 24–5, Hero compares Beatrice to a lapwing, a bird that searches for food by running along close to the ground, stopping and leaning forward to look for insects, then running on again.

a Write a brief explanation of what this metaphor suggests about the way Beatrice reaches her hiding place.

b In lines 35–6, Hero says that Beatrice's spirits are 'as coy [disdainful] and wild, / As haggards of the rock'. A 'haggard' is a wild female hawk, which is far more difficult to train than one reared in captivity. What do you think Hero means by this image? Consider the negative connections it could suggest. What might these lines reveal about the attitudes towards women in Shakespeare's time?

c Identify the other 'creature image' used in lines 26–58 to describe Beatrice. Write an explanation of how these images present her character, and suggest how easy or difficult you think it will be to trick her.

Stagecraft 导演技巧
Beatrice's reactions (in threes, then whole class)

Some productions create a more serious mood by 'hiding' Beatrice in full view of the audience, so they can see her pained reaction to her friends' criticism.

a Stage lines 26–58 so that Beatrice's expressions and gestures can be seen by the audience. Show her by turns shocked, guilty, puzzled, dismayed, angry and delighted. Present your version to the rest of the class.

b As a class, discuss how this 'gulling' mixes seriousness and humour. Would it work if it was entirely straight-faced, or played only for laughs?

1 angling 钓鱼
2 couchèd 躲藏
3 woodbine 忍冬属的一种灌木，类似金银花
4 coverture 遮蔽处，隐藏处
5 coy 高傲轻蔑
6 haggard 雌野鹰（这种鹰很难驯服，比喻碧翠平时高傲的气质；这种比喻用法同第65页的 lapwing）
7 trothèd 订婚的，有婚约的
8 bid 请求
9 entreat 乞求，请求
10 acquaint 告知
11 wish him wrestle with 愿他与……搏斗
12 as full … bed 上天赐福的婚床（指幸福快乐的婚姻）
13 couch 躺下
14 framed 塑造，造就
15 Misprising 低估，看不起
16 weak 无聊，乏味
17 take … affection 表现出任何爱意
18 self-endeared 自满，以自我为中心
19 lest … sport 以免她拿它开玩笑

Much Ado About Nothing Act 3 Scene 1
虚惊一场

URSULA	The pleasant'st angling[1] is to see the fish
	Cut with her golden oars the silver stream,
	And greedily devour the treacherous bait:
	So angle we for Beatrice, who even now,
	Is couchèd[2] in the woodbine[3] coverture[4]. 30
	Fear you not my part of the dialogue.
HERO	Then go we near her, that her ear lose nothing
	Of the false sweet bait that we lay for it:
	No truly, Ursula, she is too disdainful,
	I know her spirits are as coy[5] and wild, 35
	As haggards[6] of the rock.
URSULA	But are you sure,
	That Benedick loves Beatrice so entirely?
HERO	So says the prince, and my new trothèd[7] lord.
URSULA	And did they bid[8] you tell her of it, madam?
HERO	They did entreat[9] me to acquaint[10] her of it, 40
	But I persuaded them, if they loved Benedick,
	To wish him wrestle with[11] affection,
	And never to let Beatrice know of it.
URSULA	Why did you so? Doth not the gentleman
	Deserve as full as fortunate a bed[12], 45
	As ever Beatrice shall couch[13] upon?
HERO	Oh God of love! I know he doth deserve,
	As much as may be yielded to a man:
	But nature never framed[14] a woman's heart
	Of prouder stuff than that of Beatrice: 50
	Disdain and scorn ride sparkling in her eyes,
	Misprising[15] what they look on, and her wit
	Values itself so highly, that to her
	All matter else seems weak[16]: she cannot love,
	Nor take no shape nor project of affection[17], 55
	She is so self-endeared[18].
URSULA	Sure I think so,
	And therefore certainly it were not good,
	She knew his love, lest she'll make sport at it[19].

Hero and Ursula talk about how Beatrice will never admit the true worth of any man, and how she would mock Benedick unmercifully if she knew he loved her. They then praise Benedick's virtues.

剧情简介：希柔和阿秀菈谈论起碧翠永远不会承认男人的真正价值，说她一旦得知本尼迪爱自己，一定会无情地嘲笑他。接着她们又赞美起本尼迪的优点。

1 Beatrice: No pleasing her! (in fours)

In lines 59–70, Hero says that Beatrice loves to 'spell backward' every man she meets, which suggests that she ridicules them by turning their virtues into faults. The examples Hero gives of physical attributes many find attractive, but Beatrice would turn into flaws are: the fair-faced (light-complexioned), the black (dark-complexioned), the tall, the low (short), the speaking, the silent.

Improvise a short imagined scene in which Hero introduces a range of different men to Beatrice in the style of a speed-dating evening. After Hero enthusiastically describes each man's qualities, Beatrice should turn these positive attributes into reasons why he is unsuitable. You could use some of the examples from lines 59–70 as a starting point.

Themes 主题分析

Deception: 'How much an ill word may empoison liking'

Lines 84–6, with their reference to 'honest' (harmless) deceptions and 'ill' (slanderous) words poisoning 'liking' (affection), are an ominous reminder for the audience of Don John and Borachio's plot in Act 2 Scene 2 to ruin Hero's reputation. Here we see Hero herself engaging in a more harmless deception, but using somewhat similar language and imagery to suggest a 'poisoning'. Turn back to Act 2 Scene 2 and find the 'poison' imagery that Hero's words unwittingly echo here.

a Draw up a table like the one below to list examples of both 'harmful' and 'harmless' deceptions in the play so far. Identify a quotation for each example.

Harmful ('ill') deceptions	Harmful ('ill') quotations	Harmless ('honest') deceptions	Harmless ('honest') quotations

b In groups, discuss how Shakespeare uses language to demonstrate the differences between harmful deceptions and the more harmless ones.

---

1 **rarely** 稀有，难得
2 **spell him backward** 反过来看他（即把他的优点看成缺点）
3 **antic** 丑八怪
4 **blot** 污点，瑕疵
5 **lance ill-headed** 银样镴枪头
6 **agate** 玛瑙
7 **vilely cut** 拙劣地雕刻
8 **vane** 风向标
9 **gives** 允许；承认
10 **simpleness** 淳朴
11 **purchaseth** 应得
12 **carping** 挑毛病
13 **from all fashions** 与所有人都不合拍
14 **press me** 压倒我
15 **waste** 缩小，减弱
16 **counsel** 建议，劝
17 **honest** 无辜
18 **empoison** = destroy
19 **Always excepted** 除了，不包括

Much Ado About Nothing Act 3 Scene 1
虚惊一场

HERO	Why you speak truth, I never yet saw man,
	How wise, how noble, young, how rarely[1] featured,
	But she would spell him backward[2]: if fair-faced,
	She would swear the gentleman should be her sister:
	If black, why Nature drawing of an antic[3],
	Made a foul blot[4]: if tall, a lance ill-headed[5]:
	If low, an agate[6] very vilely cut[7]:
	If speaking, why a vane[8] blown with all winds:
	If silent, why a block moved with none:
	So turns she every man the wrong side out,
	And never gives[9] to truth and virtue, that
	Which simpleness[10] and merit purchaseth[11].
URSULA	Sure, sure, such carping[12] is not commendable.
HERO	No, not to be so odd, and from all fashions[13],
	As Beatrice is, cannot be commendable:
	But who dare tell her so? If I should speak,
	She would mock me into air, oh she would laugh me
	Out of myself, press me[14] to death with wit:
	Therefore let Benedick like covered fire,
	Consume away in sighs, waste[15] inwardly:
	It were a better death, than die with mocks,
	Which is as bad as die with tickling.
URSULA	Yet tell her of it, hear what she will say.
HERO	No rather I will go to Benedick,
	And counsel[16] him to fight against his passion,
	And truly I'll devise some honest[17] slanders,
	To stain my cousin with, one doth not know
	How much an ill word may empoison[18] liking.
URSULA	Oh do not do your cousin such a wrong,
	She cannot be so much without true judgement,
	Having so swift and excellent a wit,
	As she is prized to have, as to refuse
	So rare a gentleman as Signor Benedick.
HERO	He is the only man of Italy,
	Always excepted[19] my dear Claudio.

After more praise of Benedick, Hero and Ursula go inside to choose Hero's head-dress for tomorrow's wedding. Beatrice is amazed by what she has heard, and resolves to return Benedick's love.

 剧情简介：希柔和阿秀菈继续夸了本尼迪一通后，进屋挑选次日婚礼上希柔的头饰。听了这些话，碧翠非常吃惊，决定回报本尼迪的爱。

Stagecraft 导演技巧

A Beatrice for the time (in threes)

Shakespeare's writing reflects the social and literary influences of his time. Similarly, the ways that his plays are performed often reflect contemporary tastes. In the early nineteenth century, Beatrice's final soliloquy (lines 107–16) was often given a comic flavour to parallel Benedick's conversion in Act 2 Scene 3. Most modern Beatrices have instead used it to reveal the serious and tender side of her character. Complete the activities below to explore how this scene might be played.

a Take it in turns to speak Beatrice's soliloquy in different ways (e.g. shocked, deeply moved, comically romantic). Discuss which is the most effective, and why.

b Beatrice speaks for the first time in verse. Does her soliloquy resemble an Elizabethan love **sonnet** (小歌，十四行诗) in any way (see p. 189)? Work out the **quatrain** (四行诗节，四行诗) and **couplet** (对句，二行连句) rhyme patterns, and remember that 'I' and '-ly' rhymed in Elizabethan times. Do you think Beatrice is consciously, or perhaps even self-consciously and ironically, speaking in a changed style? Explore how you might show this in performance.

c Compare your interpretations with another group. If you have arrived at different ideas, why do you think that this is?

1 Speaking my fancy　恕我直言
2 shape　体形
3 bearing　姿势，举止
4 argument　谈吐
5 every day tomorrow　明日之后永远
6 attires　衣服
7 furnish　装扮
8 limed　粘住，钩上
9 by haps　偶然
10 adieu　再见
11 No … such　这种行为没有什么可称道的
12 incite thee　鼓励你
13 band　婚约，婚姻
14 reportingly　听别人说的

Write about it 写作练习

Mirroring scenes

Beatrice's response to what she has overheard is very similar to Benedick's (Act 2 Scene 3, lines 181–200). But why are they similar and yet different? Draw a table to organise your ideas – two suggestions are given below, along with an example quote for Beatrice, but add more to develop a detailed picture.

	Beatrice	Benedick
Belief in what they hear	'What fire is in mine ears?'	
Fear being mocked for being in love		

Once you have your ideas, write 200 words answering the question: How does Shakespeare compare and contrast Beatrice and Benedick's reactions to the idea that they are secretly admired?

MUCH ADO ABOUT NOTHING ACT 3 SCENE 1
虚惊一场

URSULA	I pray you be not angry with me, madam,
	Speaking my fancy[1]: Signor Benedick,	95
	For shape[2], for bearing[3], argument[4] and valour,
	Goes foremost in report through Italy.
HERO	Indeed he hath an excellent good name.
URSULA	His excellence did earn it, ere he had it:
	When are you married, madam?	100
HERO	Why every day tomorrow[5]: come go in,
	I'll show thee some attires[6], and have thy counsel,
	Which is the best to furnish[7] me tomorrow.
URSULA	She's limed[8] I warrant you, we have caught her, madam.
HERO	If it prove so, then loving goes by haps[9],	105
	Some Cupid kills with arrows, some with traps.

Exeunt Hero and Ursula

BEATRICE	What fire is in mine ears? Can this be true?
	Stand I condemned for pride and scorn so much?
	Contempt, farewell, and maiden pride, adieu[10],
	No glory lives behind the back of such[11].	110
	And Benedick, love on, I will requite thee,
	Taming my wild heart to thy loving hand:
	If thou dost love, my kindness shall incite thee[12]
	To bind our loves up in a holy band[13],
	For others say thou dost deserve, and I	115
	Believe it better than reportingly[14].	*Exit*

Don Pedro plans to return to Arragon as soon as Claudio and Hero are married. The prince, Claudio and Leonato feign amazement at Benedick's lovelorn appearance and behaviour.

剧情简介： 唐佩卓计划在克劳丢和希柔完婚后立刻返回阿若岗。亲王、克劳丢、列纳托假装对本尼迪深陷爱河的模样和举止大为吃惊。

Characters 人物分析

'I am not as I have been' (in pairs)

The transformation of Benedick, especially his entrance in this scene, can be an opportunity for an actor and a director to explore visual comedy. Some productions have chosen to show this through a change in costume: military clothing has been swapped for fashionable civilian (平民百姓) fashion. One production saw the bearded Benedick sporting a freshly shaven appearance. Other productions have focused instead on the behaviours of Benedick, who appears more lovelorn (害相思病) or blissfully (充满喜悦) in love.

a Work by yourself first. Find the lines that refer to Benedick's clothing and mood, then draw 'before' and 'after' pictures of Benedick. You can use the examples below for inspiration.

b Swap your pictures with a partner and ask them to label the diagrams with lines from the script opposite. Swap back and see whether your partner has correctly identified the script references in your drawing.

1 consummate 完成
2 vouchsafe me 允许我
3 soil 污点
4 gloss 光彩；喜悦
5 hangman 混混，流氓
6 clapper 钟锤，铃舌
7 Gallants 绅士们
8 Hang him, truant 绞死他，流浪汉
9 Draw 拔掉
10 Hang 忘掉
11 a humour or a worm 体液或蛀虫（旧时认为龋齿里积累了这两种东西会导致牙痛，这里的用法同第42页的 melancholy）
12 grief 疼痛
13 fancy 恋爱；心血来潮
14 Dutchman ... Frenchman ... （见第171页 "时尚与外貌"）
15 slops 灯笼裤
16 old signs 常见的迹象
17 a brushes = he brushes
18 a-mornings = in the mornings
19 bode 象征，表示

▼ This is how one artist pictures Benedick's changed appearance. List the differences between these 'before' and 'after' Benedicks.

Benedick before

Benedick after

Act 3 Scene 2
Leonato's house

Enter DON PEDRO, CLAUDIO, BENEDICK *and* LEONATO

DON PEDRO I do but stay till your marriage be consummate[1], and then go I toward Arragon.

CLAUDIO I'll bring you thither, my lord, if you'll vouchsafe me[2].

DON PEDRO Nay that would be as great a soil[3] in the new gloss[4] of your marriage, as to show a child his new coat and forbid him to wear it: I will only be bold with Benedick for his company, for from the crown of his head, to the sole of his foot, he is all mirth: he hath twice or thrice cut Cupid's bow-string, and the little hangman[5] dare not shoot at him: he hath a heart as sound as a bell, and his tongue is the clapper[6], for what his heart thinks, his tongue speaks.

BENEDICK Gallants[7], I am not as I have been.

LEONATO So say I, methinks you are sadder.

CLAUDIO I hope he be in love.

DON PEDRO Hang him, truant[8], there's no true drop of blood in him to be truly touched with love: if he be sad, he wants money.

BENEDICK I have the tooth-ache.

DON PEDRO Draw[9] it.

BENEDICK Hang[10] it.

CLAUDIO You must hang it first, and draw it afterwards.

DON PEDRO What, sigh for the tooth-ache?

LEONATO Where is but a humour or a worm[11].

BENEDICK Well, everyone cannot master a grief[12], but he that has it.

CLAUDIO Yet say I, he is in love.

DON PEDRO There is no appearance of fancy[13] in him, unless it be a fancy that he hath to strange disguises, as to be a Dutchman today, a Frenchman[14] tomorrow, or in the shape of two countries at once, as a German from the waist downward, all slops[15], and a Spaniard from the hip upward, no doublet: unless he have a fancy to this foolery, as it appears he hath, he is no fool for fancy, as you would have it appear he is.

CLAUDIO If he be not in love with some woman, there is no believing old signs[16]: a brushes[17] his hat a-mornings[18], what should that bode[19]?

Benedick's friends continue to joke at his expense. Benedick takes Leonato aside for a private word. Don John interrupts Don Pedro and Claudio's amusement with an ominous-sounding declaration.

 剧情简介：本尼迪的朋友们继续开他的玩笑。本尼迪把列纳托叫到一旁单独说话。唐约翰带来不祥的消息，打断了唐佩卓和克劳丢的欢声笑语。

1 A change of mood (in fours)

Don John's arrival on stage appears to change the atmosphere of the scene.

a Take parts and read lines 48–69. Use your voices to create a sharp change of mood when Don John enters.

b Do you think Don Pedro and Claudio's exhilaration (欢欣) at their teasing of Benedick disappears immediately on Don John's entrance, or at a point some lines later? Perform the scene twice and experiment by changing the point at which the tone shifts.

c Choose five lines from the script opposite as captions (说明文字) for tableaux that show the changes in atmosphere. In your groups, stage each tableau and invite others to guess the line that is the caption.

d Decide which character is which in the photograph below, and then stage it. What do you think is the caption for this tableau?

1 stuffed 填塞（伊丽莎白时期的网球里填塞的是毛发）
2 civet 麝香
3 melancholy （指本尼迪因相思而忧郁的模样）
4 wont 常常
5 paint himself 擦化妆品
6 For … him 我听说人们议论他就是因为这个
7 Nay but his 不，是因为他的
8 lute-string 鲁特琴的琴弦（当时情歌多以鲁特琴伴奏）
9 governed 被命令，被管辖
10 stops 品（弦乐器指板上凸起的横道，用来将指板分为多个区间，演奏时帮助找音和定音）
11 heavy 伤心
12 conclude 停止；总结
13 ill conditions 坏品质
14 dies for him 想他想得要死
15 hobby-horses 捣蛋鬼，傻瓜蛋
16 Good den = Good e'en = Good evening
17 If your leisure served 如果您方便
18 Means your lordship to 殿下您是否打算
19 impediment 阻止这场婚姻的理由
20 discover 表露，揭露

MUCH ADO ABOUT NOTHING ACT 3 SCENE 2

虚惊一场

DON PEDRO   Hath any man seen him at the barber's?
CLAUDIO   No, but the barber's man hath been seen with him, and the old ornament of his cheek hath already stuffed[1] tennis balls.
LEONATO   Indeed he looks younger than he did, by the loss of a beard.
DON PEDRO   Nay, a rubs himself with civet[2], can you smell him out by that?
CLAUDIO   That's as much as to say, the sweet youth's in love.
DON PEDRO   The greatest note of it is his melancholy[3].
CLAUDIO   And when was he wont[4] to wash his face?
DON PEDRO   Yea, or to paint himself[5]? For the which I hear what they say of him[6].
CLAUDIO   Nay but his[7] jesting spirit, which is now crept into a lute-string[8], and now governed[9] by stops[10].
DON PEDRO   Indeed that tells a heavy[11] tale for him: conclude[12], conclude, he is in love.
CLAUDIO   Nay but I know who loves him.
DON PEDRO   That would I know too, I warrant one that knows him not.
CLAUDIO   Yes, and his ill conditions[13], and in despite of all, dies for him[14].
DON PEDRO   She shall be buried with her face upwards.
BENEDICK   Yet is this no charm for the tooth-ache: old signor, walk aside with me, I have studied eight or nine wise words to speak to you, which these hobby-horses[15] must not hear.

[*Exeunt Benedick and Leonato*]

DON PEDRO   For my life, to break with him about Beatrice.
CLAUDIO   'Tis even so: Hero and Margaret have by this played their parts with Beatrice, and then the two bears will not bite one another when they meet.

Enter DON JOHN *the Bastard*

DON JOHN   My lord and brother, God save you.
DON PEDRO   Good den[16], brother.
DON JOHN   If your leisure served[17], I would speak with you.
DON PEDRO   In private?
DON JOHN   If it please you, yet Count Claudio may hear, for what I would speak of, concerns him.
DON PEDRO   What's the matter?
DON JOHN   Means your lordship to[18] be married tomorrow?
DON PEDRO   You know he does.
DON JOHN   I know not that, when he knows what I know.
CLAUDIO   If there be any impediment[19], I pray you discover[20] it.

75

Don John claims that he has proof of Hero's infidelity. He invites Claudio and Don Pedro to witness Hero's unfaithful behaviour. They vow to shame her in public if she is proved unchaste.

 剧情简介：唐约翰说他有希柔不贞的证据，并邀请克劳丢和唐佩卓见证希柔的不贞行为。他们发誓如果希柔果真不守贞操，必将当众羞辱她。

Language in the play 剧中语言

Hear the male anger (in threes)

As Shakespeare's plays have few stage directions, it is the language that gives the actor an idea of how to play the part.

a How does the language and structure of Don John's speech opposite direct the manner in which he addresses the other two characters?

b In a copy of the script opposite, highlight or underline the hard consonants used in lines 91–100. Read the exchange aloud, sounding angry and vengeful (图谋报复). Spit out the consonants (especially the 'd's, 'p's, 't's and 's's) for emphasis.

c Discuss the way questions, complex sentences and exclamations create a sense of growing hostility (敌意) in lines 74–100. Notice how the three men are quickly united in their anger at Hero's presumed infidelity.

d Perform the scene, exploring how the delivery of the sentence types listed above influences the mood/atmosphere in the scene.

Themes 主题分析

Deception: why trust Don John? (in small groups)

In line 88, Don John seems to be saying, 'if you are not prepared to trust the evidence of your own eyes, then you can never say that you know anything'. The prince's brother has already provoked a war and attempted to spoil Claudio's betrothal (婚约) to Hero, yet both Claudio and Don Pedro seem all too ready to believe what they are about to 'see' at Hero's bedroom window.

a On sticky notes or small pieces of paper, write down the reasons why you think they are so easily convinced by Don John. Arrange your sticky notes into a ranked order of the ideas or words you think are most significant. Compare your order with that of another group, and discuss any differences.

b Identify or highlight the key words Don John uses in lines 78–85 to wound the pride of these powerful men.

1 aim better at me 更好地评价我
2 manifest 解释
3 holp to effect 帮着促成 (holp = helped)
4 suit ill-spent 白费力气
5 ill-bestowed 使用不当，滥用
6 circumstances shortened 长话短说
7 too long a-talking of 议论得太多
8 paint out 刻画出，描绘出
9 title 说法，称呼
10 fit 适合，配上
11 warrant 证据
12 in the congregation 在教堂
13 disparage 批评
14 bear it coldly 冷静对待
15 issue 后果
16 untowardly 不利，不祥
17 mischief 不幸
18 thwarting 挫败，阻挠
19 sequel 后续的事

MUCH ADO ABOUT NOTHING ACT 3 SCENE 2
虚惊一场

DON JOHN   You may think I love you not, let that appear hereafter, and aim better at me[1] by that I now will manifest[2], for my brother (I think he holds you well, and in dearness of heart) hath holp to effect[3] your ensuing marriage: surely suit ill-spent[4], and labour ill-bestowed[5].

DON PEDRO   Why what's the matter?

DON JOHN   I came hither to tell you, and circumstances shortened[6] (for she has been too long a-talking of[7]), the lady is disloyal.

CLAUDIO   Who Hero?

DON JOHN   Even she, Leonato's Hero, your Hero, every man's Hero.

CLAUDIO   Disloyal?

DON JOHN   The word is too good to paint out[8] her wickedness, I could say she were worse, think you of a worse title[9], and I will fit[10] her to it: wonder not till further warrant[11]: go but with me tonight, you shall see her chamber window entered, even the night before her wedding day: if you love her, then tomorrow wed her: but it would better fit your honour to change your mind.

CLAUDIO   May this be so?

DON PEDRO   I will not think it.

DON JOHN   If you dare not trust that you see, confess not that you know: if you will follow me, I will show you enough: and when you have seen more, and heard more, proceed accordingly.

CLAUDIO   If I see anything tonight, why I should not marry her tomorrow in the congregation[12], where I should wed, there will I shame her.

DON PEDRO   And as I wooed for thee to obtain her, I will join with thee, to disgrace her.

DON JOHN   I will disparage[13] her no farther, till you are my witnesses: bear it coldly[14] but till midnight, and let the issue[15] show itself.

DON PEDRO   Oh day untowardly[16] turned!

CLAUDIO   Oh mischief[17] strangely thwarting[18]!

DON JOHN   Oh plague right well prevented! So will you say, when you have seen the sequel[19].

Exeunt

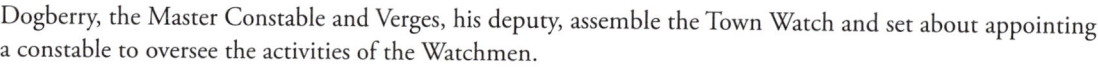

Dogberry, the Master Constable and Verges, his deputy, assemble the Town Watch and set about appointing a constable to oversee the activities of the Watchmen.

剧情简介：治安官道博瑞和他的副官瓦吉召集镇上的巡夜人，打算任命一名警官来监督他们的日常工作。

Characters 人物分析

Enter the clowns (in groups of five or more)

No sooner has Don John begun to weave his evil plot, than Shakespeare introduces the simple, ordinary men whose dramatic function it will be to bring the villain and his henchmen (帮凶) to justice.

The Watch were the policemen of Shakespeare's day, and their incompetence was a standing joke with Elizabethan playwrights. Shakespeare's Watchmen are very English, with English names and attitudes, and they are spectacularly inept (无能).

Will Kemp, the resident comedian in Shakespeare's company, was probably the first to play the part of Dogberry. Kemp employed techniques such as clowning, grimaces (扮怪相) and ad lib (即兴) remarks to accentuate the comedy and make the audience laugh.

a Share out the parts of Dogberry, Verges, Seacoal, Watchman 1 and Watchman 2, and read through lines 1–77.

b For each of these characters, select a single line that you feel is most 'typical' of their behaviour. Give each character a different (comical) facial expression and a single gesture for emphasis when delivering that line.

c Decide upon a distinctive and humorous accent or vocal style that each character could use. Improvise a short scene based on a long, tedious and ineffective 'Watch', and use it to develop a range of interesting and funny voices.

1 Mangler of words (in small groups)

Dogberry attempts to give his words an imposing ring (装腔作势的特点), but the results are often baffling (令人困惑). His talent is for **malapropisms** (词语误用，搞笑误听) (the mistaken use of words – see pp. 184–5). For example, he says 'desartless' (line 8) when he means 'deserving'.

a Use the glossary to the right to find other malapropisms. Then devise your own version of lines 1–22, entitled 'Dogberry Corrected', in which Dogberry delivers his lines while the others in the group find ways of intervening to correct his mistakes and comically respond to what he has actually said.

b Stage the scene, and pay homage (敬意) to Will Kemp and other Shakespearean clowns by including comic 'business' (actions designed to make people laugh, but not necessarily scripted). Examples of this might include falling over each other, distracted behaviour, nose-picking or ridiculous facial expressions.

1 **it were pity but** = it would be a pity if
2 **salvation** 救赎（瓦吉想说 damnation [下地狱]，他和道博瑞经常词不达意）
3 **allegiance** 效忠，忠诚（道博瑞想说 disloyalty [不忠诚]）
4 **give them their charge** 说说他们的职责
5 **neighbour**（一种友好亲近的称呼，此处意思相当于"老兄，老弟"）
6 **desartless** = desertless (不够格)
7 **Seacoal ... name** (Seacoal 即今天的煤 [coal]，前面加 sea 是为了区别于炭 [charcoal]；炭是人工生产的，煤在当时被认为是上天赐予人类的)
8 **well-favoured** 长相好
9 **Fortune** 好运
10 **nature** 自然（道博瑞想说 nurture [教养]）
11 **favour** 长相
12 **senseless** 无知（道博瑞想说 sensible [明智]）
13 **charge** 工作
14 **comprehend** 了解（道博瑞想说 apprehend [逮捕]）
15 **vagrom** 流浪（道博瑞想说 vagrant [无赖]）
16 **stand** 站住

Act 3 Scene 3
Near Leonato's house

Enter DOGBERRY *and his partner* VERGES *with* SEACOAL, WATCHMAN 1, WATCHMAN 2 *and the rest of the Watch*

DOGBERRY Are you good men and true?

VERGES Yea, or else it were pity but[1] they should suffer salvation[2] body and soul.

DOGBERRY Nay, that were a punishment too good for them, if they should have any allegiance[3] in them, being chosen for the prince's watch.

VERGES Well, give them their charge[4], neighbour[5] Dogberry.

DOGBERRY First, who think you the most desartless[6] man to be constable?

WATCHMAN 1 Hugh Oatcake, sir, or George Seacoal, for they can write and read.

DOGBERRY Come hither, neighbour Seacoal, God hath blessed you with a good name[7]: to be a well-favoured[8] man, is the gift of Fortune[9], but to write and read, comes by nature[10].

SEACOAL Both which, master constable —

DOGBERRY You have: I knew it would be your answer: well, for your favour[11], sir, why give God thanks, and make no boast of it, and for your writing and reading, let that appear when there is no need of such vanity: you are thought here to be the most senseless[12] and fit man for the constable of the watch: therefore bear you the lantern: this is your charge[13], you shall comprehend[14] all vagrom[15] men, you are to bid any man stand[16], in the prince's name.

Dogberry outlines the duties required of the Watch in maintaining law and order. He advises them to avoid getting involved with criminals and troublemakers, and tells them that it's far better to go to sleep!

剧情简介：道博瑞给巡夜人讲了他们在维护法律和秩序方面的职责，他建议他们要避免跟犯罪分子和捣乱分子接触，最好是整夜睡大觉。

1 The 'farces' (笑剧，闹剧) of law and order (in small groups)

The production pictured below had women playing the parts of the Watch as Victorian ladies. Unlike a stereotypical onstage police force, this group is neither 'uniform' nor wearing a typical uniform. Instead, they are all different shapes and sizes, are wearing variously decorated hats and carrying handbags, and are armed with umbrellas!

a Can you identify the characters in the picture below? List the costume elements and props that you can see, and suggest how this company might have staged a farcical approach to the scene.

b Celebrities and well-known comedians of movies and television often like to have a go at performing Shakespearean roles. The comic roles are often perfect for celebrities, but comic actors are sometimes given serious roles and vice versa. What impact might this reverse casting have on the audience's response? Why might this be effective for the play? Decide who you would cast in these roles, and why. What would they look like? Produce some annotated sketches.

c Dress up one member of your group to accompany a class presentation about staging the Watch's appearance. Show how the costume and props you have chosen produce a comedic effect, perhaps through gesture and action as well as visual impact.

1 **How ... stand?** 如果他不站住怎么办？
2 **bidden** 被下令要……
3 **tolerable** 可容忍（道博瑞想说intolerable [不可容忍]）
4 **belongs to** 适合；是……应该做的
5 **ancient** 经验丰富
6 **bills** 矛或戟之类的武器
7 **let them alone** 不管他们
8 **make ... answer** 不能好好回答问题，不能做出明确的答复
9 **office** 职责，本分
10 **true** 诚实
11 **meddle or make** 打交道
12 **the more ... honesty** 对保持你们的好名声越有利
13 **pitch** 沥青
14 **defiled** 弄脏
15 **steal out of your company** 在你们面前逃走
16 **hang a dog** 吊死一只狗（在16世纪，动物伤害人类要受到相应的惩罚）
17 **much more** 更不要说

Much Ado About Nothing Act 3 Scene 3
虚惊一场

SEACOAL How if a will not stand?[1]

DOGBERRY Why then take no note of him, but let him go, and presently call the rest of the watch together, and thank God you are rid of a knave.

VERGES If he will not stand when he is bidden[2], he is none of the prince's subjects.

DOGBERRY True, and they are to meddle with none but the prince's subjects: you shall also make no noise in the streets: for, for the watch to babble and to talk, is most tolerable[3] and not to be endured.

WATCHMAN 2 We will rather sleep than talk, we know what belongs to[4] a watch.

DOGBERRY Why you speak like an ancient[5] and most quiet watchman, for I cannot see how sleeping should offend: only have a care that your bills[6] be not stolen: well, you are to call at all the alehouses, and bid those that are drunk get them to bed.

SEACOAL How if they will not?

DOGBERRY Why then let them alone[7] till they are sober: if they make you not then the better answer[8], you may say, they are not the men you took them for.

SEACOAL Well, sir.

DOGBERRY If you meet a thief, you may suspect him, by virtue of your office[9], to be no true[10] man: and for such kind of men, the less you meddle or make[11] with them, why the more is for your honesty[12].

SEACOAL If we know him to be a thief, shall we not lay hands on him?

DOGBERRY Truly by your office you may, but I think they that touch pitch[13] will be defiled[14]: the most peaceable way for you, if you do take a thief, is, to let him show himself what he is, and steal out of your company[15].

VERGES You have been always called a merciful man, partner.

DOGBERRY Truly I would not hang a dog[16] by my will, much more[17] a man who hath any honesty in him.

After giving more advice, Dogberry and Verges leave. As the Watch make themselves comfortable on the church bench, Borachio and Conrade enter, unaware that they are being observed.

剧情简介：道博瑞和瓦吉又给了一些忠告之后离开，巡夜人在教堂的长凳上舒服地坐下。此时鲍拉丘和康拉上场，没意识到有人正在盯着他们。

Stagecraft 导演技巧
Stage the eavesdropping and capture

The picture below shows a model of the reconstructed Shakespeare's Globe in London (see the 'Much Ado About Nothing in performance' section, p. 190). Thanks to the open roof and the English weather, the theatre very often does 'drizzle rain' (lines 86–7)! Notice the two pillars supporting the 'penthouse' (overhanging roof), and the actors' entrance doors left and right. The central section can also be opened to reveal a small 'inner room'.

Draw a stage plan with notes detailing props, movements and so on, indicating how you would use this theatre to present the moment when the plot to ruin Hero is overheard (lines 70–147).

1 still 使安静
2 ewe 母羊
3 bleats 哞哞叫
4 present 出现（道博瑞想说 represent [代表]）
5 stay 叫住并盘问
6 by'r Lady 圣母在上（发誓用语）
7 Five … on't 我拿5先令赌他1个先令
8 statutes 法规
9 and … chances 如果发生什么大事
10 keep … own 你们要谨言慎行
11 coil 热闹
12 vigitant （道博瑞想说 vigilant [警觉]）
13 Mass 老天在上（发誓用语）
14 scab 伤疤（也有"恶棍"的意思）
15 I … that 回头再找你算这笔账
16 penthouse 外廊
17 true drunkard 真醉鬼

1 Seacoal overhears

In lines 70–147, Seacoal overhears the plotters' conversation. Although in full view of the audience, he has little to say.

a Read through these lines and then write notes so that the actor playing the part knows how to move around this stage.

b Link directions for actions (non-verbal communication) to specific lines in the script, so that the actor has 'cues' for movements, gestures and facial expressions.

c Add adverbs that describe how lines should be delivered for maximum comic effect. Again, link these adverbs to particular lines so that your directions are clear.

MUCH ADO ABOUT NOTHING ACT 3 SCENE 3
虚惊一场

VERGES   If you hear a child cry in the night, you must call to the nurse and bid her still¹ it.   55
WATCHMAN 2   How if the nurse be asleep and will not hear us?
DOGBERRY   Why then depart in peace, and let the child wake her with crying, for the ewe² that will not hear her lamb when it baas, will never answer a calf when he bleats³.
VERGES   'Tis very true.   60
DOGBERRY   This is the end of the charge: you, constable, are to present⁴ the prince's own person, if you meet the prince in the night, you may stay⁵ him.
VERGES   Nay by'r Lady⁶ that I think a cannot.
DOGBERRY   Five shillings to one on't⁷ with any man that knows the statutes⁸, he may stay him: marry, not without the prince be willing, for indeed the watch ought to offend no man, and it is an offence to stay a man against his will.   65
VERGES   By'r Lady I think it be so.
DOGBERRY   Ha, ah ha! Well, masters, good night: and there be any matter of weight chances⁹, call up me: keep your fellows' counsels, and your own¹⁰, and good night: come, neighbour.   70
SEACOAL   Well masters, we hear our charge, let us go sit here upon the church bench till two, and then all to bed.
DOGBERRY   One word more, honest neighbours, I pray you watch about Signor Leonato's door, for the wedding being there tomorrow, there is a great coil¹¹ tonight: adieu, be vigitant¹² I beseech you.   75

Exeunt [*Dogberry and Verges*]

Enter BORACHIO *and* CONRADE

BORACHIO   What, Conrade?
SEACOAL   Peace, stir not.
BORACHIO   Conrade, I say.   80
CONRADE   Here, man, I am at thy elbow.
BORACHIO   Mass¹³ and my elbow itched, I thought there would a scab¹⁴ follow.
CONRADE   I will owe thee an answer for that¹⁵, and now forward with thy tale.   85
BORACHIO   Stand thee close then under this penthouse¹⁶, for it drizzles rain, and I will, like a true drunkard¹⁷, utter all to thee.

The drunken Borachio starts to tell Conrade about the villainous deed he has done that very night. He then digresses to talk about the influence of fashion on wealthy young gentlemen. The Watch listen, bemused.

剧情简介：醉酒的鲍拉丘跟康拉说他当天晚上做了一件坏事，之后跑题说起时装对阔少爷们的影响。巡夜人听到这些话，莫名其妙。

Themes 主题分析
Fashion (in pairs)

The drunken Borachio has just seen a rich villain (Don John) buy the kind of 'truth' he wants. Now he considers the young aristocrats of the day, giddily (发狂) seeking the latest fashions. Borachio's remarks in lines 89–117 are not just about fashion, and his words puzzle Conrade, the Watch – and the audience.

a Discuss with your partner what you think Shakespeare is saying about clothes and fashion here. Make a list of points, and find quotations from the script opposite to support your ideas.

b Compare your list with another pair, then discuss and debate the similarities and differences between your ideas.

Language in the play 剧中语言
Deformed words

In lines 101–7, it is remarked twice and echoed a third time 'what a deformed thief this fashion is'. This repetition of the statement means that the audience is meant to 'note' it.

a Elizabethan fashions, with their padding (衬垫) and strange shapes (see pp. 171–3), certainly 'de-formed' the human figure. But what other meanings might this remark have? For example, what has fashion or costume 'stolen' from Hero and Benedick?

b Shakespeare's careful choice of language allows for ambiguity and creates vivid images. Below is a diagram exploring relevant definitions of the word 'deformed'. Potential explanations of the use are linked to quotations from the scene that evidence this meaning. Complete the *de-forming* of 'deformed' or complete a similar breakdown of the word 'fashion'. Use a good dictionary to help you get started on identifying relevant definitions.

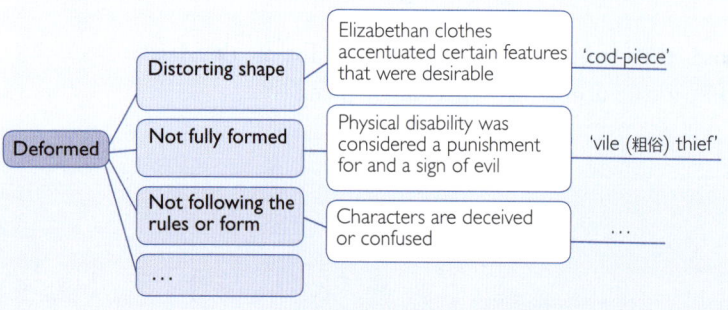

1 **stand close** 站着别动
2 **be so rich** 花这么多钱
3 **make** 要（价）
4 **unconfirmed** 没有经验，无知
5 **nothing to a man** 不能说明这个人到底怎么样
6 **apparel** 衣服
7 **fashion** 方式；时尚
8 **Tush** 胡说
9 **this seven year** 这7年来
10 **vane** 风向标（与vain谐音，也可表示像风一样变化多端）
11 **hot-bloods** 热血青年
12 **reechy** 肮脏，被烟熏脏的
13 **god Bel** 柏尔神（巴比伦神话中的一个神，当时被看作异教的神）
14 **smirched** 弄脏的，损坏的
15 **cod-piece** 遮羞袋（旧时男士裆前起遮挡作用的布袋，与半截裤连在一起，起装饰作用）
16 **massy** 粗大

SEACOAL	Some treason, masters, yet stand close[1].	
BORACHIO	Therefore know, I have earned of Don John a thousand ducats.	90
CONRADE	Is it possible that any villainy should be so dear?	
BORACHIO	Thou shouldst rather ask if it were possible any villainy should be so rich[2]. For when rich villains have need of poor ones, poor ones may make[3] what price they will.	
CONRADE	I wonder at it.	95
BORACHIO	That shows thou art unconfirmed[4]: thou knowest that the fashion of a doublet, or a hat, or a cloak, is nothing to a man[5].	
CONRADE	Yes, it is apparel[6].	
BORACHIO	I mean the fashion[7].	
CONRADE	Yes, the fashion is the fashion.	100
BORACHIO	Tush[8], I may as well say the fool's the fool, but seest thou not what a deformed thief this fashion is?	
WATCHMAN 1	I know that Deformed, a has been a vile thief, this seven year[9], a goes up and down like a gentleman: I remember his name.	
BORACHIO	Didst thou not hear somebody?	105
CONRADE	No, 'twas the vane[10] on the house.	
BORACHIO	Seest thou not, I say, what a deformed thief this fashion is, how giddily a turns about all the hot-bloods[11], between fourteen and five and thirty, sometimes fashioning them like Pharaoh's soldiers in the reechy[12] painting, sometime like god Bel's[13] priests in the old church window, sometime like the shaven Hercules in the smirched[14] worm-eaten tapestry, where his cod-piece[15] seems as massy[16] as his club?	110
CONRADE	All this I see, and I see that the fashion wears out more apparel than the man: but art not thou thyself giddy with the fashion too, that thou hast shifted out of thy tale into telling me of the fashion?	115

Borachio tells Conrade the details of how he deceived Don Pedro and Claudio. The Watch arrest the two villains and lead them away.

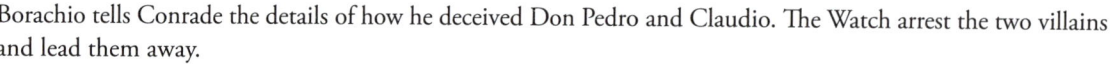

剧情简介：鲍拉丘告诉康拉他如何蒙骗了唐佩卓和克劳丢。巡夜人逮捕了这两个恶棍并把他们带走。

Write about it 写作练习

Comic or dramatic arrest?

Although the Watch are often regarded as an incompetent bunch and are the source of much fun, on this occasion they successfully capture criminals. Playing this scene therefore requires striking the right balance between comedy and drama.

Elizabethan gentlemen carried swords and often used them. The Watch (despite Dogberry's advice) could be brave and determined, and the villains prepared to fight and kill. In one production, a huge, hulking watchman accidentally felled (打倒) two of his companions before beating Borachio and Conrade into submission (臣服).

a Make notes in a table like the one below, to gather evidence about how the scene should be played. What actions should accompany the lines? Is there action that should be included but is not covered by what the characters say? Add this to the 'Action' columns of the table as well.

Comic		Dramatic	
Line	Action	Line	Action

b Once you have completed your table, write a detailed outline of how the scene should be played. You could structure this by:

- using your ideas to in turn explore how the scene could be played in a comic or dramatic way
- supporting your ideas by quoting lines from the text
- analysing possible meanings of each line and describing the accompanying actions
- making some recommendations about how you think the scene ought to be played and why
- explaining what your intention was and saying how you hope the audience will react.

1 leans me out 朝我探出身子
2 possessed 被摄魂，被蒙骗
3 amiable 温存
4 appointed 安排好
5 o'er night 前一天晚上
6 stand 起立
7 right 尊贵，尊敬
8 recovered / lechery （他想说discovered [发现] 和 treachery [背叛]；lechery意为"好色"）
9 commonwealth 邦国
10 Deformed （他误以为Deformed 是其中一个阴谋策划者的名字，让人感觉他知道这人的相貌）
11 lock 一缕长发（参见第172页）
12 obey 服从（他想说order [命令]）
13 commodity 商品，货物
14 in question 紧俏

Much Ado About Nothing Act 3 Scene 3
虚惊一场

BORACHIO Not so neither, but know that I have tonight wooed Margaret, the Lady Hero's gentlewoman, by the name of Hero: she leans me out¹ at her mistress' chamber window, bids me a thousand times good night: I tell this tale vilely, I should first tell thee how the prince, Claudio and my master planted, and placed, and possessed², by my master Don John, saw afar off in the orchard this amiable³ encounter. 120

CONRADE And thought they Margaret was Hero? 125

BORACHIO Two of them did, the prince and Claudio, but the devil my master knew she was Margaret, and partly by his oaths, which first possessed them, partly by the dark night which did deceive them, but chiefly, by my villainy, which did confirm any slander that Don John had made – away went Claudio enraged, swore he would meet her as he was appointed⁴ next morning at the temple, and there, before the whole congregation shame her, with what he saw o'er night⁵, and send her home again without a husband. 130

SEACOAL We charge you in the prince's name, stand⁶.

WATCHMAN 2 Call up the right⁷ master constable, we have here recovered⁸ the most dangerous piece of lechery⁸, that ever was known in the commonwealth⁹. 135

WATCHMAN 1 And one Deformed¹⁰ is one of them, I know him, a wears a lock¹¹.

CONRADE Masters, masters. 140

WATCHMAN 1 You'll be made bring Deformed forth I warrant you.

SEACOAL Masters, never speak, we charge you, let us obey¹² you to go with us.

BORACHIO We are like to prove a goodly commodity¹³, being taken up of these men's bills. 145

CONRADE A commodity in question¹⁴ I warrant you: come, we'll obey you.

Exeunt

It is the morning of the wedding and Hero, with Margaret to help her, prepares herself. At first the talk is of fashion, but Margaret turns the conversation to sex.

 剧情简介：婚礼当天的早上，希柔在玛格蕊的帮助下梳妆待嫁。二人聊着服饰样式，后来玛格蕊把话题转到性事上。

1 The height of fashion

Wealthy Elizabethans wore extravagant, fashionable clothing – and, of course, Queen Elizabeth I wore the most sumptuous (奢华) garments of them all. In the portrait below, the rich fabrics of Elizabeth's dress are woven with gold and silver thread ('cloth o'gold'), on which are sewn jewels and pearls. In places there are 'cuts' in the material to show off the contrasting fabrics beneath. Note the wired neck ruff (皱领) or 'rebato', the 'tire' (wired head-dress decorated with jewels and false curls) and the wide 'down sleeves'. The down sleeves and the V-shaped stomacher (束腰) are heavily padded. The huge skirt is 'round underborne' (stiffened with material on the inside) and shaped with padding and wire supports.

a Are any of these features reminiscent of (让人回忆起) Borachio's observation in the previous scene (line 107) that fashion is 'a deformed thief'? Use books or the Internet to research Elizabethan fashions. Copy or sketch a range of images of extreme or unusual fashions from the period to support Borachio's point.

b Fashion in the twenty-first century can be equally over the top (过分). List or sketch a range of examples of contemporary fashions that might be said to be extreme.

c Create a collage (拼贴画) or presentation showing how much (or perhaps how little) fashion has changed since the play was written. Suggest what twenty-first-century costumes particular characters might wear in a contemporary production of the play. Explain your choices and the effect that you want the costumes to have on the audience.

1 **desire her** 请她
2 **rebato** 大立褶领（17世纪早期英格兰流行的一种用蕾丝边、硬质材料做的宽竖领）
3 **By my troth's** = By my troth it is
4 **I warrant** 我认为；我保证
5 **within** （褶领）里面（16—17世纪英格兰流行白色厚褶领）
6 **a thought** 一点点
7 **rare** 稀有，不寻常
8 **exceeds** 胜过，极好
9 **night-gown** 睡袍，梳妆袍
10 **in respect of** 比起……来
11 **round ... tinsel** 下面用金丝布镶了一圈边
12 **quaint** 高雅精巧
13 **on't** = of it
14 **weight of a man** 一个男人的重量（既指婚姻的压力，又指房事）
15 **Fie** 呸（表示嫌恶，震惊等）
16 **bad thinking** 歪念头
17 **wrest** 扭曲，曲解
18 **and it be** = if it be
19 **light** 轻浮
20 **else** 否则

Act 3 Scene 4
Hero's dressing room

Enter HERO *and* MARGARET *and* URSULA

HERO	Good Ursula, wake my cousin Beatrice, and desire her[1] to rise.
URSULA	I will, lady.
HERO	And bid her come hither.
URSULA	Well. [*Exit*]
MARGARET	Troth I think your other rebato[2] were better.
HERO	No pray thee, good Meg, I'll wear this.
MARGARET	By my troth's[3] not so good, and I warrant[4] your cousin will say so.
HERO	My cousin's a fool, and thou art another, I'll wear none but this.
MARGARET	I like the new tire within[5] excellently, if the hair were a thought[6] browner: and your gown's a most rare[7] fashion i'faith. I saw the Duchess of Milan's gown that they praise so.
HERO	Oh, that exceeds[8] they say.
MARGARET	By my troth's but a night-gown[9] in respect of[10] yours, cloth o'gold and cuts, and laced with silver, set with pearls, down sleeves, side sleeves, and skirts, round underborne with a bluish tinsel[11] – but for a fine quaint[12] graceful and excellent fashion, yours is worth ten on't[13].
HERO	God give me joy to wear it, for my heart is exceeding heavy.
MARGARET	'Twill be heavier soon by the weight of a man[14].
HERO	Fie[15] upon thee, art not ashamed?
MARGARET	Of what, lady? Of speaking honourably? Is not marriage honourable in a beggar? Is not your lord honourable without marriage? I think you would have me say, saving your reverence, a husband: and bad thinking[16] do not wrest[17] true speaking, I'll offend nobody: is there any harm in the heavier for a husband? None I think, and it be[18] the right husband, and the right wife, otherwise 'tis light[19] and not heavy: ask my Lady Beatrice else[20], here she comes.

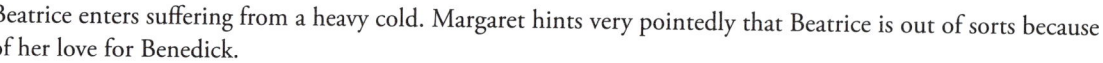

Beatrice enters suffering from a heavy cold. Margaret hints very pointedly that Beatrice is out of sorts because of her love for Benedick.

剧情简介：碧翠上场，患了重感冒。玛格蕊直言不讳地说碧翠这么难受是因为她爱上了本尼迪。

Language in the play 剧中语言
Quick-witted women (in threes)

This scene echoes the mockery of Benedick in Act 3 Scene 2. Love has given Benedick toothache and it has given Beatrice a cold. Margaret takes the lead in teasing Beatrice, hoping perhaps to match Beatrice's wit while she is temporarily off form (状态不佳).

a Take parts and rehearse a comic version of lines 33–70. Use the following explanations of the wordplay to help you deliver the lines with the intended tone and emphasis:

- *Light o'Love* (meaning 'joy of love') was a popular dance song of the day (lines 33–7). Margaret claims to want Beatrice to sing it because it needs no bass (男低音) or male accompaniment ('goes without a burden'). This continues the pun on 'lightness', because 'light o'love' could also mean 'loose woman'. Beatrice takes up the hint with her use of 'heels' and 'barns'. Kicking up your heels also suggested sexual promiscuity (乱交), while 'barns' puns on 'bairns' (children).

- *Carduus benedictus* is the Latin name for Holy Thistle (line 60), a popular and fashionable remedy for many complaints, especially 'perilous diseases of the heart'. In lines 52–61, one Beatrice covered her head as she said, 'by my troth I am sick', popped her head out in surprise at Margaret's joke about getting some 'distilled *Carduus benedictus*' for her cold, then hid again when Margaret said, 'you may think perchance that I think you are in love' (lines 60–1).

b Act out your version for the rest of the class, and watch the other groups' efforts. Decide as a class which performance raises the most laughs at the expense of the pathetic Beatrice. You could vote or use score cards to determine the best one.

1 Good morrow = Good morning
2 coz 堂姐（cousin的昵称）
3 Why how now? 怎么啦？
4 in the sick tune 病恹恹
5 Clap's into 拍手演唱
6 illegitimate construction 误解意思
7 heigh ho 咳（也指狩猎时对马或鹰发号施令）
8 H （即ache；也读作aitch）
9 and … Turk 如果您不变成土耳其人（指皈依伊斯兰教，即转变信仰，从不爱转为爱）
10 there's … star 那么航海时我们连北极星都不能相信了
11 trow = I wonder
12 stuffed 鼻塞（也指怀孕）
13 catching of cold 感冒传染
14 apprehension 才智
15 cap = fool's cap
16 *Carduus benedictus* 水飞蓟（拉丁文，英文为Holy Thistle，可入药，清热解毒）
17 qualm 突发病
18 thistle 蓟（野生植物，多刺）
19 *Benedictus* （既指赞美耶稣的拉丁祈祷文的名字，也指剧中的本尼迪）
20 moral 寓意；从故事里学到的东西

1 'What means the fool, trow?' (in threes)

Beatrice puts up a good fight in response to Margaret and Hero's teasing in lines 29–70, but what is she really thinking?

Take parts and read the lines. Each time Beatrice speaks a line, pause the action afterwards and take turns to voice her *real* thoughts and emotions. Consider that she is not used to being the butt of the joke, so might be annoyed by this; also, she may be in love but desperate to conceal it.

MUCH ADO ABOUT NOTHING ACT 3 SCENE 4

虚惊一场

Enter BEATRICE

HERO   Good morrow[1], coz[2].
BEATRICE Good morrow, sweet Hero.
HERO   Why how now?[3] Do you speak in the sick tune[4]?
BEATRICE I am out of all other tune, methinks.
MARGARET Clap's into[5] *Light o'Love*: that goes without a burden: do you sing it and I'll dance it.
BEATRICE Ye light o'love with your heels, then if your husband have stables enough, you'll see he shall lack no barns.
MARGARET Oh illegitimate construction[6]! I scorn that with my heels.
BEATRICE 'Tis almost five o'clock, cousin, 'tis time you were ready: by my troth I am exceeding ill, heigh ho[7].
MARGARET For a hawk, a horse, or a husband?
BEATRICE For the letter that begins them all, H[8].
MARGARET Well, and you be not turned Turk[9], there's no more sailing by the star[10].
BEATRICE What means the fool, trow[11]?
MARGARET Nothing I, but God send everyone their heart's desire.
HERO   These gloves the count sent me, they are an excellent perfume.
BEATRICE I am stuffed[12], cousin, I cannot smell.
MARGARET A maid and stuffed! There's goodly catching of cold[13].
BEATRICE Oh God help me, God help me, how long have you professed apprehension[14]?
MARGARET Ever since you left it: doth not my wit become me rarely?
BEATRICE It is not seen enough, you should wear it in your cap[15]: by my troth I am sick.
MARGARET Get you some of this distilled *Carduus benedictus*[16], and lay it to your heart, it is the only thing for a qualm[17].
HERO   There thou prick'st her with a thistle[18].
BEATRICE *Benedictus*[19], why *benedictus?* You have some moral[20] in this *benedictus.*

Margaret chatters teasingly to Beatrice about love and Benedick. Ursula returns with the news that the men have arrived to take Hero to the church.

剧情简介：玛格蕊拿爱情和本尼迪来跟碧翠开玩笑。阿秀菈带回消息，男士们已到，要接希柔去教堂。

1 Thoughts triangle (in threes)

Despite the humour of the teasing, there are other emotions and feelings in this scene.

a List the different moods and attitudes to marriage expressed by Beatrice, Hero and Margaret in this scene.

b Decide who is who in the photograph below, and look at their facial expressions. What do they tell you of the characters' unspoken thoughts? How would you describe the range of moods in this scene? How might these be shown in your performances?

c Each of you should assume the role and the pose of one of the women in the photo. Run through the scene with each of you reading one of the women's lines. When you feel ready, clap your hands to freeze the action and tell the audience what your character is really thinking. It might be very different from what they are saying. Are they secretly scared, sad or excited?

d Perform your version of the scene, with the actual lines from the script and the added spoken-aloud thoughts, to another group or to your class.

1 **perchance** 也许
2 **list** 喜欢，想要
3 **such another** 另一个这种人（同样不会坠入爱河）
4 **in despite** = in spite
5 **eats his meat without grudging** 毫无怨言地接受他（要结婚）的命运
6 **converted** 改主意，改信仰
7 **Not a false gallop** 不迈错一步，不说一句假话
8 **withdraw** 移步

MUCH ADO ABOUT NOTHING ACT 3 SCENE 4
虚惊一场

MARGARET   Moral? No by my troth, I have no moral meaning, I meant
plain Holy Thistle, you may think perchance[1] that I think you are in   60
love, nay by'r Lady I am not such a fool to think what I list[2], nor I list
not to think what I can, nor indeed I cannot think, if I would think
my heart out of thinking, that you are in love, or that you will be in
love, or that you can be in love: yet Benedick was such another[3], and
now is he become a man, he swore he would never marry, and yet   65
now in despite[4] of his heart he eats his meat without grudging[5], and
how you may be converted[6] I know not, but methinks you look with
your eyes as other women do.

BEATRICE   What pace is this that thy tongue keeps?

MARGARET   Not a false gallop[7].   70

Enter URSULA

URSULA   Madam, withdraw[8], the prince, the count, Signor Benedick,
Don John, and all the gallants of the town are come to fetch you to
church.

HERO   Help to dress me, good coz, good Meg, good Ursula.

[*Exeunt*]

Leonato is busy with the last-minute preparations for the wedding. Dogberry and Verges come to inform him of the arrest of Borachio and Conrade, but their ramblings exasperate the impatient Leonato.

 剧情简介：列纳托忙着婚礼的最后准备工作。道博瑞和瓦吉前来向他禀告鲍拉丘和康拉已被捕，他们词不达意、东拉西扯，让不耐烦的列纳托非常恼火。

Characters 人物分析

What does he mean now? (in pairs)

Whenever Dogberry is on stage, one of the great sources of amusement for the audience is trying to work out what he is attempting to say – and matching that against the impact of his actual words on the other characters.

a Below are two lists of words that Dogberry uses completely incorrectly. Read through lines 1–51 and come up with a range of possible meanings for these words. Aim to have three definitions for each word in one of the lists below:

- one that is sensible, describing what you think Dogberry actually means
- one that is plausible, but clearly not correct
- one that is wildly imaginative.

List A	List B
decerns (line 3)	blunt (line 9)
odorous (line 13)	exclamation (line 20)
comprehended (line 35)	aspitious (line 36)
suffigance (line 40)	examination (line 46)

b Once you have your definitions, team up with a pair who worked on definitions for the other list. Read through the scene with your partner. When you get to one of your words, shout 'What does he mean now?' to freeze the scene. You and your partner take it in turns to read out the three possible definitions, and the other pair tries to guess which one is correct. If they choose the correct explanation, they score a point. If they do not, your pair scores a point. The pair with the most points at the end is the winner.

c As you read the lines, experiment with the way in which you say them. Is Dogberry playful with the lines, or is it actually funnier if he delivers his lines with complete sincerity? Think about the reactions of characters who may not have scripted lines – should they laugh openly or attempt to keep straight faces? Might some of them not even notice Dogberry's mistakes?

1 *Headborough* 镇长
2 Marry 确实
3 confidence 私人谈话
4 decerns 辨别（道博瑞想说 concerns [关系到]）
5 nearlys 密切
6 Brief 长话短说
7 Goodman 贤士（比 gentleman低一等的称谓）
8 odorous 难闻（道博瑞想说 odious [讨厌]）
9 palabras 话语（西班牙语，道博瑞故意卖弄）
10 poor duke's officers （道博瑞想说the duke's poor officers）
11 tedious 啰唆（道博瑞误以为 tedious是"富有"的意思）
12 of your worship = on your worship
13 exclamation on 对……大声斥责（道博瑞想说 acclamtion [称赞；喝彩]）
14 fain know 很高兴知道

Act 3 Scene 5
The hall of Leonato's house

Enter LEONATO *and* DOGBERRY *the Constable and* VERGES *the Headborough*[1]

LEONATO   What would you with me, honest neighbour?
DOGBERRY   Marry[2], sir, I would have some confidence[3] with you, that decerns[4] you nearly[5].
LEONATO   Brief[6] I pray you, for you see it is a busy time with me.
DOGBERRY   Marry this it is, sir.   5
VERGES   Yes in truth it is, sir.
LEONATO   What is it, my good friends?
DOGBERRY   Goodman[7] Verges, sir, speaks a little off the matter, an old man, sir, and his wits are not so blunt, as God help I would desire they were, but in faith honest, as the skin between his brows.   10
VERGES   Yes I thank God, I am honest as any man living, that is an old man, and no honester than I.
DOGBERRY   Comparisons are odorous[8], palabras[9], neighbour Verges.
LEONATO   Neighbours, you are tedious.
DOGBERRY   It pleases your worship to say so, but we are the poor duke's   15
officers[10], but truly for mine own part, if I were as tedious[11] as a king, I could find in my heart to bestow it all of your worship[12].
LEONATO   All thy tediousness on me, ah?
DOGBERRY   Yea, and 'twere a thousand pound more than 'tis, for I hear as good exclamation on[13] your worship as of any man in the city, and   20
though I be but a poor man, I am glad to hear it.
VERGES   And so am I.
LEONATO   I would fain know[14] what you have to say.

Leonato cannot wait for Dogberry to get to the point. He instructs Dogberry to conduct the trial, not realising the significance for himself and his daughter of the crime that has been uncovered.

剧情简介：列纳托没等道博瑞说到正题就命令他去审案，因此没有意识到案中人所犯的罪对他本人以及他女儿多么重要。

1 Don't interrupt me now (in threes)

Ironically, in his anxiety to get to his daughter's wedding, Leonato is unaware of the importance of this interview. For their part, Dogberry and Verges are equally unaware of how vital their news is. Take a part each (ignore lines 42–4) and read the scene through.

- Dogberry and Verges should be very respectful, but rambling and 'tedious'.
- Leonato should be flustered (慌乱), irritable, anxious to leave, but also displaying an amused sarcasm.
- Decide where Dogberry talks to Leonato and where he talks to Verges. Dogberry sees himself as far superior to his partner, so show Dogberry's patronising (居高临下) self-importance.

▼ Is this how you imagined these three men might look? Find the line in this scene that suggests Dogberry is physically larger than Verges. Think about how you can use physical comedy in your performance of the scene.

1 **excepting** （瓦吉想说 respecting [尊重]）
2 **ha' ta'en** = have taken
3 **arrant** 彻头彻尾
4 **world** 奇迹，奇观
5 **and ... horse** 如果两人骑一匹马（势必一前一后，即只能有一个领头的）
6 **as ever broke bread** 总是乐善好施
7 **comprehended** （道博瑞其实想说apprehended [拘捕]）
8 **aspitious** （道博瑞其实想说suspicious [可疑]）
9 **suffigance** （道博瑞想说sufficient [足够]）
10 **stay** 等待
11 **Francis Seacoal** （不确定道博瑞是否指第3幕第3场出现的George Seacoal）
12 **ink-horn** 墨水瓶
13 **goal** = jail
14 **to a noncome** （拉丁文 *non compos mentis* [昏头昏脑] 的错误略语）
15 **only** 只管
16 **excommunication** 逐出教会 （道博瑞想说communication [口供]）

Write about it 写作练习

The police (mis-)report

As he makes such a mess of actually telling Leonato what has been planned, consider what a hash (糟乱) Dogberry would make of writing up these events for the formal record!

As Dogberry, write a report of your visit to Leonato. Include Dogberry's malapropisms (refer to the list on the previous page and the glossaries on each page), taking particular care to use them according to his intended definitions in the script. You might begin: 'Decerning that most tedious Signor Leonato, his daughter and the aspitious persons that were comprehended …'

Much Ado About Nothing Act 3 Scene 5

虚惊一场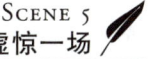

VERGES Marry, sir, our watch tonight, excepting[1] your worship's presence, ha' ta'en[2] a couple of as arrant[3] knaves as any in Messina.

DOGBERRY A good old man, sir, he will be talking as they say, when the age is in, the wit is out, God help us, it is a world[4] to see: well said i'faith, neighbour Verges, well, God's a good man, and two men ride of a horse[5], one must ride behind, an honest soul i'faith, sir, by my troth he is, as ever broke bread[6], but God is to be worshipped, all men are not alike, alas, good neighbour.

LEONATO Indeed, neighbour, he comes too short of you.

DOGBERRY Gifts that God gives.

LEONATO I must leave you.

DOGBERRY One word, sir, our watch, sir, have indeed comprehended[7] two aspitious[8] persons, and we would have them this morning examined before your worship.

LEONATO Take their examination yourself, and bring it me, I am now in great haste, as it may appear unto you.

DOGBERRY It shall be suffigance[9].

[Enter MESSENGER*]*

LEONATO Drink some wine ere you go: fare you well.

MESSENGER My lord, they stay[10] for you, to give your daughter to her husband.

LEONATO I'll wait upon them, I am ready.

Exit [Leonato with Messenger]

DOGBERRY Go, good partner, go get you to Francis Seacoal[11], bid him bring his pen and ink-horn[12] to the gaol[13]: we are now to examination these men.

VERGES And we must do it wisely.

DOGBERRY We will spare for no wit I warrant you: here's that shall drive some of them to a noncome[14], only[15] get the learned writer to set down our excommunication[16], and meet me at the gaol.

Exeunt

Much Ado About Nothing
虚惊一场

Looking back at Act 3 第3幕回顾
Activities for groups or individuals

1 Themes: Keeping track of deception

Act 3 contains much plotting and trickery; some is light-hearted, but other intrigues are altogether more sinister (邪恶). When you write about a theme, it is important to consider all the instances in which it appears, how the characters are involved, and the impact on them and the play as a whole.

Make some medium-sized cards, and label three of them with the deceptions that are now up and running in the play:

- the 'gulling' of Benedick
- Don John's plot to destroy the reputation of Hero
- tricking the eavesdropping Beatrice.

Arrange these three cards on a piece of paper so that they form a triangle with a lot of space in the middle. Now consider the characters involved in these deceptions. Make some smaller cards and write a character's name on each one. Arrange these in a circle within the triangle – see the diagram opposite. Draw lines between the 'character' and 'deception' cards to link the characters to the deceptions in which they are involved. Along the lines, write key quotations that explain the nature of this involvement and its impact on the character and/or the play.

You might colour-code (以颜色标记) the deceptions and the lines, so you can see each 'web of intrigue' more clearly. Similarly, you could highlight comic and serious effects in different colours. Some deceptions may appear wholly comic or wholly serious, but there could be contrasting elements involved. For example, Dogberry is involved in the deception of Hero, but he is trying to stop it and is making a real mess of things, adding an element of comedy to an upsetting episode.

2 Beatrice's dream

Act out Beatrice's dream on the night before Hero's wedding. Who might visit her in her dream, and what might they say? Think about how her subconscious mind might explore her feelings for Benedick, and Hero's 'criticism'.

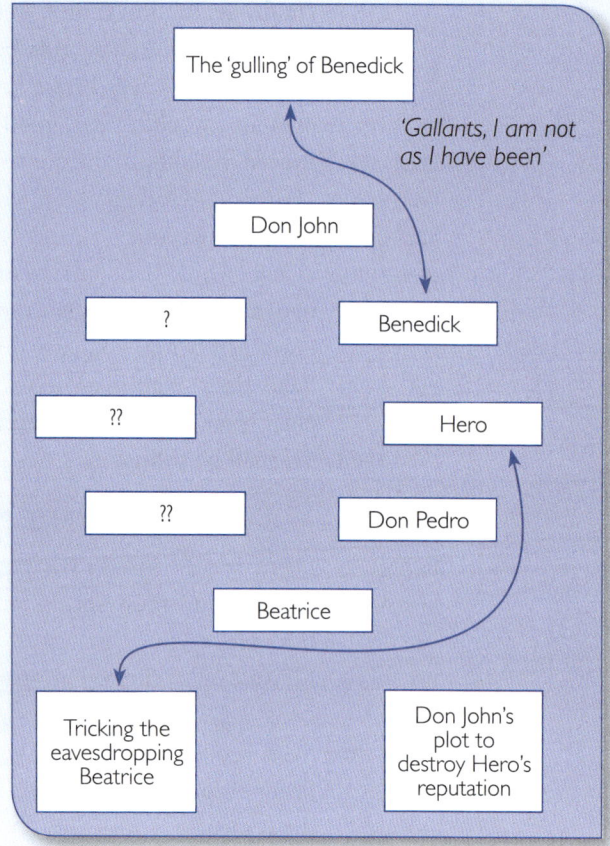

3 Dark and light

As the play moves towards its crisis, Shakespeare alternates lighter (Beatrice–Benedick) and darker (Hero–Claudio) plots. He thus continually shifts the mood of the play from comedy to potential tragedy.

In groups of six, present a five-minute version of Act 3. Speed up the comic moments and make the threatening or serious moments seem slow and intense. Be careful to note that within the lighter plot there are some darker moments, and that there is some lighter material in the darker plot.

You might divide the scene so that some in the group play the 'light' and some the 'dark'. Use costume or lighting to signal this divide.

Dogberry and his men did not feature (给予特写) in the play until this act. This image shows them at their best (or possibly worst)! Use this picture and the notes on pages 180–1 to explain why these characters are now so prominent in the plot. How do they add to the play and help develop it as a comedy?

The guests assemble for the wedding of Hero and Claudio. As Friar Francis begins the marriage ceremony, Claudio refuses to accept Hero as his bride and hands her back to Leonato.

 剧情简介：希柔和克劳丢婚礼的宾客到齐。福冉希修士宣布婚礼开始，克劳丢却拒绝希柔做他的新娘，把她退回给列纳托。

Write about it 写作练习

'this rotten orange'

In line 27, Claudio uses a metaphor to compare Hero to a rotten orange. An orange is sweet and nourishing before it rots to become ugly and sour. It is also thought that prostitutes sold oranges in and around the Globe Theatre in Shakespeare's time.

a Write an explanation of the different interpretations or connotations of this 'rotten orange' theme.

b The theme is extended and further explored in lines 28–104. Identify any words or phrases connected to the theme of sweetness turning to ugliness, and write a second paragraph explaining how Shakespeare develops the idea.

1 **''Tis pity she's a whore'** (in sixes)

One person speaks Claudio's opening accusations of Hero (lines 25–55). The others express their reactions in the following ways:

- **Disbelief** Claudio speaks his lines face to face with Hero. The rest act as family and friends. Echo the words and phrases you find unbelievable. At the end, ask Hero to say what she is thinking.
- **Support** Repeat the exercise, but now the group members are, like Don Pedro, supporters of Claudio. They echo words that emphasise Claudio's anger and disgust. At the end, ask Hero how she feels.

Stagecraft 导演技巧

A very public rejection (in large groups)

The dramatic impact of this scene is made stronger by the public nature of Claudio's rejection. Hero is dressed as a bride and all of Messina is present to witness her humiliation. On the next few pages, you will see how different productions have staged the wedding.

a Rehearse the dramatic opening moments of this scene (lines 1–31). Show the change from a happy and holy atmosphere to one of shock and dismay (沮丧) as Claudio begins his denunciation (谴责).

b Sketch a stage plan showing where you would position the different characters. The scene should resemble a formal wedding occasion, and the audience must be able to see characters' reactions.

---

1 plain form 简单的仪式
2 recount their particular duties 详细列出夫妻各自的责任
3 inward impediment 内部（即不为人知的）阻碍
4 Interjections 插话，插曲
5 Stand thee by 请你站在一旁
6 unconstrainèd 无拘束
7 maid 处女
8 counterpoise 使等值，抵得上
9 render her 将她归还
10 learn me 教会我
11 semblance 外表
12 what … truth 权威和真诚的外表

MUCH ADO ABOUT NOTHING ACT 4 SCENE 1
虚惊一场

Act 4 Scene 1
A church

Enter DON PEDRO, DON JOHN, LEONATO, FRIAR FRANCIS, CLAUDIO, BENEDICK, HERO *and* BEATRICE; *Wedding Guests*

LEONATO   Come, Friar Francis, be brief, only to the plain form[1] of marriage, and you shall recount their particular duties[2] afterwards.
FRIAR FRANCIS   You come hither, my lord, to marry this lady?
CLAUDIO   No.
LEONATO   To be married to her: friar, you come to marry her.   5
FRIAR FRANCIS   Lady, you come hither to be married to this count?
HERO   I do.
FRIAR FRANCIS   If either of you know any inward impediment[3] why you should not be conjoined, I charge you on your souls to utter it.
CLAUDIO   Know you any, Hero?   10
HERO   None, my lord.
FRIAR FRANCIS   Know you any, count?
LEONATO   I dare make his answer, none.
CLAUDIO   Oh what men dare do! What men may do! What men daily do, not knowing what they do!   15
BENEDICK   How now! Interjections[4]? Why then, some be of laughing, as, ah, ha, he.
CLAUDIO   Stand thee by[5], friar: father, by your leave,
Will you with free and unconstrainèd[6] soul
Give me this maid[7] your daughter?   20
LEONATO   As freely, son, as God did give her me.
CLAUDIO   And what have I to give you back, whose worth
May counterpoise[8] this rich and precious gift?
DON PEDRO   Nothing, unless you render her[9] again.
CLAUDIO   Sweet prince, you learn me[10] noble thankfulness: 25
There, Leonato, take her back again,
Give not this rotten orange to your friend,
She's but the sign and semblance[11] of her honour:
Behold how like a maid she blushes here!
Oh what authority and show of truth[12]   30
Can cunning sin cover itself withal!

101

Claudio declares that he will not marry Hero. Leonato assumes that Hero has lost her virginity to Claudio, but Claudio denies this. Don Pedro denounces Hero as a common prostitute.

 剧情简介：克劳丢宣布他不会娶希柔为妻。列纳托以为希柔已失身于克劳丢，但克劳丢否认。唐佩卓指责希柔是粗俗的娼妇。

1 Speak your thoughts (in sixes)

Take a part each and read or perform lines 18–88. As you finish each speech, freeze the action and express in a few words the emotions that the character who has spoken feels at that moment. For example, at some point Leonato might be 'anxious and puzzled', Hero 'scared and confused', Claudio 'savagely angry', and Don John 'excited and delighted'. Try this activity several times and see if your reactions/emotions change.

As an extension, have Don Pedro and Claudio try to explain or justify their public humiliation of Hero and her father. Perform this as a 'hot-seat'* activity, where the group asks questions of the characters.

1	**Comes not that blood** 那抹红潮不正像……
2	**luxurious** 充满肉欲
3	**approvèd wanton** 已被证实的荡妇
4	**vanquished** 战胜，征服
5	**known** 与……发生性关系
6	**extenuate the forehand sin** 为之前的罪恶（即我破了她的贞操）找理由
7	**large** 不当
8	**Bashful sincerity** 羞涩的真诚
9	**comely** 本分，合适
10	**Dian** = Diana（荻阿娜，贞洁与月亮女神）
11	**orb** 天体（这里指月亮）
12	**blown** 盛开，怒放
13	**intemperate** 放纵，无节制
14	**Venus** 维纳斯（性爱女神）
15	**pampered animals** 吃得过饱/纵欲的禽兽
16	**wide** 弄错，不着边际
17	**stale** 野鸡，娼妇
18	**nuptial** 婚礼

Themes 主题分析

Appearance and reality: 'Sir, they are spoken and these things are true'

Don John claims to know the truth (line 61): Hero is unchaste and dishonest.

a List what each of the characters present appears to know, or believes they know, about Hero. Note down where this information has come from.

b To what extent do you sympathise with the characters' mistaken beliefs? List and rank them, providing a brief justification for your feelings.

* **hot-seat** 热座位，一种课堂游戏，玩法是请一位同学坐到讲台上的一把椅子上，其他同学轮番给他/她出难题，哪个问题他/她回答不出就算输。

▼ Who's who in this painting? Can you identify the different characters?

Much Ado About Nothing Act 4 Scene 1
虚惊一场

      Comes not that blood[1], as modest evidence,
      To witness simple virtue? Would you not swear
      All you that see her, that she were a maid,
      By these exterior shows? But she is none: 35
      She knows the heat of a luxurious[2] bed:
      Her blush is guiltiness, not modesty.
LEONATO What do you mean, my lord?
CLAUDIO   Not to be married,
      Not to knit my soul to an approvèd wanton[3].
LEONATO Dear my lord, if you in your own proof,   40
      Have vanquished[4] the resistance of her youth,
      And made defeat of her virginity –
CLAUDIO I know what you would say: if I have known[5] her,
      You will say, she did embrace me as a husband,
      And so extenuate the forehand sin[6]: no, Leonato,   45
      I never tempted her with word too large[7],
      But as a brother to his sister, showed
      Bashful sincerity[8], and comely[9] love.
HERO And seemed I ever otherwise to you?
CLAUDIO Out on thee seeming, I will write against it!   50
      You seem to me as Dian[10] in her orb[11],
      As chaste as is the bud ere it be blown[12]:
      But you are more intemperate[13] in your blood,
      Than Venus[14], or those pampered animals[15],
      That rage in savage sensuality.   55
HERO Is my lord well, that he doth speak so wide[16]?
LEONATO Sweet prince, why speak not you?
DON PEDRO   What should I speak?
      I stand dishonoured that have gone about
      To link my dear friend to a common stale[17].
LEONATO Are these things spoken, or do I but dream?   60
DON JOHN Sir, they are spoken, and these things are true.
BENEDICK This looks not like a nuptial[18].
HERO   True, oh God!
CLAUDIO Leonato, stand I here?
      Is this the prince? Is this the prince's brother?
      Is this face Hero's? Are our eyes our own?   65
LEONATO All this is so, but what of this, my lord?

Claudio questions Hero about the man he saw at her window. Hero denies there was any man. Don Pedro and his brother confirm the truth of Claudio's accusation.

 剧情简介：克劳丢质问希柔他在希柔窗前看到的男人是谁，希柔否认有任何男人。唐佩卓和他的弟弟证明克劳丢的指控是真的。

Characters 人物分析
Hero – 'answer truly to your name'

The first question in the Christian catechism (教义问答) (a series of questions testing knowledge of the Christian faith) is 'What is your name?' In Shakespeare's time, the name Hero would have suggested faithfulness in love. In Greek legend, Hero was the true love of Leander, who drowned whilst swimming across the Hellespont to meet her. She, in turn, drowned herself for love of him.

Use this information to write a paragraph explaining the significance of the dialogue between Hero and Claudio in lines 72–76. Suggest how knowledge of the legend might change the way an audience views the scene.

Language in the play 剧中语言
Claudio's farewell to Hero (in pairs)

a Read aloud lines 93–101 several times. Try to identify all the examples of **alliteration*** (repeating the same letter or sound at the start of a sequence of words), wordplay (using double or hidden/suggested meanings in words) and **oxymoron** (矛盾修辞法) (placing two contradictory ideas side by side).

b Read aloud these lines again, over-emphasising the consonants that Claudio uses to create the alliteration. Discuss, or describe in writing, the effect of these harsh consonants on the way an actor delivers the speech.

c Discuss how the language used by Shakespeare in this speech helps create sympathy for Hero.

d Shakespeare often uses wordplay and oxymorons for comic effect. Write director's notes for an actor playing Claudio, explaining how these elements should be used in this speech, and what they might tell us about Claudio's state of mind.

1 **kindly power**　（作为父亲）天赋的权力
2 **catechising**　询问，盘问
3 **answer truly to your name**　（基督教教义问答手册中的第一个问题就是"What is your name？"）
4 **blot**　玷污，败坏（名声）
5 **reproach**　责难，谴责
6 **Hero itself** = Hero herself
7 **no maiden**　不是处女
8 **grievèd**　委屈，悲哀
9 **ruffian**　流氓，无赖
10 **liberal**　粗俗，放肆
11 **vile encounters**　令人作呕的会面
12 **much misgovernment**　太不自重，太不检点
13 **counsels**　意图
14 **impiety**　不敬畏，不自重
15 **conjecture**　猜疑
16 **never … gracious**　（美貌）不再令人心动

* **alliteration**　头韵，指诗句里两个或多个词的第一个辅音相同，如 sing a song of sixpence，类似中文的双声。

1 'Hath no man's dagger here a point for me?'

This is a desperate line from Leonato, expressing his shame, despair and implied belief in what he has just been told about his daughter.

Try delivering this line in a number of different ways to see what works best. What do you want the audience to feel at this point?

MUCH ADO ABOUT NOTHING ACT 4 SCENE 1

虚惊一场

CLAUDIO   Let me but move one question to your daughter,
           And by that fatherly and kindly power[1],
           That you have in her, bid her answer truly.
LEONATO   I charge thee do so, as thou art my child.   70
HERO   Oh God defend me, how am I beset!
           What kind of catechising[2] call you this?
CLAUDIO   To make you answer truly to your name[3].
HERO   Is it not Hero? Who can blot[4] that name
           With any just reproach[5]?
CLAUDIO   Marry that can Hero,   75
           Hero itself[6] can blot out Hero's virtue.
           What man was he, talked with you yesternight,
           Out at your window betwixt twelve and one?
           Now if you are a maid, answer to this.
HERO   I talked with no man at that hour, my lord.   80
DON PEDRO Why then are you no maiden[7]. Leonato,
           I am sorry you must hear: upon mine honour,
           Myself, my brother, and this grievèd[8] count
           Did see her, hear her, at that hour last night,
           Talk with a ruffian[9] at her chamber window,   85
           Who hath indeed most like a liberal[10] villain,
           Confessed the vile encounters[11] they have had
           A thousand times in secret.
DON JOHN   Fie, fie, they are
           Not to be named my lord, not to be spoke of,
           There is not chastity enough in language,   90
           Without offence to utter them: thus, pretty lady,
           I am sorry for thy much misgovernment[12].
CLAUDIO   Oh Hero! What a hero hadst thou been,
           If half thy outward graces had been placed
           About thy thoughts and counsels[13] of thy heart?   95
           But fare thee well, most foul, most fair, farewell
           Thou pure impiety[14], and impious purity,
           For thee I'll lock up all the gates of love,
           And on my eyelids shall conjecture[15] hang,
           To turn all beauty into thoughts of harm,   100
           And never shall it more be gracious[16].
LEONATO   Hath no man's dagger here a point for me?
                    [*Hero faints*]

105

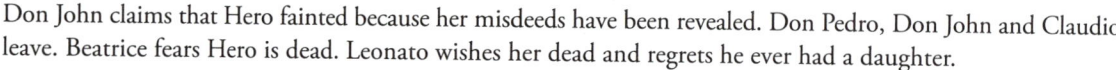

Don John claims that Hero fainted because her misdeeds have been revealed. Don Pedro, Don John and Claudio leave. Beatrice fears Hero is dead. Leonato wishes her dead and regrets he ever had a daughter.

剧情简介：唐约翰声称希柔昏倒是因为丑行被揭穿。唐佩卓、唐约翰、克劳丢离开。碧翠担心希柔已死。列纳托但愿她死了，后悔自己有女儿。

Characters 人物分析
Why does Benedick stay?

This is a crucial moment of decision for Benedick. Should he leave with his friends or stay with Hero and Beatrice?

a List the reasons why Benedick might be tempted to leave, and his possible reasons for staying.

b Use this information to write a 'duologue' (二人对白剧) in which the two halves of Benedick's mind explain his dilemma and his decision.

1 A father's anger and shame (in small groups)

Leonato's feelings (lines 113–36) are intense. He reflects upon the love and pride he felt for Hero, and the shame he feels now that her honour 'is fallen / Into a pit of ink'.

a One of you is Hero, one Leonato. Sit Hero on a chair. Leonato and the rest of the group circle Hero. As Leonato addresses his unconscious daughter, the group should violently and angrily echo the 'accusing' words (e.g. 'Wherefore?', 'Cry shame', 'Do not live', 'thy shames').

b One person mimes Leonato's gestures while another reads his words. How can Leonato use his face and body to express anguish?

c Divide the speech into smaller sections and distribute it among the group. Have Hero walk slowly down a line of you as you each deliver a section of the speech in a different tone. Try to make the delivery sound like Leonato's mind debating with itself. This should reveal the complexity of his feelings.

Themes 主题分析
Male power

Leonato's speech is very similar to Capulet's tirade (长篇激烈讲话) against Juliet in *Romeo and Juliet* (Act 3 Scene 5, lines 149–95). It reflects the way that daughters were viewed as possessions of value, with the ability to create powerful alliances between families. Hero's treatment also shows how important and how fragile a woman's reputation could be in Elizabethan times.

   Write a note or letter from Beatrice to a close friend, in which she describes what Leonato says to Hero here and tries to explain the attitude he adopts.

1 spirits 活力
2 look up 睁开眼睛
3 printed in her blood 她羞臊脸红
4 on the rearward of reproaches 就在痛骂之后
5 Strike at thy life 了结你的性命
6 frugal 吝啬
7 Chid … frame? 我埋怨老天吝啬只给我一个孩子了吗？
8 issue 儿女，子女
9 smirchèd 有污点
10 mired 沾上泥，弄脏
11 infamy 恶名，声名狼藉
12 unknown loins 不知父母是谁
13 salt … season （给肉加盐可防腐）

Much Ado About Nothing Act 4 Scene 1
虚惊一场

BEATRICE	Why how now, cousin, wherefore sink you down?	
DON JOHN	Come let us go: these things come thus to light,	
	Smother her spirits[1] up.	
	[*Exeunt Don Pedro, Don John and Claudio*]	
BENEDICK	How doth the lady?	105
BEATRICE	Dead I think, help, uncle!	
	Hero, why Hero: uncle: Signor Benedick: friar!	
LEONATO	Oh Fate! Take not away thy heavy hand,	
	Death is the fairest cover for her shame	
	That may be wished for.	
BEATRICE	How now, cousin Hero?	110
FRIAR FRANCIS	Have comfort, lady.	
LEONATO	Dost thou look up[2]?	
FRIAR FRANCIS	Yea, wherefore should she not?	
LEONATO	Wherefore? Why doth not every earthly thing	
	Cry shame upon her? Could she here deny	
	The story that is printed in her blood[3]?	115
	Do not live, Hero, do not ope thine eyes:	
	For did I think thou wouldst not quickly die,	
	Thought I thy spirits were stronger than thy shames,	
	Myself would on the rearward of reproaches[4]	
	Strike at thy life[5], Grieved I, I had but one?	120
	Chid I for that at frugal[6] nature's frame?[7]	
	Oh one too much by thee! Why had I one?	
	Why ever wast thou lovely in my eyes?	
	Why had I not with charitable hand,	
	Took up a beggar's issue[8] at my gates,	125
	Who smirchèd[9] thus, and mired[10] with infamy[11],	
	I might have said, no part of it is mine,	
	This shame derives itself from unknown loins[12]:	
	But mine, and mine I loved, and mine I praised,	
	And mine that I was proud on, mine so much,	130
	That I myself, was to myself not mine,	
	Valuing of her: why she, oh she is fallen	
	Into a pit of ink, that the wide sea	
	Hath drops too few to wash her clean again,	
	And salt too little, which may season[13] give	135
	To her foul tainted flesh.	

Benedick asks Beatrice if she had kept Hero company that night. When Beatrice says no, Leonato is immediately convinced of his daughter's guilt and wishes her dead. Friar Francis believes Hero is innocent.

剧情简介：本尼迪问碧翠那天晚上是否和希柔在一起，碧翠说没有，列纳托立刻确信希柔有罪过，但愿她去死，福冉希修士相信希柔是清白的。

▼ In this production, the women form a protective group around Hero as Leonato rants (叫嚷). How do you interpret Benedick's expression here? Discuss his conflicted feelings at this point in the play.

1 **attired** 被包裹
2 **belied** 被冤枉
3 **Hence from her** 离她远点儿
4 **given … fortune** 旁观事态的发展
5 **apparitions** 迹象，表露
6 **with experimental seal** 再加上我的人生阅历
7 **warrant … book** 保证我书本知识的可靠性
8 **divinity** 神职，神职人员
9 **biting error** 重大失误
10 **perjury** 作伪证
11 **proper nakedness** 赤裸裸的事实

Write about it 写作练习

'by noting of the lady'

Beatrice trusts Hero and knows in her 'soul' (line 139) that she is innocent. Other characters desperately attempt to 'know' the truth by judging or 'noting' the outward signs. Leonato and Friar Francis are two such people.

a After reading lines 113–168, write in role as Leonato. Describe the outward signs you have observed in both Hero and Claudio, and explain what this has led you to believe:

- By noting of Claudio/Hero I have marked …
- I am therefore convinced that …

b Try the same activity in role as Friar Francis. List what you have noticed about Hero, what your conclusions are, and justify why you should be trusted in this matter:

- By noting of the lady I have marked …
- I can only conclude that …
- My words should be listened to because …

BENEDICK	Sir, sir, be patient. For my part I am so attired[1] in wonder, I know not what to say.	
BEATRICE	Oh on my soul my cousin is belied[2].	
BENEDICK	Lady, were you her bedfellow last night?	140
BEATRICE	No truly not, although until last night, I have this twelve month been her bedfellow.	
LEONATO	Confirmed, confirmed, oh that is stronger made, Which was before barred up with ribs of iron. Would the two princes lie, and Claudio lie, Who loved her so, that speaking of her foulness, Washed it with tears? Hence from her[3], let her die.	145
FRIAR FRANCIS	Hear me a little, for I have only been Silent so long, and given way unto This course of fortune[4], by noting of the lady. I have marked A thousand blushing apparitions[5], To start into her face, a thousand innocent shames, In angel whiteness beat away those blushes, And in her eye there hath appeared a fire, To burn the errors that these princes hold Against her maiden truth: call me a fool, Trust not my reading, nor my observations, Which with experimental seal[6] doth warrant The tenure of my book[7]: trust not my age, My reverence, calling, nor divinity[8], If this sweet lady lie not guiltless here, Under some biting error[9].	150 155 160
LEONATO	Friar, it cannot be, Thou seest that all the grace that she hath left, Is that she will not add to her damnation A sin of perjury[10], she not denies it: Why seek'st thou then to cover with excuse, That which appears in proper nakedness[11]?	165

Hero is prepared to suffer torture and death if proven guilty. Benedick begins to suspect his friends have been deceived. Leonato swears revenge if this is true. Friar Francis advises them to pretend that Hero has died.

 剧情简介：希柔做好了准备，如果她被证明有罪，她宁愿受酷刑甚至去死。本尼迪怀疑他的朋友们可能受骗了。列纳托发誓如果这是一场骗局，他定将报复。福冉希修士建议他们先假装希柔已死。

1 Show their reactions (in fives)

The accusations of Claudio and the princes have left everyone in turmoil, with Hero innocent and distraught (心急如焚) at the centre of it all (see the picture below and the one on page 108).

a Devise a tableau to illustrate a line or sentence from the script opposite. Show your tableau to the rest of the class. Be prepared to hold the freeze for at least thirty seconds, so the others can identify each character and guess the line your group is portraying.

b Take a photograph of each of the tableaux and prepare a slide show or presentation titled 'Hero Accused', showing each of the images along with a line of text as a caption. You could even record some of the text and insert the recording as a sound file to accompany the images.

1	maiden modesty	少女的贞操
2	unmeet	不适当，不合礼法
3	Refuse me	把我撵走
4	misprision	误会，误解
5	have … honour	秉性正派
6	practice	策划，谋划
7	Whose … villainies	他总是唯恐天下不乱
8	hear of it	为此负责
9	invention	谋划事情的能力
10	havoc	浩劫，大破坏
11	means	财富
12	reft me	剥夺我
13	policy of mind	睿智
14	To … throughly	好好算总账
15	counsel sway you	用建议引导您
16	kept in	深居简出
17	mourning ostentation	悼念仪式
18	monument	坟墓
19	epitaphs	悼文，祭文
20	rites	仪式
21	appertain unto	属于

2 'publish it, that she is dead indeed' (in sixes)

Act out the plan that Friar Francis urges Leonato to adopt (lines 193–201). One person narrates the events, which the others mime. Make sure you show every part of Friar Francis's plan through your mime.

MUCH ADO ABOUT NOTHING ACT 4 SCENE 1
虚惊一场

FRIAR FRANCIS Lady, what man is he you are accused of?
HERO   They know that do accuse me, I know none: 170
        If I know more of any man alive
        Than that which maiden modesty¹ doth warrant,
        Let all my sins lack mercy. Oh my father,
        Prove you that any man with me conversed,
        At hours unmeet², or that I yesternight 175
        Maintained the change of words with any creature,
        Refuse me³, hate me, torture me to death.
FRIAR FRANCIS There is some strange misprision⁴ in the princes.
BENEDICK Two of them have the very bent of honour⁵,
        And if their wisdoms be misled in this, 180
        The practice⁶ of it lives in John the bastard,
        Whose spirits toil in frame of villainies⁷.
LEONATO I know not: if they speak but truth of her,
        These hands shall tear her, if they wrong her honour,
        The proudest of them shall well hear of it⁸. 185
        Time hath not yet so dried this blood of mine,
        Nor age so eat up my invention⁹,
        Nor fortune made such havoc¹⁰ of my means¹¹,
        Nor my bad life reft me¹² so much of friends,
        But they shall find, awaked in such a kind, 190
        Both strength of limb, and policy of mind¹³,
        Ability in means, and choice of friends,
        To quit me of them throughly¹⁴.
FRIAR FRANCIS   Pause awhile,
        And let my counsel sway you¹⁵ in this case:
        Your daughter here the princes left for dead, 195
        Let her awhile be secretly kept in¹⁶,
        And publish it, that she is dead indeed:
        Maintain a mourning ostentation¹⁷,
        And on your family's old monument¹⁸
        Hang mournful epitaphs¹⁹, and do all rites²⁰, 200
        That appertain unto²¹ a burial.
LEONATO What shall become of this? What will this do?

111

Friar Francis outlines what he hopes will be the healing effect on Claudio when he hears of Hero's 'death'. If his plan fails, Hero will have to enter a nunnery.

 剧情简介：福冉希修士简要说明，他希望克劳丢听到希柔的"死讯"能对抚慰他的感情创伤有作用。如果他的计划失败，希柔将不得不进修道院。

Language in the play 剧中语言
'Change slander to remorse'

This is a detailed and considered speech, reflecting the complexity of the Friar's plan and the uncertain outcome.

a There is a **lexical field** (词汇场，有语义关联的一组词) (group of words) relating to death in this speech. Make a list of all these words.

b There is a corresponding field relating to the vitality of life and of birth. Make a parallel list of these words to compare and contrast.

c How is language used in lines 203–36 to reflect Friar Francis's hopes that Hero can move from darkness (denunciation) into light (reconciliation and the restoration of love and reputation)? Write an explanation, either a single paragraph or a more extended analysis. You may also want to draw or create a diagram to illustrate this change.

1 well carried 进展顺利
2 slander to remorse 化指责为悔恨
3 on this travail 由于这样做
4 lamented 哀悼，怀念
5 prize not to the worth 不好好珍惜
6 rack 扩大，夸大
7 study of imagination 冥思苦想
8 every … life 她身体和灵魂的每一部分
9 apparelled 穿戴上
10 habit 服饰
11 moving 令人激动
12 liver 肝脏（常被认为是身体的激情中心）
13 success 后果
14 all aim but 所有目标，除……外
15 be levelled false 不能实现
16 supposition 假设
17 quench 熄灭，终止
18 sort not well 不太顺利

1 'And if it sort not well' (in sixes)

In *Romeo and Juliet*, Friar Lawrence devises a desperately dangerous scheme to help the young lovers. Here, Shakespeare again gives the Church the difficult job ('this travail') of trying to turn tragedy into something positive ('greater birth'). Friar Francis envisages (设想) four possible outcomes to his plan:

- News of Hero's death will make her accusers feel pity (lines 203–4).
- Hero's death will bring new life to Claudio's love (lines 207–29).
- Hero's death will cleanse her of her tarnished reputation (lines 230–2).
- If the plan fails, Hero can be sent to a nunnery (lines 233–6).

Select one person to narrate these lines. Plan a short scene (or improvise one), showing what might happen in each of these outcomes. You could mime this scene while the narrator delivers the Friar's lines, or you could use the Friar's lines as an introduction to a scene in contemporary language. Ask the audience to decide which outcome they would prefer to see, or which they think is most plausible.

Much Ado About Nothing Act 4 Scene 1
虚惊一场

FRIAR FRANCIS   Marry, this well carried[1], shall on her behalf,
Change slander to remorse[2], that is some good,
But not for that dream I on this strange course,   205
But on this travail[3] look for greater birth:
She dying, as it must be so maintained,
Upon the instant that she was accused,
Shall be lamented[4], pitied, and excused
Of every hearer: for it so falls out,   210
That what we have, we prize not to the worth[5],
Whiles we enjoy it; but being lacked and lost,
Why then we rack[6] the value, then we find
The virtue that possession would not show us
Whiles it was ours: so will it fare with Claudio: 215
When he shall hear she died upon his words
Th'idea of her life shall sweetly creep
Into his study of imagination[7],
And every lovely organ of her life[8],
Shall come apparelled[9] in more precious habit[10],   220
More moving[11]-delicate, and full of life,
Into the eye and prospect of his soul
Than when she lived indeed: then shall he mourn,
If ever love had interest in his liver[12],
And wish he had not so accusèd her: 225
No, though he thought his accusation true:
Let this be so, and doubt not but success[13]
Will fashion the event in better shape
Than I can lay it down in likelihood.
But if all aim but[14] this be levelled false[15],   230
The supposition[16] of the lady's death,
Will quench[17] the wonder of her infamy.
And if it sort not well[18], you may conceal her,
As best befits her wounded reputation,
In some reclusive and religious life,   235
Out of all eyes, tongues, minds and injuries.

Benedick advises Leonato to accept Friar Francis's advice and promises secrecy. Alone with Beatrice, he asks how he can help to prove Hero's innocence and tells Beatrice that he loves her.

 剧情简介：本尼迪建议列纳托同意福冉希修士的安排并承诺严守秘密。众人离开，本尼迪问碧翠怎样才能帮着证明希柔的清白，并告诉碧翠他爱她。

1 'The smallest twine may lead me'

Leonato describes himself as being 'in grief' in line 242. Feelings are running very high at this crucial point in the play. It is important that members of the audience decide where they think the most blame and, consequently, the most shame lies for what has happened.

- Sketch simple images of Hero and Don John. Cut out a piece of string ('twine'), and attach one image to each end. Hero represents the most blameless and shame-free of the characters, Don John the opposite.

- Create similar pictures of the other key characters, and write 'example' quotations underneath each sketch to show the character's part (behaviour/actions) in these events. Place the images along the piece of string, in order of how much blame/shame you think each character merits. The order of this line will reflect your sympathies and opinions of the positions adopted by various characters. Debate the order as a class.

1	inwardness 亲密关系
2	deal in this 在这件事情上会做得……
3	Being ... grief 我过于悲伤（而六神无主）
4	twine 细线
5	'Tis well consented 您这就是同意了
6	presently away 立刻行动起来
7	to ... cure 非常之症需要非常之法来医治
8	but prolonged 只是推迟了
9	I will not desire that 我不想让您这样
10	right her 还她清白
11	even 直截了当
12	confess 承认

Stagecraft 导演技巧
Hero's exit

```
                    STAGE
  X Margaret                      X Leonato
  X Beatrice
          X Benedick   X Hero       X Ursula
  X Friar Francis
  Stage Right                     Stage Left
                    AUDIENCE
```

a Above is an example of how a director might position the different characters on the stage during lines 105–247. Do you agree with this arrangement? Design your own stage proxemics (戏台调度) (positions) sketch – either for the whole scene or for one particular section of it.

b Write a set of director's notes to describe how Hero should exit. Does anyone accompany or support Hero? Explain how you would arrange for Beatrice and Benedick to be left alone on the stage, and write these instructions for the actors.

Much Ado About Nothing Act 4 Scene 1
虚惊一场

BENEDICK   Signor Leonato, let the friar advise you,
And though you know my inwardness[1] and love
Is very much unto the prince and Claudio,
Yet, by mine honour, I will deal in this[2],   240
As secretly and justly as your soul
Should with your body.

LEONATO   Being that I flow in grief[3],
The smallest twine[4] may lead me.

FRIAR FRANCIS   'Tis well consented[5], presently away[6]:
For to strange sores, strangely they strain the cure[7]:   245
Come, lady, die to live, this wedding day
Perhaps is but prolonged[8]: have patience and endure.

Exeunt [Friar Francis, Leonato and Hero]

BENEDICK   Lady Beatrice, have you wept all this while?

BEATRICE   Yea, and I will weep a while longer.

BENEDICK   I will not desire that[9].   250

BEATRICE   You have no reason, I do it freely.

BENEDICK   Surely I do believe your fair cousin is wronged.

BEATRICE   Ah, how much might the man deserve of me that would right her[10]!

BENEDICK   Is there any way to show such friendship?   255

BEATRICE   A very even[11] way, but no such friend.

BENEDICK   May a man do it?

BEATRICE   It is a man's office, but not yours.

BENEDICK   I do love nothing in the world so well as you, is not that strange?   260

BEATRICE   As strange as the thing I know not: it were as possible for me to say, I loved nothing so well as you, but believe me not, and yet I lie not, I confess[12] nothing, nor I deny nothing: I am sorry for my cousin.

Beatrice reluctantly admits that she loves Benedick. He swears he will do anything to prove his love for her, but refuses her order to kill Claudio. Beatrice wishes she were a man so she could take revenge herself.

剧情简介：碧翠无奈地承认她爱本尼迪。本尼迪发誓会为她做任何事以证明他爱她，但拒绝执行她的命令去杀克劳丢。碧翠希望她自己是个男人，这样就能亲自去为希柔报仇。

Language in the play 剧中语言

Annotating actors need adverbs

Actors will often annotate a script with adverbs to suggest the tone of delivery. Experiment with different ways of saying each line in the script opposite. Create a table showing a range of adverbs to sum up different ways of delivering lines (see example below). Have a go at delivering the lines in these different ways!

Line 265	Excitedly, fondly, assertively
Line 266	Dismissively, cautiously, affectionately

Themes 主题分析

A crucial test of love (in pairs)

Beatrice risks losing Benedick's love when she asks him to challenge his friend Claudio. He in turn risks his very life if he accepts. What Don Pedro began as an amusing 'sport' is sport no longer.

a **Freeze-frames** Create six tableaux (one for each sentence in lines 278–84) that capture the emotions and intentions of Beatrice and Benedick. Show them in sequence to another pair.

b **'Kill Claudio'** Benedick suddenly realises the price he must pay for Beatrice's love. How might Beatrice deliver line 279, and how might Benedick respond? Experiment with different tones of voice and facial expressions. Do *you* think he should kill Claudio?

1 Eating words, eating swords, eating hearts

Now, even the wordplay becomes deadly serious. When Benedick swears by his sword (line 265), Beatrice warns him not to 'swear and eat it' (meaning 'do not go back on your oath', or perhaps 'do not eat your sword by getting yourself wounded in combat').

a Identify and note down the wordplay in the script opposite that concerns swearing/protesting love and eating words/swords.

b Write a paragraph (or an extended and further developed piece) analysing how the wordplay in this section reflects the tensions between Benedick and Beatrice, and the seriousness of what Beatrice asks.

1 **By my sword** 以我的佩剑起誓（佩剑往往是绅士们名誉气节的象征）
2 **protest** 宣布
3 **stayed ... hour** 止住我的时机恰到好处
4 **protest** 坦承
5 **bid me** 吩咐我
6 **not for the wide world** 说破天也不行
7 **Tarry** 等等
8 **Is a not** = Is he not
9 **approved ... villain** 充分证明（他）是一个大坏蛋
10 **bear her in hand** 哄骗她
11 **unmitigated rancour** 毫不留情的恶意、仇恨

Much Ado About Nothing Act 4 Scene 1
虚惊一场

BENEDICK By my sword[1], Beatrice, thou lovest me. 265
BEATRICE Do not swear and eat it.
BENEDICK I will swear by it that you love me, and I will make him eat it that says I love not you.
BEATRICE Will you not eat your word?
BENEDICK With no sauce that can be devised to it: I protest[2] I love thee. 270
BEATRICE Why then God forgive me.
BENEDICK What offence, sweet Beatrice?
BEATRICE You have stayed me in a happy hour[3], I was about to protest I loved you.
BENEDICK And do it with all thy heart. 275
BEATRICE I love you with so much of my heart, that none is left to protest[4].
BENEDICK Come bid me[5] do anything for thee.
BEATRICE Kill Claudio.
BENEDICK Ha, not for the wide world[6]. 280
BEATRICE You kill me to deny it, farewell.
BENEDICK Tarry[7], sweet Beatrice.
BEATRICE I am gone, though I am here, there is no love in you, nay, I pray you let me go.
BENEDICK Beatrice. 285
BEATRICE In faith I will go.
BENEDICK We'll be friends first.
BEATRICE You dare easier be friends with me, than fight with mine enemy.
BENEDICK Is Claudio thine enemy? 290
BEATRICE Is a not[8] approved in the height a villain[9], that hath slandered, scorned, dishonoured my kinswoman? Oh that I were a man! What, bear her in hand[10], until they come to take hands, and then with public accusation, uncovered slander, unmitigated rancour[11]? Oh God that I were a man! I would eat his heart in the market place. 295

Beatrice despairs of finding a man brave enough to take up her cause. Benedick is convinced by her belief that Hero has been wronged, and he determines to challenge Claudio.

剧情简介：碧翠因找不到男人有勇气替她报仇而绝望。她的信念让本尼迪相信希柔是被冤枉的，于是他决定挑战克劳丢。

▲ Beatrice is seen here snarling (咆哮) with rage and indignation (愤怒) at the injustice visited upon Hero. Which line from the script opposite do you think this image corresponds with?

1 a proper saying 编得有模有样的故事
2 undone 被毁了
3 testimony 证词
4 a goodly count 义正词严的控告
5 Count Comfect 糖果伯爵（表示克劳丢是个善于甜言蜜语的人）
6 for his sake 和他较量
7 curtsies 请安礼
8 valour 英勇
9 turned into tongue 变成如簧巧舌
10 trim 圆滑世故
11 with wishing 只靠愿望
12 this hand （思考第308行和第314行中的hand具体指谁的手）
13 some other way 用在别的事情上（暗指与克劳丢决斗）
14 engaged 承诺
15 render me a dear account 给我付出昂贵的代价

1 Changing relationships of power (in pairs)

Even Beatrice is forced to realise her limitations. Three times in this scene she wishes she were a man, because only a man can challenge Claudio to single combat. Explore how the control, initiative and power moves from Beatrice to Benedick by performing the scene in the following ways.

a **The seat of power** Place two chairs facing each other. Beatrice stands in front of her chair as the scene is performed, and Benedick sits. Every time Benedick tries to rise, Beatrice pushes him back down. Decide at which point he becomes determined enough to stand and push Beatrice down.

b **The circle of power** Draw a circle of chalk on the floor (ties or jumpers would do the job too!) and perform the scene. Beatrice remains in the circle as she speaks. Benedick tries to enter but Beatrice physically stops him. At which point in the script should he eventually gain entry?

c **The glove of power** Beatrice holds a glove as she speaks and uses it to emphasise her anger throughout this exchange. Eventually, Benedick takes the glove from her. How does he do this, at which point, and what could this symbolise?

Much Ado About Nothing Act 4 Scene 1
虚惊一场

BENEDICK   Hear me, Beatrice.
BEATRICE   Talk with a man out at a window, a proper saying[1].
BENEDICK   Nay, but Beatrice.
BEATRICE   Sweet Hero, she is wronged, she is slandered, she is undone[2].
BENEDICK   Beat –   300
BEATRICE   Princes and counties! Surely a princely testimony[3], a goodly count[4], Count Comfect[5], a sweet gallant surely, oh that I were a man for his sake[6]! Or that I had any friend would be a man for my sake! But manhood is melted into curtsies[7], valour[8] into compliment, and men are only turned into tongue[9], and trim[10] ones too: he is now as valiant as Hercules, that only tells a lie, and swears it: I cannot be a man with wishing[11], therefore I will die a woman with grieving.   305
BENEDICK   Tarry, good Beatrice, by this hand[12] I love thee.
BEATRICE   Use it for my love some other way[13] than swearing by it.
BENEDICK   Think you in your soul the Count Claudio hath wronged Hero?   310
BEATRICE   Yea, as sure as I have a thought, or a soul.
BENEDICK   Enough, I am engaged[14], I will challenge him. I will kiss your hand, and so I leave you: by this hand, Claudio shall render me a dear account[15]: as you hear of me, so think of me: go comfort your cousin, I must say she is dead, and so farewell.   315

[Exeunt]

Dogberry, Verges and the Sexton take evidence from Borachio and Conrade. Dogberry commences his blundering cross-examination.

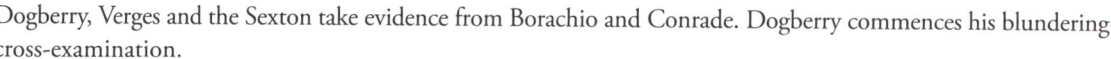

剧情简介：道博瑞、瓦吉、教堂司事审问鲍拉丘和康拉。道博瑞的当堂审问错误百出。

1	SEXTON 教堂司事
2	dissembly （道博瑞想说 assembly [集会]）
3	malefactors 案犯
4	exhibition （瓦吉想说 permission）
5	come before 回答
6	sirrah 小子（对仆人的称呼）
7	we hope 我们这么觉得
8	God defend 上帝不允许
9	knaves 无赖，流氓
10	it … shortly 这很快就会被证实
11	go about with 有办法对付
12	in a tale = in collusion（编同一个故事）
13	writ down 记下来

▲ Can you identify Dogberry, Verges, Borachio, Conrade and the Sexton in this image? Discuss the potential for comedy you think there might be in the way that Borachio and Conrade are gagged (封嘴) and bound together here.

1 Dogberry has a cunning plan! (in eights)

Although this scene should be played for comedy, there is a very important and serious plot element involved. Dogberry and Verges, despite their idiocy (愚蠢行为), need to bring the truth to light in order for Hero to be exonerated (证明无罪) (cleared of charges).

Stage and act out this amateurish (外行的) court examination (法庭审问) of the villains (lines 1–55). Consider the following points:

- Dogberry tries, and fails, to catch out Conrade and Borachio by interrogating them separately (lines 16–27) in the hope that they will say different things. Why does this fail, and how could you make it physically and verbally amusing?
- The Sexton is the only character with any sense of how to properly conduct the questioning and trial. How and when will he intervene to keep matters on track, and how might he respond to Dogberry?
- Dogberry calls Conrade 'sirrah' (line 11), a customary way of addressing servants. How should he and Borachio react to being ordered about by such socially inferior fools?

Act 4 Scene 2
Messina A courtroom

Enter the Constables DOGBERRY *and* VERGES *and the* SEXTON[1] *as Town Clerk in gowns,* CONRADE *and* BORACHIO

DOGBERRY Is our whole dissembly[2] appeared?
VERGES Oh a stool and a cushion for the sexton.
SEXTON Which be the malefactors[3]?
DOGBERRY Marry that am I, and my partner.
VERGES Nay that's certain, we have the exhibition[4] to examine. 5
SEXTON But which are the offenders, that are to be examined? Let them come before master constable.
DOGBERRY Yea marry, let them come before[5] me: what is your name, friend?
BORACHIO Borachio. 10
DOGBERRY Pray write down Borachio. Yours, sirrah[6]?
CONRADE I am a gentleman, sir, and my name is Conrade.
DOGBERRY Write down Master Gentleman Conrade: masters, do you serve God?
BORACHIO } Yea, sir, we hope[7]. 15
CONRADE }
DOGBERRY Write down, that they hope they serve God: and write God first, for God defend[8] but God should go before such villains: masters, it is proved already that you are little better than false knaves[9], and it will go near to be thought so shortly[10]: how answer you for yourselves? 20
CONRADE Marry, sir, we say we are none.
DOGBERRY A marvellous witty fellow I assure you, but I will go about with[11] him: come you hither, sirrah, a word in your ear, sir: I say to you, it is thought you are false knaves.
BORACHIO Sir, I say to you, we are none. 25
DOGBERRY Well, stand aside, 'fore God they are both in a tale[12]: have you writ down[13], that they are none?

The Sexton instructs Dogberry to summon the Watch, who confirm that they overheard Borachio confess his crime. The Sexton reveals that Hero has since died and Don John secretly fled.

 剧情简介：教堂司事让道博瑞传唤巡夜人，他们证实偷听到鲍拉丘坦白罪行。教堂司事透露希柔已死，唐约翰已偷偷逃跑。

Write about it 写作练习

The Sexton's notes

Some regard the Sexton as the real hero of the play! His ability to write down and record events is central to his character.

Write in role as the Sexton, composing the personal notes (perhaps as a journal entry) you think he would make at the conclusion of these proceedings (lines 1–55). Include the Sexton's frank opinions of the other characters in the play. For example, what would be his opinion of Don John? How might he describe the way Dogberry and Verges behaved?

Language in the play 剧中语言

Dogberry: making a dog's dinner (一团糟) of language!

Dogberry continues to use numerous malapropisms (see p. 78) in this scene.

a Make a list of all the malapropisms you can find. Write a paragraph explaining both why this is funny and how you think the legal context (a semi-trial) might influence the way he mangles (损毁，糟蹋) the language.

b Another source of humour in this scene is Dogberry's tendency to apply **proper nouns** (naming words) in an insulting, inaccurate or over-the-top (夸张) way. Note down all the proper nouns that Dogberry uses. Next to each example, suggest the unintentional implication or effect of its use – for either the audience or the person to whom he is speaking.

1 you … examine 您的审问不得法
2 call forth 传来问话
3 eftest (道博瑞造词，他也许想说deftest [最巧妙])
4 charge you 命令你们
5 flat perjury 完全是伪证
6 of = from
7 burglary (道博瑞想说bribery [贿赂])
8 by mass = by the Holy Mass (以神圣弥撒发誓)
9 upon his words 听信他的话
10 redemption (道博瑞想说damnation [遭天谴])
11 upon the grief 由于悲愤交加
12 bound 绑起来
13 show him their examination 让他看审问他们的结果

1 How should the villains react? (in pairs)

Discuss how you think Borachio and Conrade might react to the Sexton informing them of Hero's death and Don John's sudden departure (lines 51–55). Explore some possibilities through different performances:

- The two men are hard-hearted and react unfeelingly. They are callous (麻木不仁), perhaps even amused.
- Borachio is worried and guilt-stricken (愧疚). Both men are obviously struck with remorse.
- Improvise a short dialogue between the two characters, in which they share their true thoughts and feelings.

Decide which response works best, and share your views as a class..

SEXTON   Master constable, you go not the way to examine¹, you must call forth² the watch that are their accusers.

DOGBERRY   Yea marry, that's the eftest³ way, let the watch come forth.   30

[*Enter* SEACOAL, WATCHMAN, *and the rest of the Watch*]

Masters, I charge you⁴ in the prince's name, accuse these men.

SEACOAL   This man said, sir, that Don John the prince's brother was a villain.

DOGBERRY   Write down, Prince John a villain: why this is flat perjury⁵, to call a prince's brother villain.   35

BORACHIO   Master constable.

DOGBERRY   Pray thee, fellow, peace, I do not like thy look I promise thee.

SEXTON   What heard you him say else?

WATCHMAN 2   Marry that he had received a thousand ducats of⁶ Don John, for accusing the Lady Hero wrongfully.   40

DOGBERRY   Flat burglary⁷ as ever was committed.

VERGES   Yea by mass⁸ that it is.

SEXTON   What else, fellow?

SEACOAL   And that Count Claudio did mean upon his words⁹, to disgrace Hero before the whole assembly, and not marry her.   45

DOGBERRY   Oh villain! Thou wilt be condemned into everlasting redemption¹⁰ for this.

SEXTON   What else?

SEACOAL   This is all.   50

SEXTON   And this is more, masters, than you can deny: Prince John is this morning secretly stolen away: Hero was in this manner accused, in this very manner refused, and upon the grief¹¹ of this, suddenly died: master constable, let these men be bound¹², and brought to Leonato's: I will go before and show him their examination¹³.   [*Exit*]   55

As the Watch escort the prisoners away, Conrade offers some resistance. Exasperated beyond endurance, he calls Dogberry an ass, an insult that mortally offends Dogberry.

 剧情简介：巡夜人欲将囚犯押走，康拉试图抵抗。他怒不可遏，骂道博瑞是头蠢驴，这句侮辱的话深深伤害了道博瑞。

Characters 人物分析

Dogberry: 'remember that I am an ass' (in pairs)

Many of Shakespeare's comic characters inspire sympathy as much as ridicule. Being called an 'ass' by Conrade wounds Dogberry greatly, and he is still angry about it the next time we see him.

Explore different ways of physically presenting Dogberry for maximum comic effect.

- **Smug and self-assured** Perform lines 57–71, presenting Dogberry as being very pompous (自命不凡) and furiously angry with Conrade. He should be shouting, huffing and puffing (气喘吁吁), with his hands on his hips and his chest thrust upwards and forwards.

- **Strangely sympathetic** Perform the same lines again, this time presenting Dogberry more sympathetically. He is genuinely sensitive and insecure about his position. Emphasise that he *can't* write down what has been said. Have Conrade loudly mock him. Dogberry should be physically less confident, hunching (耸起) his shoulders and gesturing weakly with his hands.

Decide as a class or group which version is funniest, and which you think is most effective or interesting. What Dogberry is saying should remain ridiculous (he is ridiculous!), but decide exactly *how* Shakespeare wants us to laugh at this character.

1. opinioned （瓦吉想说 pinioned [捆绑]）
2. coxcomb 自负的蠢货
3. God's my life 老天在上（语气温和的发誓语）
4. naughty 邪恶，缺德
5. varlet 小人，奴才
6. suspect （道博瑞想说 respect）
7. piety （道博瑞想说 impiety [对神不敬]）
8. householder 有家有房的人
9. go to 老子要让你知道
10. had losses 丢过钱（但照样活了下来）

▼ Dogberry is clearly a comically ridiculous character, but does he deserve to be called an 'ass'? What does Dogberry bring to the play? Discuss why you think he is an important character.

MUCH ADO ABOUT NOTHING ACT 4 SCENE 2
虚惊一场

VERGES   Come, let them be opinioned¹.
CONRADE   Let them be in the hands of coxcomb².
DOGBERRY   God's my life³, where's the sexton? Let him write down the prince's officer coxcomb: come, bind them, thou naughty⁴ varlet⁵.
CONRADE   Away, you are an ass, you are an ass.   60
DOGBERRY   Dost thou not suspect⁶ my place? Dost thou not suspect my years? Oh that he were here to write me down an ass! But masters, remember that I am an ass, though it be not written down, yet forget not that I am an ass: no, thou villain, thou art full of piety⁷ as shall be proved upon thee by good witness: I am a wise fellow, and which is more, an officer, and which is more, a householder⁸, and which is more, as pretty a piece of flesh as any is in Messina, and one that knows the law, go to⁹, and a rich fellow enough, go to, and a fellow that hath had losses¹⁰, and one that hath two gowns, and everything handsome about him: bring him away: oh that I had been writ down an ass!

                                                                         Exeunt

Much Ado About Nothing 虚惊一场

Looking back at Act 4 第4幕回顾
Activities for groups or individuals

1 Scandal!

The 'death' of Hero has everything the celebrity-obsessed contemporary media loves: sex, death, betrayal and powerful, beautiful young people. Report the 'story' of Hero's death as it might have been presented to the people of Messina at the end of Act 4 Scene 1. Write in one of the following forms:

- a front-page feature in a gossipy celebrity magazine
- a sensationalised (引起轰动) article in a tabloid newspaper (小报)
- a sober, factual report in a broadsheet newspaper (大报)
- a 'personal' account from an anonymous blogger 'close' to events.

Try to include typical journalistic features such as puns, hyperbole, opinion presented as fact, incidental details, quotations/opinions of eyewitnesses and dramatic language.

2 Appearance and reality

Many characters in Act 4 try to judge inner truths by outward signs. Leonato, Don Pedro, Claudio and the Friar all 'note' different things about Hero. Leonato notes Claudio's tears as a sign of his sincerity (Act 4 Scene 1, line 147). Dogberry wants people to note his wealth and dignity.

Use a table like the one below to record the disparity between appearance and reality.

What is noted?	What is the truth?
Don Pedro believes he is dishonoured by Hero's behaviour.	Don Pedro is dishonoured by the way he is so easily tricked by Don John.

As an extension, try to present these ideas in a creative way – perhaps as a diagram, a short film or a collage.

3 Being Beatrice

The events of Act 4 are traumatic (让人痛苦) for many characters, but perhaps for none more so than Beatrice. She had probably anticipated the wedding would be a difficult time for her. She had been 'exceeding ill' that morning, and faced her first meeting with Benedick since learning of his love for her.

a In a pair, make a chronological list of all the things that happen to Beatrice in Act 4. Next to each event, jot down how you think she feels. Focus upon developing a range of words to describe her emotions.

b Use this list to help you write a 'Beatrice monologue' in contemporary language. The monologue should be candid (honest), exploring her feelings about what happened in the church and about what she has asked Benedick to do. Perform this monologue in class.

4 Messina, a man's world

The men in this play are the cause of many of the problems! Form small groups and assign each person in the group one male character from Act 4.

a Use your body and facial expressions to prepare three poses that sum up the actions and attitudes adopted by your character in Act 4.

b Write down three adjectives to describe your character in Act 4, and write down one quotation (be careful not to make it too obvious!) that sums him up. Lay it at your feet.

c When each member of your group has prepared their poses and quotations, invite another group to walk around your 'living statue garden'. They should guess which character each person represents, and write the name on the piece of paper at their feet. Discuss how the other group arrived at their guesses, and say whether they are correct or incorrect.

LOOKING BACK AT ACT 4

Beatrice, Margaret, Hero and Leonato react in shock to Claudio's rejection in this outdoor production from Shakespeare's Globe. In groups, adopt the pose of each character in the image and then take it in turns to speak their thoughts at this significant moment.

Antonio attempts to console his brother, but the loss of his daughter's reputation continues to hit Leonato hard. He says that only a man who has suffered as he has is entitled to offer him counsel.

剧情简介：安托纽努力安慰兄长，但女儿名声的败坏仍让列纳托痛心。他说只有跟他有相同遭遇的人才有资格劝说他。

1 Is Leonato self-indulgent (自我放纵)? (in pairs)

Some directors have cut parts of Leonato's speech (lines 3–32), possibly feeling his grief to be overly 'tragic' or melodramatic (戏剧化，过于夸张).

a With your partner, decide on Leonato's most self-indulgent phrase or sentence – the one that might have provoked his gesture in the image below.

b Join with another pair and discuss the similarities and differences between your choices. Consider whether Leonato's behaviour here is over the top. Keep in mind the following points during your discussion:

- Has anything happened at the wedding to make you somewhat sceptical about Leonato's love for his daughter and his current sense of loss?
- Messina is a patriarchal (male-dominated) society with male values (honour, allegiance and so on). Might you, therefore, sympathise with Leonato's anguish at Hero's ruined reputation?

In your pair, decide whether or not you would cut Leonato's speech. Explain your decision to another pair, and give reasons. Think about the effect that it might have on the audience.

1 second 加强，加深
2 sieve 筛子
3 suit 和（我的痛苦）相当
4 lineament 容貌
5 stroke his beard 捋胡须（自我满足的神态）
6 wag 装愚卖傻
7 cry hem 咳嗽一声
8 make … candle-wasters 夜晚燃烛看书以忘记悲伤
9 preceptial medicine 道德药汤
10 Fetter 戴上镣铐，限制
11 'tis all men's office 每人都认为他能……
12 wring 疼得打滚
13 sufficiency 能力
14 advertisement 忠告

Much Ado About Nothing Act 5 Scene 1
虚惊一场

Act 5 Scene 1
Outside Leonato's house

Enter LEONATO *and his brother* ANTONIO

ANTONIO	If you go on thus, you will kill yourself,
	And 'tis not wisdom thus to second[1] grief,
	Against yourself.
LEONATO	I pray thee cease thy counsel,
	Which falls into mine ears as profitless,
	As water in a sieve[2]: give not me counsel, 5
	Nor let no comforter delight mine ear,
	But such a one whose wrongs do suit[3] with mine.
	Bring me a father that so loved his child,
	Whose joy of her is overwhelmed like mine,
	And bid him speak of patience, 10
	Measure his woe the length and breadth of mine,
	And let it answer every strain for strain,
	As thus for thus, and such a grief for such,
	In every lineament[4], branch, shape and form:
	If such a one will smile and stroke his beard[5], 15
	And sorrow; wag[6], cry hem[7], when he should groan;
	Patch grief with proverbs, make misfortune drunk
	With candle-wasters[8]: bring him yet to me,
	And I of him will gather patience:
	But there is no such man, for, brother, men 20
	Can counsel and speak comfort to that grief,
	Which they themselves not feel, but tasting it,
	Their counsel turns to passion, which before,
	Would give preceptial medicine[9] to rage,
	Fetter[10] strong madness in a silken thread, 25
	Charm ache with air, and agony with words –
	No, no, 'tis all men's office[11], to speak patience
	To those that wring[12] under the load of sorrow,
	But no man's virtue nor sufficiency[13]
	To be so moral, when he shall endure 30
	The like himself: therefore give me no counsel,
	My griefs cry louder than advertisement[14].

As Leonato's mind turns to thoughts of revenge, the sight of Claudio and Don Pedro hurrying past, apparently unconcerned about the grief they have caused him, quickly arouses his anger.

剧情简介：列纳托想到了复仇，此时看到克劳丢和唐佩卓匆匆路过。他们给自己带来了悲痛却视而不见，这让他一时怒火中烧。

1 Feelings are running high (in pairs)

There are many powerful outbursts in this scene. Consider the way in which Leonato and Antonio talk together, the manner of Don Pedro and Claudio's entrance, how each reacts on seeing Leonato, and the response of the two old men.

a Read through lines 1–57 and identify the moments when the characters' moods change. Decide how to emphasise the meaning of Leonato's remarks in lines 47–57.

b Create a set of graph axes (轴) that show how characters' positive or negative 'feelings' develop over 'time' in this scene (see below). Plot each character's emotional changes through the scene, as has been done for Leonato and Don Pedro in the examples below. Use a quotation to support each point that you plot on the graph. Join the quotations into a curve, using a different colour for each character. What does this reveal about the characters' feelings in this scene? How are the characters related? Discuss your ideas with another pair.

c Use the graph to help you write director's notes for an actor playing one of the characters in this scene.

1 However 不论多少
2 writ the style of gods 写作时如神一样洞察一切
3 made a push at 嘲弄
4 sufferance 苦难
5 bend 把……指向
6 have some haste 有急事要办
7 all is one 都一样
8 lie low 不得不小心
9 dissembler 骗子，伪君子
10 beshrew 诅咒
11 nothing to 根本没有想移向

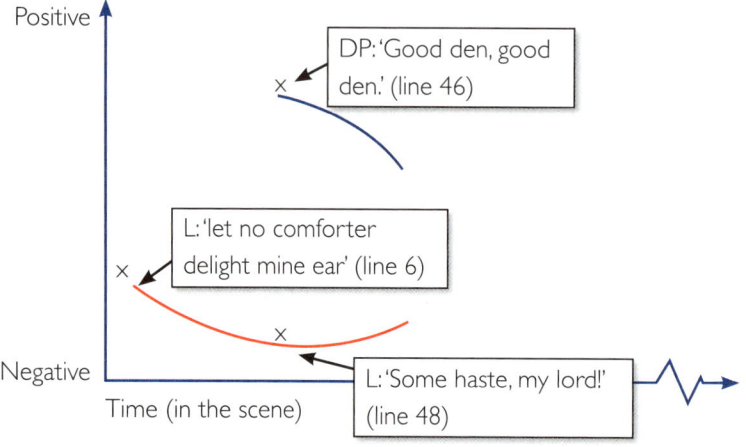

Language in the play 剧中语言

'thou dissembler, thou' (in pairs)

You will remember how Leonato addressed his guests in the opening scene of the play using the polite 'you' form. Use of the 'thou' form is a sign of friendship, but it can also signal contempt.

Take it in turns to tell Claudio what you think of him (lines 52–7, from 'Who wrongs him?' onwards). Stress all the 'thee/thou' words. Try it in different ways: mockingly, smilingly or angrily.

Much Ado About Nothing Act 5 Scene 1
虚惊一场

ANTONIO	Therein do men from children nothing differ.
LEONATO	I pray thee peace, I will be flesh and blood,
	For there was never yet philosopher,
	That could endure the tooth-ache patiently,
	However[1] they have writ the style of gods[2],
	And made a push at[3] chance and sufferance[4].
ANTONIO	Yet bend[5] not all the harm upon yourself,
	Make those that do offend you suffer too.
LEONATO	There thou speak'st reason, nay I will do so,
	My soul doth tell me, Hero is belied,
	And that shall Claudio know, so shall the prince,
	And all of them that thus dishonour her.

Enter DON PEDRO *and* CLAUDIO

ANTONIO	Here comes the prince and Claudio hastily.
DON PEDRO	Good den, good den.
CLAUDIO	Good day to both of you.
LEONATO	Hear you, my lords?
DON PEDRO	We have some haste[6], Leonato.
LEONATO	Some haste, my lord! Well, fare you well, my lord,
	Are you so hasty now? Well, all is one[7].
DON PEDRO	Nay do not quarrel with us, good old man.
ANTONIO	If he could right himself with quarrelling,
	Some of us would lie low[8].
CLAUDIO	Who wrongs him?
LEONATO	Marry thou dost wrong me, thou dissembler[9], thou:
	Nay, never lay thy hand upon thy sword,
	I fear thee not.
CLAUDIO	Marry beshrew[10] my hand,
	If it should give your age such cause of fear,
	In faith my hand meant nothing to[11] my sword.

Despite his age, Leonato challenges Claudio to single combat, but Claudio refuses to fight a duel with the old man. Then Antonio challenges Claudio so fiercely that even Leonato is surprised.

剧情简介：列纳托不顾年事已高，向克劳丢发出挑战，克劳丢拒绝和这位老人决斗。此时安托纽挺身而出挑战克劳丢，义愤填膺，连列纳托都很吃惊。

1 Challenges and responses (in fours)

a Take up the positions of the characters of Leonato and Antonio opposite Claudio and Don Pedro as in the picture below. Read aloud lines 58–90. Consider the likely attitudes and reactions of the characters in the scene, and how this might affect your performance:

- Tempers are running high, so the men may gesture vigorously as they speak. Leonato and Antonio could prod (戳，捅) Claudio firmly with their fingers on each relevant word (e.g. 'Claudio', 'thy', 'thee', 'Sir Boy', 'braggarts').
- How should Claudio and Don Pedro respond to this aggression? Are they surprised, amused, hostile, sneering, unnerved (紧张不安)?
- Think about the tensions relating to status in this scene. Respect should be shown for the older Antonio and Leonato. However, the positions of Don Pedro, a prince, and Claudio, a count, potentially outrank this consideration of their age.
- In the picture below, Claudio is laughing as he faces Antonio's challenge. This may challenge the audience's expectations of the characters. Claudio appears arrogant and rude, and Antonio also behaves uncharacteristically.

b Freeze the action at line 90, and speak aloud the thoughts of each character. Consider whether they are in two minds about what they are saying and doing.

c Perform your version to another group, and discuss the similarities and differences between your interpretations.

1	Tush = Hush	（含有轻蔑的语气）
2	fleer	虚情假意地微笑
3	dotard	老糊涂
4	brag	炫耀
5	to thy head	当着你的面
6	reverence	对（达官贵人的）尊敬
7	trial of a man	单打独斗
8	never scandal slept	从来没有任何耻辱被掩埋
9	nice fence	娴熟的剑术
10	active practice	习武，练剑
11	May of youth	青春年华
12	lustihood	身强力壮
13	daff me	推开我，打发我
14	foining	突刺（击剑术语）
15	Content yourself	您等一下
16	apes	傻瓜
17	braggarts	说大话的人
18	Jacks	无赖
19	milksops	奶里奶气的家伙，娘娘腔

LEONATO	Tush[1], tush, man, never fleer[2] and jest at me,	
	I speak not like a dotard[3], nor a fool,	
	As under privilege of age to brag[4],	60
	What I have done, being young, or what would do,	
	Were I not old: know, Claudio, to thy head[5],	
	Thou hast so wronged mine innocent child and me,	
	That I am forced to lay my reverence[6] by,	
	And with grey hairs and bruise of many days,	65
	Do challenge thee to trial of a man[7]:	
	I say thou hast belied mine innocent child.	
	Thy slander hath gone through and through her heart,	
	And she lies buried with her ancestors:	
	Oh in a tomb where never scandal slept[8],	70
	Save this of hers, framed by thy villainy.	
CLAUDIO	My villainy?	
LEONATO	Thine, Claudio, thine I say.	
DON PEDRO	You say not right, old man.	
LEONATO	My lord, my lord,	
	I'll prove it on his body if he dare,	
	Despite his nice fence[9], and his active practice[10],	75
	His May of youth[11], and bloom of lustihood[12].	
CLAUDIO	Away, I will not have to do with you.	
LEONATO	Canst thou so daff me[13]? Thou hast killed my child,	
	If thou kill'st me, boy, thou shalt kill a man.	
ANTONIO	He shall kill two of us, and men indeed,	80
	But that's no matter, let him kill one first:	
	Win me and wear me, let him answer me,	
	Come follow me, boy, come, Sir Boy, come follow me,	
	Sir Boy, I'll whip you from your foining[14] fence,	
	Nay, as I am a gentleman, I will.	
LEONATO	Brother.	85
ANTONIO	Content yourself[15], God knows, I loved my niece,	
	And she is dead, slandered to death by villains,	
	That dare as well answer a man indeed,	
	As I dare take a serpent by the tongue.	
	Boys, apes[16], braggarts[17], Jacks[18], milksops[19].	
LEONATO	Brother Anthony.	90

Don Pedro maintains his belief that Claudio was correct in his accusation of Hero. As the two old men depart, still rumbling angrily, a grimly determined Benedick arrives on the scene.

 剧情简介：唐佩卓坚持认为克劳丢对希柔的指控是正确的。列纳托和安托纽两位老人愤然离开，这时本尼迪上场，表情凝重而坚决。

Write about it 写作练习

Claudio on trial

Antonio (lines 91–8) sees Claudio as one of those shallow, worthless fashion-conscious young men that Borachio so despises (Act 3 Scene 3, lines 107–13).

a Can you defend the young war hero's behaviour in this scene? Look at how he conducts himself with first Leonato, then Antonio and finally Benedick (lines 45–173).

b Imagine that you are Claudio's commanding officer (指挥官), sitting in a court martial (military court). A complaint has been made against Claudio for arguing and drawing a sword against two elderly men in the street. Examine his behaviour and write down your conclusions and recommendations.

c In a table like the one below, list the accusations that Leonato, Antonio and Benedick might make against Claudio – include quotations from the script. Next, list the things that Claudio might say in his defence. You will need to add your own ideas here, as Claudio's speech is quite brief at this point. Decide which parts of each side's argument you accept, and come to a judgement about who is at fault in each case.

Accuser	Accusation	Claudio's defence	Your analysis and judgement
Leonato	Claudio has ruined the reputation of his daughter and in turn injured his – 'Thou hast so wronged mine innocent child and me' (line 63).	It is my reputation that has been injured. Despite being engaged to me and about to be married, Hero was having a secret and romantic relationship with another man.	
Antonio			
Benedick			

d Write up your judgements as a speech to deliver to the court (the class or your group). Pay particular attention to:

- medium/genre (a speech)
- audience (a formal courtroom)
- purpose (to analyse and inform)
- effect (who do you want the audience to sympathise with?)

1 Hold you content 您别插手
2 scruple 一分一毫（比喻最少量）
3 Scambling 乱争抢
4 out-facing 飞扬跋扈
5 fashion-monging 赶时髦
6 cog 欺骗
7 flout 吹牛
8 deprave 侮辱
9 slander 诽谤
10 Go anticly 穿得怪模怪样
11 hideousness 可怕，唬人
12 durst 胆敢
13 wake your patience 劝你们要耐心
14 smart 受伤，受苦
15 fray 争斗
16 with two = by two
17 high proof 极其
18 scabbard 剑鞘

ANTONIO	Hold you content[1], what, man! I know them, yea	
	And what they weigh, even to the utmost scruple[2]:	
	Scambling[3], out-facing[4], fashion-monging[5] boys,	
	That lie, and cog[6], and flout[7], deprave[8] and slander[9],	
	Go anticly[10], and show outward hideousness[11],	95
	And speak off half a dozen dangerous words,	
	How they might hurt their enemies, if they durst[12],	
	And this is all.	
LEONATO	But brother Anthony –	
ANTONIO	Come 'tis no matter,	
	Do not you meddle, let me deal in this.	100
DON PEDRO	Gentlemen both, we will not wake your patience[13],	
	My heart is sorry for your daughter's death:	
	But on my honour she was charged with nothing	
	But what was true, and very full of proof.	
LEONATO	My lord, my lord –	
DON PEDRO	I will not hear you.	105
LEONATO	No come, brother, away, I will be heard.	
ANTONIO	And shall, or some of us will smart[14] for it.	

Exeunt Leonato and Antonio

DON PEDRO	See, see, here comes the man we went to seek.	

Enter BENEDICK

CLAUDIO	Now, signor, what news?	
BENEDICK	Good day, my lord.	
DON PEDRO	Welcome, signor, you are almost come to part almost a fray[15].	110
CLAUDIO	We had like to have had our two noses snapped off with two[16] old men without teeth.	
DON PEDRO	Leonato and his brother: what think'st thou? Had we fought, I doubt we should have been too young for them.	115
BENEDICK	In a false quarrel there is no true valour: I came to seek you both.	
CLAUDIO	We have been up and down to seek thee, for we are high proof[17] melancholy, and would fain have it beaten away, wilt thou use thy wit?	120
BENEDICK	It is in my scabbard[18], shall I draw it?	

Don Pedro and Claudio welcome Benedick's arrival as much-needed light relief. The deadly serious Benedick, unmoved by their mockery, challenges Claudio for causing the death of Hero.

 剧情简介： 唐佩卓和克劳丢欢迎本尼迪的到来，希望他能带来轻松愉快。表情严肃的本尼迪不为他们的嘲讽所动，说希柔的死是克劳丢造成的，因此向他提出决斗。

Characters 人物分析

The tables are turned (in threes)

As the play progresses and the audience thinks it knows a character, Shakespeare often uses a 'twist' in the story to reveal another aspect of their personality.

Don Pedro and Claudio look to Benedick to cheer themselves up after their bruising (激烈) encounter with Leonato and Antonio. However, Benedick has 'another subject' that he wishes to explore. Through this conversation, Shakespeare reveals a caring side to Benedick: he acts on behalf of Beatrice, but also shows a great deal of empathy for Hero. The 'flat' character of Benedick, the wit and joker, becomes 'rounded' into a character who has principles and morality. Similarly, the previously good impressions of Don Pedro and Claudio become sullied (败坏), as we realise that they are prepared to put their reputations above those of others.

a Explore how Shakespeare develops 'flat' characters into 'round' ones. Each group member draws an outline of a man on a big piece of paper, and labels it either Benedick, Don Pedro or Claudio. Inside the outline, write words that describe – and quotations that illustrate – your chosen character's normal behaviour. Now draw a circle around the shape. Into the space between the outline and the circle, write words and quotations about any unexpected behaviour – the 'twist' in their presentation.

b Compare your work with other groups, and develop your ideas by annotating each other's drawings with additional suggestions.

Language in the play 剧中语言

A warning signal

Elizabethans might well have sensed very quickly that all was not right with Benedick. Whilst ordinarily he is overly familiar with his noble friends, he is now very formal. Read the information on the use of 'thou' and 'you' on page 166.

1 **beside their wit** 发疯
2 **minstrels** 吟游诗人
3 **draw** 拔出（剑）
4 **care killed a cat** 忧愁害死猫（源自谚语 "Care'll kill a cat."）
5 **mettle** 韧性
6 **in the career** 急冲下去，全力以赴
7 **staff … cross**（staff 指矛杆，broke cross 的意思是"折断"；对决中矛杆折断是骑士懦弱的表现，这里克劳丢指责本尼迪拒绝做他俩的开心果）
8 **how to turn his girdle** 该如何处理（turn his girdle 字面义是"转动他的腰带"，引申义是"准备拔剑应战"）
9 **God bless me** 上帝保佑我
10 **calf / capon / woodcock** 小牛、阉鸡、山鹬（均为无攻击能力的动物）
11 **curiously** 手艺精湛
12 **ambles** 蹒跚（该词用来形容女士骑马的速度，这里本尼迪暗示克劳丢像个嘴硬的妇女）
13 **fine** 极好，精致
14 **wise gentleman** 自作聪明的人
15 **hath the tongues** 会说几种语言
16 **forswore** 收回（誓言）
17 **trans-shape** 歪曲，使走样
18 **properest** 最英俊

Much Ado About Nothing Act 5 Scene 1
虚惊一场

DON PEDRO Dost thou wear thy wit by thy side?

CLAUDIO Never any did so, though very many have been beside their wit[1]: I will bid thee draw, as we do the minstrels[2], draw[3] to pleasure us.

DON PEDRO As I am an honest man, he looks pale, art thou sick, or angry?

CLAUDIO What, courage, man: what though care killed a cat[4], thou hast mettle[5] enough in thee to kill care.

BENEDICK Sir, I shall meet your wit in the career[6], and you charge it against me: I pray you choose another subject.

CLAUDIO Nay then, give him another staff, this last was broke cross[7].

DON PEDRO By this light, he changes more and more, I think he be angry indeed.

CLAUDIO If he be, he knows how to turn his girdle[8].

BENEDICK Shall I speak a word in your ear?

CLAUDIO God bless me[9] from a challenge.

BENEDICK You are a villain, I jest not, I will make it good how you dare, with what you dare, and when you dare: do me right, or I will protest your cowardice: you have killed a sweet lady, and her death shall fall heavy on you: let me hear from you.

CLAUDIO Well I will meet you, so I may have good cheer.

DON PEDRO What, a feast, a feast?

CLAUDIO I'faith I thank him, he hath bid me to a calf's[10] head and a capon[10], the which if I do not carve most curiously[11], say my knife's naught: shall I not find a woodcock[10] too?

BENEDICK Sir, your wit ambles[12] well, it goes easily.

DON PEDRO I'll tell thee how Beatrice praised thy wit the other day: I said thou hadst a fine[13] wit, true said she, a fine little one: no said I, a great wit: right says she, a great gross one: nay said I, a good wit: just said she, it hurts nobody: nay said I, the gentleman is wise: certain said she, a wise gentleman[14]: nay said I, he hath the tongues[15]: that I believe said she, for he swore a thing to me on Monday night, which he forswore[16] on Tuesday morning, there's a double tongue, there's two tongues: thus did she an hour together trans-shape[17] thy particular virtues, yet at last she concluded with a sigh, thou wast the properest[18] man in Italy.

Benedick resigns from Don Pedro's service. He informs the prince that Don John has fled and accuses his former friends of bringing about the death of Hero. Don John's men are brought in under guard.

剧情简介：本尼迪提出不再为唐佩卓效力，并告知亲王唐约翰已逃，并指责昔日好友导致了希柔的死。唐约翰的手下被看守押了上来。

Language in the play 剧中语言

Echoes (in pairs)

This play is full of resonances (共鸣). As each scene unfolds, we start to hear echoes of language that has been used before.

a **Cuckolds again** In lines 158–66, Don Pedro and Claudio hint at the trick they played on Benedick, and mock him with the cuckolded (戴绿帽) husband joke. Find the remarks Benedick made in Act 1 Scene 1, which are echoed here when Don Pedro and Claudio talk of the 'savage bull's horns' and 'Benedick the married man'. Is their jesting here somewhat ironic considering what has happened in Acts 3 and 4? Explain why.

b **'Lord Lack-beard there'** List the insults that Benedick aims at Claudio in this scene. Compare them with the comments Beatrice has made about him (Act 2 Scene 1, lines 222–4 and Act 4 Scene 1, lines 291–307). Are there any similarities? Write them under your list of insults.

1 **deadly** 直到她死（这里指恨之入骨）
2 **among** = between
3 **Lord Lack-beard** 无须勋爵（本尼迪嘲笑克劳丢年轻不经事）
4 **pretty** 肤浅，外表光鲜
5 **doublet and hose** 小双衣和紧腿裤（即平常的穿戴）
6 **giant** 大英雄
7 **doctor** 智者
8 **sad** 严肃，认真
9 **more reasons** 更多的证据
10 **balance** 秤
11 **once** 彻底、永久（证明）
12 **Hearken after** 询问

1 Hurling abuse (in threes)

Take parts and speak the lines 157–73, in which the former friends trade (你来我往) insults. Pause at each punctuation mark for the reaction of the person who has just been insulted. Imagine (*don't enact!*) that each clause is a punch fight. A comma delivers a small blow. A full stop lands a punch that sends the opponent flying. Decide what effect other punctuation marks should have, such as the colons that litter (随处可见) Benedick's parting words (lines 167–73). Who emerges battered and bruised from this 'fight'?

◀ 'Here dwells Benedick the married man' – Claudio mocks Benedick.

CLAUDIO   For the which she wept heartily, and said she cared not.
DON PEDRO   Yea that she did, but yet for all that, and if she did not hate him deadly[1], she would love him dearly, the old man's daughter told us all.
CLAUDIO   All, all, and moreover, God saw him when he was hid in the garden.
DON PEDRO   But when shall we set the savage bull's horns on the sensible Benedick's head?
CLAUDIO   Yea and text underneath, 'Here dwells Benedick the married man'?
BENEDICK   Fare you well, boy, you know my mind, I will leave you now to your gossip-like humour: you break jests as braggarts do their blades, which God be thanked hurt not: my lord, for your many courtesies I thank you: I must discontinue your company: your brother the bastard is fled from Messina: you have among[2] you killed a sweet and innocent lady: for my Lord Lack-beard[3] there, he and I shall meet, and till then peace be with him.   [*Exit*]
DON PEDRO   He is in earnest.
CLAUDIO   In most profound earnest, and I'll warrant you, for the love of Beatrice.
DON PEDRO   And hath challenged thee?
CLAUDIO   Most sincerely.
DON PEDRO   What a pretty[4] thing man is, when he goes in his doublet and hose[5], and leaves off his wit!
CLAUDIO   He is then a giant[6] to an ape, but then is an ape a doctor[7] to such a man.
DON PEDRO   But soft you, let me be, pluck up my heart, and be sad[8], did he not say my brother was fled?

Enter DOGBERRY *and* VERGES, CONRADE *and* BORACHIO [*with Watchmen*]

DOGBERRY   Come you, sir, if justice cannot tame you, she shall ne'er weigh more reasons[9] in her balance[10], nay, and you be a cursing hypocrite once[11], you must be looked to.
DON PEDRO   How now, two of my brother's men bound? Borachio one.
CLAUDIO   Hearken after[12] their offence, my lord.
DON PEDRO   Officers, what offence have these men done?

As Dogberry begins his repetitive and garbled account of the trial, Don Pedro questions Borachio, who immediately and shamefacedly confesses the whole plot to disgrace Hero.

 剧情简介：道博瑞开始啰里啰唆、颠三倒四地讲述审案过程。唐佩卓质问鲍拉丘，鲍拉丘立刻面露惭色，将陷害希柔的过程和盘托出。

Stagecraft 导演技巧

Comedy at the heart of the play (in groups of four or more)

The deception and the false accusations against Hero are actually revealed twice in the script opposite: Borachio's speech (lines 203–13) clarifies Dogberry's earlier garbled report (lines 191–4).

Don Pedro and Claudio's mocking of Dogberry delays the truth coming out, and increases the anticipation of this revelation. At the same time, it provides more opportunity for comedy – some productions really draw this out.

a Experiment with ways of delivering lines 185–202, alternately emphasising:
  - the serious and pompous Dogberry
  - the confused but amused Don Pedro
  - the dismissive (轻蔑) Claudio.

b How do you think the other characters, who do not speak in the lines above, would respond to the action? Think about how to show their reactions through gestures, expressions and movement.

1 **in his own division**　像道博瑞那样分出几条
2 **bound to your answer**　被传唤来接受审问
3 **cunning**　聪明，狡猾
4 **go … answer**　直截了当地回答
5 **shallow**　浅薄，愚蠢
6 **incensed**　煽动，蛊惑
7 **seal**　结束，终结
8 **whiles**　在……的同时
9 **set thee on**　指使你
10 **the practice of it**　办好此事
11 **rare semblance**　百里挑一的长相
12 **plaintiffs**　原告（道博瑞想说 **defendants** [被告]）
13 **reformed**　改变（道博瑞想说 **informed** [告知]）

Themes 主题分析

Deception at the heart of the play (in pairs)

Borachio's account of how he deceived Claudio and Don Pedro is deeply perceptive (目光敏锐). One of the play's key themes is the difficulty that people have in distinguishing truth from illusion, appearance from reality.

a Discuss the quotations below. What do they suggest to the other characters and/or the audience about the problem of discerning what is true or false? Write out the quotations on a piece of paper, and annotate them with your thoughts – focusing on either the characters' or the audience's response:
  - 'I have deceived even your very eyes'
  - 'what your wisdoms could not discover, these shallow fools have brought to light'
  - 'you … saw me court Margaret in Hero's garments'.

b Join with a pair that chose a different focus (audience/other characters) to your own, and discuss your ideas.

Much Ado About Nothing Act 5 Scene 1
虚惊一场

DOGBERRY Marry, sir, they have committed false report, moreover they have spoken untruths, secondarily, they are slanders, sixth and lastly, they have belied a lady, thirdly they have verified unjust things, and to conclude, they are lying knaves.

DON PEDRO First I ask thee what they have done, thirdly I ask thee what's their offence, sixth and lastly why they are committed, and to conclude, what you lay to their charge?

CLAUDIO Rightly reasoned, and in his own division[1], and by my troth there's one meaning well suited.

DON PEDRO Who have you offended, masters, that you are thus bound to your answer[2]? This learned constable is too cunning[3] to be understood: what's your offence?

BORACHIO Sweet prince, let me go no farther to mine answer[4]: do you hear me, and let this count kill me: I have deceived even your very eyes: what your wisdoms could not discover, these shallow[5] fools have brought to light, who in the night overheard me confessing to this man, how Don John your brother incensed[6] me to slander the Lady Hero, how you were brought into the orchard, and saw me court Margaret in Hero's garments, how you disgraced her when you should marry her: my villainy they have upon record, which I had rather seal[7] with my death, than repeat over to my shame: the lady is dead upon mine and my master's false accusation: and briefly I desire nothing but the reward of a villain.

DON PEDRO Runs not this speech like iron through your blood?

CLAUDIO I have drunk poison whiles[8] he uttered it.

DON PEDRO But did my brother set thee on[9] to this?

BORACHIO Yea, and paid me richly for the practice of it[10].

DON PEDRO He is composed and framed of treachery,
And fled he is upon this villainy.

CLAUDIO Sweet Hero, now thy image doth appear
In the rare semblance[11] that I loved it first.

DOGBERRY Come, bring away the plaintiffs[12], by this time our sexton hath reformed[13] Signor Leonato of the matter: and masters, do not forget to specify when time and place shall serve, that I am an ass.

VERGES Here, here comes Master Signor Leonato, and the sexton too.

Leonato returns. Claudio and the prince, full of remorse, beg to be able to make amends. Leonato orders Claudio to mourn Hero's death that night at her tomb and later marry his niece.

剧情简介：列纳托回来，克劳丢和唐佩卓亲王悔恨不已，恳求列纳托能让他们做出补偿。列纳托命令克劳丢当晚到希柔的墓前哀悼，随后娶他的侄女为妻。

▲ An angry Leonato turns away from Borachio to confront Claudio and Don Pedro. Which line do you think he is about to speak?

1 when I note 当我注意到
2 with thy breath 用你的言辞
3 beliest thyself 委屈你自己
4 bethink you of it 你们想一想
5 Impose … sin 让我因为自己的罪恶而受到您能想到的任何惩罚
6 bend under 承担，接受（任何重罚）
7 enjoin 责令
8 Possess 告知，昭告
9 labour aught in sad invention 写下一篇悼词
10 epitaph 墓志铭
11 Give her the right 给她应有的权力（即娶她为妻）
12 wring tears from me 让我感动得落泪

1 A pair of 'honourable men'? (in fours)

A thin line divides Shakespearean comedy from tragedy. In this play, the suspicions, jealousies, deceptions and revenges that take hold of the characters could easily lead to a tragic outcome. Claudio and Don Pedro have behaved badly, and the audience needs to believe their remorse in this scene in order to enjoy the 'happy' ending of the play.

Act out lines 226–62 and try to emphasise the following elements:

- Leonato needs to appear genuinely angry, sarcastic and vengeful. However, the audience also knows (**dramatic irony** [戏剧反讽]) that he is playing with Claudio and Don Pedro's feelings of guilt and remorse, and this can be funny. Find ways of showing both sides to his character in this scene.
- Don Pedro and Claudio are clearly deeply remorseful. How far can you take this in performance? Would they be literally on their knees? Are there any lines where they might express surprise or concern at what Leonato suggests? Is there comedy to be found in their reactions to Leonato, or perhaps in their responses to Borachio? Use exaggerated body language and facial expressions to highlight the remorse they are feeling.

Much Ado About Nothing Act 5 Scene 1
虚惊一场

Enter LEONATO, *his brother* [ANTONIO] *and the Sexton*

LEONATO	Which is the villain? Let me see his eyes,
	That when I note[1] another man like him,
	I may avoid him: which of these is he?
BORACHIO	If you would know your wronger, look on me.
LEONATO	Art thou the slave that with thy breath[2] hast killed
	Mine innocent child?
BORACHIO	Yea, even I alone.
LEONATO	No, not so, villain, thou beliest thyself[3],
	Here stand a pair of honourable men,
	A third is fled that had a hand in it:
	I thank you, princes, for my daughter's death,
	Record it with your high and worthy deeds,
	'Twas bravely done, if you bethink you of it[4].
CLAUDIO	I know not how to pray your patience,
	Yet I must speak, choose your revenge yourself,
	Impose me to what penance your invention
	Can lay upon my sin[5], yet sinned I not,
	But in mistaking.
DON PEDRO	By my soul nor I,
	And yet to satisfy this good old man,
	I would bend under[6] any heavy weight,
	That he'll enjoin[7] me to.
LEONATO	I cannot bid you bid my daughter live,
	That were impossible, but I pray you both,
	Possess[8] the people in Messina here,
	How innocent she died, and if your love
	Can labour aught in sad invention[9],
	Hang her an epitaph[10] upon her tomb,
	And sing it to her bones, sing it tonight:
	Tomorrow morning come you to my house,
	And since you could not be my son-in-law,
	Be yet my nephew: my brother hath a daughter,
	Almost the copy of my child that's dead,
	And she alone is heir to both of us,
	Give her the right[11] you should have given her cousin,
	And so dies my revenge.
CLAUDIO	Oh noble sir!
	Your over kindness doth wring tears from me[12],

Borachio assures Leonato of Margaret's innocence in the whole affair. Dogberry leaves, still very much concerned that it should be recorded in writing that he has been called an ass.

 剧情简介： 鲍拉丘向列纳托保证玛格蕊在整件事中是无辜的。道博瑞离开，仍旧耿耿于怀，认为他被骂作蠢驴这件事应该记录在案。

Language in the play 剧中语言
Dogberry's speech in black and white prose

The change from blank verse to prose (line 270–1) is very obvious. Dogberry interrupts and spouts (滔滔不绝) forth his (by now familiar) rambling (长篇大论) and sometimes incoherent accusations.

a Do a group reading of Dogberry's two major speeches on this page (lines 271–8 and 285–9). Move to a new speaker at every punctuation mark or clause. This should emphasise the chaotic and long-winded (啰唆，絮叨) nature of Dogberry's speech.

b Write a paragraph explaining why you think Shakespeare shifts from verse to prose on line 271, and how Dogberry's sentence structures help an actor to deliver a comic performance.

1 'we'll talk with Margaret' (in pairs)

It isn't fully explained why Margaret did not tell anyone that it was she who was at Hero's bedroom window. Read the beginning of Act 5 Scene 2 (p. 147) before attempting the following activities:

a Improvise one scene in which Leonato asks Margaret to explain her behaviour, and one scene in which Margaret tries to explain to Hero what happened.

b Decide upon three possible motives Margaret may have had for not telling anyone. Try to justify these motives with evidence from the script.

Write about it 写作练习
'The watch heard them talk of one Deformed'

In passing through the brain of Dogberry, the story of the notorious villain Deformed has achieved an amazing degree of distortion. It began in Act 3 Scene 3, where Borachio talked of 'a deformed thief this fashion'. The Watchman, mistaking what he heard for a reference to an actual thief, declared that Deformed wore a lovelock (美发卷) (see the 'Fashion' section on page 171). Dogberry is still pursuing this illusory villain, but what has his brain done to the lovelock?

Can you work out what Dogberry is trying to communicate about Deformed? Write a follow-up letter from Dogberry to Leonato, urging him to continue the search for Deformed and suggesting how this villain might be found. See if you can capture his chaotic style and malapropisms in your writing!

1 embrace 接受
2 dispose / For henceforth of 从今往后听您发落
3 packed 参与
4 by her 关于她
5 under white and black 白纸黑字记下来
6 pains 努力，气力
7 God save the foundation 上帝保佑本堂（这是教堂神职人员在得到教友捐赠时说的话，the foundation 指本教堂；乞丐也常用这句话表示对施舍者的感谢）
8 discharge thee 使你解脱
9 leave to depart 允许离开
10 prohibit it 禁止
11 look for you 恭候你们
12 lewd 下贱，下流

	I do embrace¹ your offer, and dispose	
	For henceforth of² poor Claudio.	
LEONATO	Tomorrow then I will expect your coming,	
	Tonight I take my leave: this naughty man	
	Shall face-to-face be brought to Margaret,	265
	Who I believe was packed³ in all this wrong,	
	Hired to it by your brother.	
BORACHIO	No by my soul she was not,	
	Nor knew not what she did when she spoke to me,	
	But always hath been just and virtuous	
	In anything that I do know by her⁴.	270
DOGBERRY	Moreover, sir, which indeed is not under white and black⁵, this plaintiff here, the offender, did call me ass, I beseech you let it be remembered in his punishment: and also the watch heard them talk of one Deformed, they say he wears a key in his ear, and a lock hanging by it, and borrows money in God's name, the which he hath used so long, and never paid, that now men grow hard hearted and will lend nothing for God's sake: pray you examine him upon that point.	275
LEONATO	I thank thee for thy care and honest pains.	
DOGBERRY	Your worship speaks like a most thankful and reverent youth, and I praise God for you.	280
LEONATO	There's for thy pains⁶.	
DOGBERRY	God save the foundation⁷.	
LEONATO	Go, I discharge thee⁸ of thy prisoner, and I thank thee.	
DOGBERRY	I leave an arrant knave with your worship, which I beseech your worship to correct yourself, for the example of others: God keep your worship, I wish your worship well, God restore you to health, I humbly give you leave to depart⁹, and if a merry meeting may be wished, God prohibit it¹⁰: come, neighbour.	285
	Exeunt [Dogberry and Verges]	
LEONATO	Until tomorrow morning, lords, farewell.	290
ANTONIO	Farewell, my lords, we look for you¹¹ tomorrow.	
DON PEDRO	We will not fail.	
CLAUDIO	Tonight I'll mourn with Hero.	
	[Exeunt Don Pedro and Claudio]	
LEONATO	Bring you these fellows on, we'll talk with Margaret, how her acquaintance grew with this lewd¹² fellow.	
	Exeunt	

Benedick seeks Margaret's help in arranging a meeting with Beatrice. As he awaits Beatrice's arrival, he attempts a love song and laments his inability to express his love in rhyme.

剧情简介：本尼迪求玛格蕊帮忙安排与碧翠见一面。他等待碧翠的到来之时，编了一首情歌，却为自己作不出押韵的情诗而悲哀。

Language in the play 剧中语言
Double meanings: warm and funny or vulgar and dark?

As she did earlier with Beatrice, Margaret attempts to match wits with Benedick in playfully bawdy language full of double entendres. Lines 1–17 are inescapably full of sexual innuendo:

come over	surpass (suggesting 'take sexually')
buckler	shield (suggesting 'belly, vagina')
swords/pikes	weapons (suggesting 'penis')
vice	clamp (suggesting 'gripping thighs').

Margaret seems strangely unconcerned about the part she has played in Hero's slander and 'death'. Neither she nor Benedick would be aware of Borachio's confession yet. Some productions play the scene for laughs, suggesting harmless cheeky fun, whereas others use it to suggest a darker side to both Margaret and Benedick.

Write a set of director's notes to the actors playing Margaret and Benedick in this scene. Suggest the extent to which you want them to interact physically, the degree of humour you'd like to draw out of the scene, and the emphasis that you want on certain words or phrases.

Write about it 写作练习
Benedick – a soldier but no poet!

The ideal Elizabethan man was both soldier and poet. Songs, sonnets and blank verse were traditional ways for a lover to express his feelings. The audience enjoys watching Benedick's lack of skill in singing and verse-making (lines 18–31), but is also touched by the genuine desire he has to please Beatrice.

Have fun with Benedick's inability to rhyme effectively. Use the poor rhymes he lists himself, and the names of the legendary lovers from mythology he cites (see below), to come up with a comically poor love poem to 'woo' Beatrice. Perform this poem in deep earnest and in as exaggerated a way as you can for comic effect!

lady … baby	Hero rhymes with …
scorn … horn	Leander rhymes with …
school … fool	Troilus rhymes with …

1 **deserve well at my hands** 值得我善待你
2 **helping … Beatrice** 让我有机会和碧翠说句话
3 **sonnet** 小歌（一般译作"十四行诗"，常以爱情为主题）
4 **come over** 超过，般配
5 **comely** 适当，相称
6 **keep blew stairs** 待在楼下（富人家的下人工作间都在地下室，这里指当一辈子下人）
7 **catches** 一口咬中（有下流含义）
8 **fencers' foils** 击剑用的钝头剑
9 **I give thee the bucklers** 我缴械投降（bucklers指一种防身用的小圆盾）
10 **pikes** 矛尖
11 **vice** 钳子
12 **panders** 媒人，牵线的人
13 **quondam** 之前
14 **carpet-mongers** 走地毯的人（经常进出小姐卧室）
15 **in festival terms** 以节日的形式（即诗歌朗诵）

Act 5 Scene 2
Leonato's garden

Enter BENEDICK *and* MARGARET

BENEDICK Pray thee, sweet Mistress Margaret, deserve well at my hands[1], by helping me to the speech of Beatrice[2].

MARGARET Will you then write me a sonnet[3] in praise of my beauty?

BENEDICK In so high a style, Margaret, that no man living shall come over[4] it, for in most comely[5] truth thou deservest it.

MARGARET To have no man come over me, why, shall I always keep below stairs[6]?

BENEDICK Thy wit is as quick as the greyhound's mouth, it catches[7].

MARGARET And yours, as blunt as the fencers' foils[8], which hit, but hurt not.

BENEDICK A most manly wit, Margaret, it will not hurt a woman: and so I pray thee call Beatrice, I give thee the bucklers[9].

MARGARET Give us the swords, we have bucklers of our own.

BENEDICK If you use them, Margaret, you must put in the pikes[10] with a vice[11], and they are dangerous weapons for maids.

MARGARET Well, I will call Beatrice to you, who I think hath legs.   *Exit*

BENEDICK And therefore will come.

[*Sings*]   The God of love
            That sits above,
            And knows me,
            And knows me:
            How pitiful I deserve.

I mean in singing, but in loving – Leander the good swimmer, Troilus, the first employer of panders[12], and a whole book full of these quondam[13] carpet-mongers[14], whose names yet run smoothly in the even road of a blank verse, why they were never so truly turned over and over as my poor self in love: marry, I cannot show it in rhyme, I have tried: I can find out no rhyme to lady but baby, an innocent rhyme: for scorn horn, a hard rhyme: for school fool, a babbling rhyme: very ominous endings. No, I was not born under a rhyming planet, nor I cannot woo in festival terms[15].

Benedick tells Beatrice that he has challenged Claudio and then asks her how she first fell in love with him. She in turn asks Benedick how he first fell in love with her.

 剧情简介：本尼迪告诉碧翠他已向克劳丢提出挑战，还问碧翠最初是如何爱上自己的，碧翠也反问本尼迪是如何爱上她的。

1 Team Benedick vs Team Beatrice! (in large groups)

Even when they are genuinely courting (恋爱), Benedick and Beatrice cannot stop arguing. 'Thou and I are too wise to woo peaceably', Benedick remarks in line 54. Their 'merry war', however, has a new playfulness to it. In their opening exchange (lines 32–5), for example, Benedick asks Beatrice to 'stay but till then' (i.e. until he asks her to go) so she jokingly replies that, since he has just said 'then', she had better be off!

a Form two groups: 'Team Benedick' and 'Team Beatrice'. Line up Team Beatrice on one side of the classroom or studio and Team Benedick on the other. Have two confident actors perform lines 32–72 very quickly, but in such a way that each character is 'playing up' to their team every time they make a 'winning' point (turning round, encouraging, winking and so on). Each team should cheer and whoop every time they think their character is 'on top' in the scene. Afterwards, discuss which 'team' had the most to cheer about and what this tells us about Benedick and Beatrice's relationship.

b Perform the scene again, more slowly and thoughtfully. This time, one team is 'Team Love' and the other 'Team War'. Pick out a few key words in the scene that reflect love or hope, and a few that reflect war or negativity. Each team should echo each word as it is spoken in the scene, to highlight the struggle between affection and conflict present in any scene with Beatrice and Benedick. Discuss which team is dominant, or at least stronger, in this scene.

1 that I came   我来见你的目的（即问本尼迪是否已向克劳丢挑战）
2 what hath passed   怎么样了
3 thereupon   因此
4 noisome   有臭味，令人恶心
5 undergoes   收到
6 subscribe   记下，认定
7 so politic a state   如此有条理的统治
8 suffer   经受，忍受
9 epithet   措辞
10 spite it   找它的麻烦，与它为敌
11 woo peaceably   平和地谈情说爱
12 there's … himself   聪明人是不会自夸的
13 instance   格言，谚语
14 that … neighbours   曾存在于与邻为善的年代
15 live no longer in monument   一旦死了很快就会被人遗忘

▶ Both Beatrice and Benedick are keen to 'suffer love', but there is still a little way to go before there can be full peace between them. Discuss how much physical contact there should be between them in this scene.

Enter BEATRICE

Sweet Beatrice, wouldst thou come when I called thee?
BEATRICE Yea, signor, and depart when you bid me.
BENEDICK Oh stay but till then.
BEATRICE Then, is spoken: fare you well now, and yet ere I go, let me go with that I came[1], which is, with knowing what hath passed[2] between you and Claudio.
BENEDICK Only foul words, and thereupon[3] I will kiss thee.
BEATRICE Foul words is but foul wind, and foul wind is but foul breath, and foul breath is noisome[4], therefore I will depart unkissed.
BENEDICK Thou hast frighted the word out of his right sense, so forcible is thy wit: but I must tell thee plainly, Claudio undergoes[5] my challenge, and either I must shortly hear from him, or I will subscribe[6] him a coward: and I pray thee now tell me, for which of my bad parts didst thou first fall in love with me?
BEATRICE For them all together, which maintained so politic a state[7] of evil, that they will not admit any good part to intermingle with them: but for which of my good parts did you first suffer[8] love for me?
BENEDICK Suffer love! A good epithet[9]: I do suffer love indeed, for I love thee against my will.
BEATRICE In spite of your heart I think: alas poor heart, if you spite it[10] for my sake, I will spite it for yours, for I will never love that which my friend hates.
BENEDICK Thou and I are too wise to woo peaceably[11].
BEATRICE It appears not in this confession, there's not one wise man among twenty that will praise himself[12].
BENEDICK An old, an old instance[13], Beatrice, that lived in the time of good neighbours[14]: if a man do not erect in this age his own tomb ere he dies, he shall live no longer in monument[15] than the bell rings and the widow weeps.

As Benedick and Beatrice talk, Ursula comes rushing in with news that Don John's plot has been discovered and Hero's good name restored. All three leave in haste for Leonato's house.

剧情简介：正当本尼迪和碧翠说话时，阿秀菈冲进来说，唐约翰的阴谋已被揭穿，希柔恢复了名誉。三人急忙奔往列纳托府上。

1 Question 问得好
2 clamour 丧钟声
3 rheum 寡妇的抽泣
4 Don Worm 唐氏良心虫（在《圣经》中良心是一只折磨人的虫子，专门蚕食人的精神）
5 no impediment to the contrary 没有阻碍地向相反方向发展
6 be ... virtues 给自己的优点吹喇叭（即自吹自擂）
7 bear witness 证实
8 Very ill 非常憔悴
9 mend 好起来
10 yonder's old coil 那儿正闹得不可开交
11 abused 被算计
12 author 教唆者，怂恿者
13 presently 立刻
14 die in thy lap 死在你怀里（有性暗示）

▲ This Beatrice and Benedick appear to have softened their expressions and body language, and to be more 'at peace'. Discuss the changing attitudes that Beatrice and Benedick have shown towards each other through the play. How would you describe their relationship in this scene?

Write about it 写作练习

Listing the reasons for love (and hate!)

In lines 78–9, Benedick lists the ways in which he will show his devotion to Beatrice. In contrast, in lines 39–40, Beatrice uses a list to describe why she won't let him kiss her.

a Write a paragraph describing how lists are used in contrasting ways in this scene. Explain why this is a useful/effective rhetorical technique, and how it can carry strong dramatic or comedic impact.

b Shakespeare sometimes uses syndetic (连接词连接的), lists (separating lists using 'and'), and sometimes uses asyndetic (无连接词连接的), listing (separating a list out using commas). Find examples in the play of these different types of lists, and compare their impact in an additional paragraph.

Much Ado About Nothing Act 5 Scene 2

虚惊一场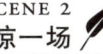

BEATRICE And how long is that think you?
BENEDICK Question[1]: why an hour in clamour[3] and a quarter in rheum[3], therefore is it most expedient for the wise, if Don Worm[4] (his conscience) find no impediment to the contrary[5], to be the trumpet of his own virtues[6], as I am to myself; so much for praising myself, who I myself will bear witness[7] is praiseworthy: and now tell me, how doth your cousin?
BEATRICE Very ill[8].
BENEDICK And how do you?
BEATRICE Very ill too.
BENEDICK Serve God, love me, and mend[9]: there will I leave you too, for here comes one in haste.

Enter URSULA

URSULA Madam, you must come to your uncle, yonder's old coil[10] at home, it is proved my Lady Hero hath been falsely accused, the prince and Claudio mightily abused[11], and Don John is the author[12] of all, who is fled and gone: will you come presently[13]?
BEATRICE Will you go hear this news, signor?
BENEDICK I will live in thy heart, die in thy lap[14], and be buried in thy eyes: and moreover, I will go with thee to thy uncle's.

Exeunt

Night. In a sombre ceremony, Claudio fulfils the first part of his promise. A tribute to Hero is read out, a solemn hymn is sung and a vow made to commemorate the anniversary of her death.

 剧情简介：夜晚，气氛阴沉的仪式中，克劳丢兑现其承诺的第一部分：念颂扬希柔的悼词，唱庄严的赞美诗，并发誓每年都来祭奠希柔。

Stagecraft 导演技巧
Creating a 'monument' in just a moment!

In Act 4, the play moved from light into dark. Now it prepares to move back from darkness into light, both literally (lines 24–8) and symbolically. Claudio's remorse and grief needs to appear genuine and moving in order to enhance the sense of joy to come. At the start of Scene 3 in one production, the lights dimmed, a tomb-like monument rose up from beneath the stage, and shadowy figures entered bearing flickering torches. However you choose to stage this scene, a significant change in mood at line 24 needs to be achieved quickly and with maximum theatrical impact.

Present a director's design brief for this scene. Either use a large sheet of paper divided into four sections, or four slides of a computer presentation program. Decide how you would like to use the following areas of stagecraft:

- **Set** How will you present the tomb? Some productions use movable scenery, whereas some modern theatres project an image of a tomb onto the back wall of the stage. Some directors have the tomb 'represented' symbolically by actors or the use of lights.
- **Lighting** Most of Shakespeare's plays were originally performed outdoors in the middle of the day, long before electric lighting was used. He may well have used actors carrying lanterns and candles to represent the dark; many outdoor productions today still do this. However, a modern theatre with coloured lighting and the ability to project images can create effects and atmosphere in many different ways. How will you use light to create a sombre (昏暗), mournful mood?
- **Music and sound** Music is specifically referred to in this scene. Will you use recorded or live music? Will you have musicians on stage? What instruments will you use? Will there be any other sound effects?
- **Speech** Shakespeare did not give any direction as to who should speak lines 3–23, so in different editions of the play they are spoken by different characters. Here it is Claudio and the Lord – one of the Attendants. One production had Claudio speaking the epithet (lines 3–10) and lines 22–3, but Balthasar singing lines 12–21. How would you allocate (分配) the lines? Are there other, more creative approaches?

1 *tapers* 点燃的蜡烛
2 *monument* 陵墓，墓地
3 *slanderous tongues* 毒舌
4 *guerdon of* 补偿
5 *with shame* = of shame
6 *dumb* 沉默，无声
7 *goddess of the night* 夜晚女神（即荻阿娜，月神和处女的守护神）
8 *virgin knight* 处女骑士（希柔是处女，所以被认为是荻阿娜的追随者）
9 *Till death be utterèd* 直到充分表达了哀思
10 *rite* 仪式

Act 5 Scene 3
Hero's monument

Enter CLAUDIO, DON PEDRO *and three or four Attendants with tapers[1] and music*

CLAUDIO	Is this the monument[2] of Leonato?
LORD	It is, my lord.
	[*He reads the*] *epitaph*
	Done to death by slanderous tongues[3],
	Was the Hero that here lies:
	Death in guerdon of[4] her wrongs,	5
	Gives her fame which never dies:
	So the life that died with shame[5],
	Lives in death with glorious fame.
	Hang thou there upon the tomb,
	Praising her when I am dumb[6].	10
CLAUDIO	Now music sound and sing your solemn hymn.
	Song
	Pardon, goddess of the night[7],
	Those that slew thy virgin knight[8],
	For the which with songs of woe,
	Round about her tomb they go:	15
	Midnight assist our moan,
	Help us to sigh and groan.
	Heavily, heavily.
	Graves yawn and yield your dead,
	Till death be utterèd[9],	20
	Heavily, heavily.
LORD	Now unto thy bones good night,
	Yearly will I do this rite[10].

As dawn breaks, Don Pedro and Claudio leave to dress suitably for the marriage. Scene 4 opens with Leonato sending the women to mask themselves in readiness for the ceremony.

 剧情简介：天刚破晓，唐佩卓与克劳丢离开，换上婚礼服。第四场开始，列纳托让女士们戴上面具参加婚礼。

▲ In this production, a door opened in the monument to reveal a ghost-image of the 'dead' Hero. Find the two lines Claudio speaks in Act 5 Scene 1 that might suggest this staging. Discuss why you think the director made this staging choice, and the impact it might have had on the audience.

1	gentle day	黎明
2	Phoebus	福珀斯（古希腊神话里太阳神阿波罗 [Apollo] 的别名；阿波罗驾驶太阳战车在天空飞驰）
3	Dapples	使……有斑点
4	several	各自，分别
5	weeds	衣服
6	Hymen	亥门（古希腊神话里的婚姻神，因婚礼上要唱圣歌 [hymn] 而得名）
7	issue	结果，结局
8	Than this	（即希柔的死）
9	rendered up	引起，造成
10	Upon the error	正是由于这个错误
11	question	审问，调查
12	sorts	结果
13	reckoning	算账，对决
14	confirmed countenance	一本正经

1 'Before the wheels of Phoebus' (in small groups)

Colour and light are very important in this play. The 1993 movie of *Much Ado About Nothing* was noted for its glorious Italian summer setting and rich use of light. Some scenes, however, shine brighter than others. Throughout Act 5 Scene 3 and into Scene 4, we are told that the night is ending and morning arriving, symbolising a new start for all the characters. Any lighting designer and director need to pay special attention to these details.

Develop a colour wheel to show which scenes you think are the lightest and darkest in the play. There is an example here, although you do not have to agree with what is shown. Draw your own wheel and annotate it with quotations from the script and any further ideas of your own. Be prepared to share, debate and justify your choices with the rest of the class.

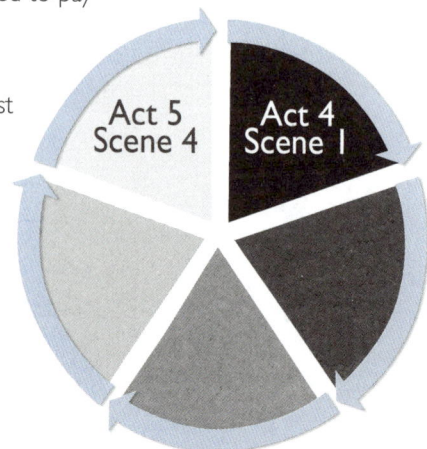

DON PEDRO	Good morrow, masters, put your torches out,	
	The wolves have preyed, and look, the gentle day[1]	25
	Before the wheels of Phoebus[2], round about	
	Dapples[3] the drowsy east with spots of grey:	
	Thanks to you all, and leave us, fare you well.	
CLAUDIO	Good morrow, masters, each his several[4] way.	

[*Exeunt Attendants*]

DON PEDRO	Come let us hence, and put on other weeds[5],	30
	And then to Leonato's we will go.	
CLAUDIO	And Hymen[6] now with luckier issue[7] speeds,	
	Than this[8] for whom we rendered up[9] this woe.	

Exeunt

Act 5 Scene 4
Leonato's house

Enter LEONATO, BENEDICK, MARGARET, URSULA, ANTONIO, FRIAR FRANCIS *and* HERO

FRIAR FRANCIS	Did I not tell you she was innocent?	
LEONATO	So are the prince and Claudio who accused her,	
	Upon the error[10] that you heard debated:	
	But Margaret was in some fault for this,	
	Although against her will as it appears,	5
	In the true course of all the question[11].	
ANTONIO	Well, I am glad that all things sorts[12] so well.	
BENEDICK	And so am I, being else by faith enforced	
	To call young Claudio to a reckoning[13] for it.	
LEONATO	Well, daughter, and you gentlewomen all,	10
	Withdraw into a chamber by yourselves,	
	And when I send for you come hither masked:	
	The prince and Claudio promised by this hour	
	To visit me: you know your office, brother,	
	You must be father to your brother's daughter,	15
	And give her to young Claudio.	

Exeunt Ladies

ANTONIO	Which I will do with confirmed countenance[14].

Benedick requests Beatrice's hand in marriage, to which Leonato willingly agrees. Claudio and Don Pedro arrive for the wedding ceremony and continue their mockery of the lovestruck Benedick.

 剧情简介：本尼迪提出想娶碧翠为妻，列纳托欣然同意。唐佩卓和克劳丢前来参加婚礼，继续拿恋爱中的本尼迪开玩笑。

Characters 人物分析

Being Benedick is 'enigmatical'! (in small groups)

Benedick formally asks permission to marry Beatrice (lines 21–31), but still cannot resist a note of sarcasm as he jokingly wonders whether what he is asking will 'undo' him (lead to his ruin). He calls Leonato's amused responses 'enigmatical' (puzzling).

a Note down precisely what in Leonato's speech is puzzling to Benedick.

b What evidence is there that Benedick is still unaware of the trick that has been played on him? Write down two lines that might suggest this. Annotate them with adverbs to suggest the tone an actor might use to deliver the lines.

c Swap your annotated lines with another group, so that they can follow your advice and perform them. Watch their performance and consider whether it was effective and achieved what you intended. Revise your annotations in light of their performance.

When Benedick, Claudio and Don Pedro last met (Act 5 Scene 1, lines 109–73), relations between them were strained. Benedick challenged Claudio, and there was considerable hostility.

d Sit in a circle in your group and read lines 40–52 (up to 'I owe you'). Try it in two ways, firstly mocking each other in a friendly/jokey fashion, and then in a more serious and aggressive way.

e Decide as a group how the script suggests Shakespeare wanted the scene performed. Do the 'thou/you' pronouns and the 'February face' image provide any clues? Discuss this and arrive at a directorial decision.

1 **intreat your pains** 给您添麻烦，求助于您
2 **undo** 毁掉
3 **eye of favour** 吸引力
4 **lent her** 鼓励她去拥有
5 **requite her** 回报她的爱
6 **sight whereof** 对其看法
7 **will** 心愿
8 **enigmatical** 令人困惑
9 **my will is …** = my will is that …
10 **conjoined** 相会，结合
11 **hold my mind** 不改初衷
12 **Ethiop** 埃塞俄比人（即今天的埃塞俄比亚人，在古希腊文里，这个词的意思是"黑脸"；当时以肤白为美，参见第184页）
13 **February face** 二月脸，冷若冰霜的脸
14 **tip thy horns with gold** 给你的角镶上金子（给你戴上一顶漂亮的绿帽子）
15 **low** 低声叫
16 **got** 生出
17 **bleat** 动物的咩咩／哞哞叫

1 Mighty Jove and the beautiful Europa (in threes)

Jupiter (Jove), king of the gods in classical mythology, took on the form of a bull in order to carry off Europa, the beautiful daughter of a Phoenician king. Europa also means Europe.

a Which of Benedick's comments in Act 1 Scene 1 is Claudio hinting at in lines 43–7 in this scene? Discuss how Benedick's reply turns the insult back onto Claudio.

b Read lines 40–52 together, keeping in mind the classical allusion (典故) described above. Think about the aggressive or bold, insulting gestures that might accompany these lines. Rehearse the sequence using such gestures to emphasise the hostility on display.

Much Ado About Nothing Act 5 Scene 4
虚惊一场

BENEDICK	Friar, I must intreat your pains[1], I think.
FRIAR FRANCIS	To do what, signor?
BENEDICK	To bind me, or undo[2] me, one of them:
	Signor Leonato, truth it is, good signor,
	Your niece regards me with an eye of favour[3].
LEONATO	That eye my daughter lent her[4], 'tis most true.
BENEDICK	And I do with an eye of love requite her[5].
LEONATO	The sight whereof[6] I think you had from me,
	From Claudio and the prince, but what's your will[7]?
BENEDICK	Your answer, sir, is enigmatical[8],
	But for my will, my will is[9], your good will
	May stand with ours, this day to be conjoined[10],
	In the state of honourable marriage,
	In which (good friar) I shall desire your help.
LEONATO	My heart is with your liking.
FRIAR FRANCIS	And my help.
	Here comes the prince and Claudio.

Enter DON PEDRO *and* CLAUDIO, *with Attendants*

DON PEDRO	Good morrow to this fair assembly.
LEONATO	Good morrow, prince, good morrow, Claudio:
	We here attend you, are you yet determined,
	Today to marry with my brother's daughter?
CLAUDIO	I'll hold my mind[11] were she an Ethiop[12].
LEONATO	Call her forth, brother, here's the friar ready.

[*Exit Antonio*]

DON PEDRO	Good morrow, Benedick, why what's the matter,
	That you have such a February face[13],
	So full of frost, of storm, and cloudiness?
CLAUDIO	I think he thinks upon the savage bull:
	Tush fear not, man, we'll tip thy horns with gold[14],
	And all Europa shall rejoice at thee,
	As once Europa did at lusty Jove,
	When he would play the noble beast in love.
BENEDICK	Bull Jove, sir, had an amiable low[15],
	And some such strange bull leaped your father's cow,
	And got[16] a calf in that same noble feat,
	Much like to you, for you have just his bleat[17].

157

Antonio brings in four masked ladies. Claudio accepts his unknown bride and discovers she is Hero. Beatrice and Benedick realise they have been tricked into believing that each was in love with the other.

 剧情简介：安托纽领来四位戴面具的女士。克劳丢接受了未曾谋面的新娘，却发现是希柔。碧翠和本尼迪明白过来之前上了当，以为彼此爱上了对方。

Themes 主题分析
Masking and unmasking

This is a serious and tense moment for Claudio and Hero. All the women who enter are in disguise (masked or veiled), so Claudio has no idea who is to be his bride. Equally, Hero cannot be sure of Claudio's reaction when she unmasks herself.

In a play where appearances are given so much importance, this final sequence is significant because Claudio must set them aside and give himself to a stranger.

a Claudio has surprisingly little to say once he discovers Hero is still alive. Write and then perform a short monologue exploring his feelings at the moment Hero 'unmasks' herself. Is he overjoyed? Does he feel ashamed? Is there a sense of relief or anxiety? What has he learned from this experience?

b Write and then perform a short monologue from Hero's perspective just prior to the unmasking. What are her feelings? Does she have any residual (遗留) anger? Is she nervous about how Claudio may react?

Language in the play 剧中语言
Taking possession of Hero (in sevens)

The language on this page is notable for the use of words relating to possession. In a sense, the 'ownership' of Hero is being settled in this scene, which may tell us a lot about attitudes towards marriage in Shakespeare's time.

a Make a list of all the words or phrases you can find in the script opposite that relate to taking possession or ownership. Try performing lines 52–66 as a group, with the women echoing these words when they arise. Think about the tone of the echo. What do they want to convey? Discuss the effect this has on the mood of the scene.

b Discuss whether this scene is dramatically satisfying for a modern audience. How do you feel about the apparent ease with which Claudio is forgiven? Suggest ways in which, through performance, a more heart-warming tone or mood can be created (a big kiss perhaps!) Use these ideas to perform this scene in a way that you think contemporary audiences will enjoy and find more realistic.

1 For this I owe you 我会还您这笔账
2 reckonings 义务
3 seize upon 娶为妻
4 defiled 被诽谤
5 but whiles 只有当……的时候
6 qualify 解释
7 largely 详细
8 let wonder seem familiar 让奇迹显得平常
9 Soft and fair 等一等
10 no more than reason 也不特别，不超乎寻常
11 wellnigh 几乎
12 but in friendly recompense 只当是做朋友
13 I'll ... upon't 我发誓

MUCH ADO ABOUT NOTHING ACT 5 SCENE 4
虚惊一场

Enter ANTONIO, HERO, BEATRICE, MARGARET [*and*] URSULA [*masked*]

CLAUDIO	For this I owe you[1]: here comes other reckonings[2].	
	Which is the lady I must seize upon[3]?	
LEONATO	This same is she, and I do give you her.	
CLAUDIO	Why then she's mine, sweet, let me see your face.	55
LEONATO	No that you shall not, till you take her hand,	
	Before this friar, and swear to marry her.	
CLAUDIO	Give me your hand before this holy friar,	
	I am your husband if you like of me.	
HERO	And when I lived I was your other wife,	60
	And when you loved, you were my other husband.	
CLAUDIO	Another Hero?	
HERO	Nothing certainer.	
	One Hero died defiled[4], but I do live,	
	And surely as I live, I am a maid.	
DON PEDRO	The former Hero, Hero that is dead.	65
LEONATO	She died, my lord, but whiles[5] her slander lived.	
FRIAR FRANCIS	All this amazement can I qualify[6],	
	When after that the holy rites are ended,	
	I'll tell you largely[7] of fair Hero's death:	
	Meantime let wonder seem familiar[8],	70
	And to the chapel let us presently.	
BENEDICK	Soft and fair[9] friar, which is Beatrice?	
BEATRICE	I answer to that name, what is your will?	
BENEDICK	Do not you love me?	
BEATRICE	Why no, no more than reason.	
BENEDICK	Why then your uncle, and the prince, and Claudio,	75
	Have been deceived, they swore you did.	
BEATRICE	Do not you love me?	
BENEDICK	Troth no, no more than reason[10].	
BEATRICE	Why then my cousin, Margaret and Ursula	
	Are much deceived, for they did swear you did.	
BENEDICK	They swore that you were almost sick for me.	80
BEATRICE	They swore that you were wellnigh[11] dead for me.	
BENEDICK	'Tis no such matter, then you do not love me?	
BEATRICE	No truly, but in friendly recompense[12].	
LEONATO	Come, cousin, I am sure you love the gentleman.	
CLAUDIO	And I'll be sworn upon't[13], that he loves her,	85

After being confronted with the love sonnets they have both written, Beatrice and Benedick agree to accept each other. Benedick and Claudio are reconciled. News comes of Don John's capture. The dancing begins.

剧情简介：面对别人拿出他们二人写过的情歌，碧翠和本尼迪同意接受对方。本尼迪和克劳丢言归于好。消息传来，唐约翰被抓获。众人开始跳舞。

▲ Benedick dominates the final moments of the play, but why is Beatrice so uncharacteristically silent? Write a short monologue outlining her thoughts as you imagine them.

1. written in his hand 他亲笔写的
2. halting sonnet 蹩脚的情歌
3. Fashioned to 专为……所写
4. by this light 老天在上
5. consumption 日渐憔悴
6. witcrackers 开玩笑的家伙
7. care for 在乎
8. epigram 箴言诗
9. a shall wear = he shall wear
10. giddy 奇怪
11. kinsman 家人，亲戚
12. cudgelled 棒打
13. double dealer 两面派
14. do … thee 没有看紧你
15. staff … horn 没有什么权杖比顶上镶了角的权杖更受尊重（有"妻子出轨"的隐含义）
16. ta'en 抓获
17. flight 逃跑

1 A happy ending (in large groups)

It is the convention in a comedy that all differences are eventually resolved. Shakespeare clearly meant for the play to end happily, but how entirely happy should this play's final moments be? Is everyone left fulfilled? Explore different interpretations of the play's ending by performing lines 91–120 in the following ways (feel free to try your own ideas too):

- **The toothache ending** (so sweet it rots your teeth!) Everyone is blissfully happy. There is lots of hugging, kissing and gazing into one another's eyes. The idea of Don John's 'brave' punishment thrills and excites all. Cheering, clapping and infectious (群情激昂) excitement greets nearly every line, and the whole cast is ready to dance wildly by the end!
- **The hesitantly happy ending** Although the ending is happy, the actors suggest the mixed emotions that, for example, Don Pedro, Hero and Beatrice may well feel. Emphasise the tension between Benedick and Claudio in lines 98–110, perhaps suggesting only an uneasy peace between them.
- **The awkward ending** None of the female characters speaks in this section, and Don Pedro's line could be interpreted in a number of ways. The staging suggests that the women are not entirely comfortable with all that is happening. Perhaps imply that Don Pedro is unhappy at the idea of Benedick devising a punishment for his brother, or that Leonato is insulted by the way Benedick dismisses him in line 114.

Discuss as a class or group which approach you feel is most effective. If you can't see a live production, consult movie versions to see how various directors have approached the end of the play. Decide how you would leave your audience satisfied.

Much Ado About Nothing Act 5 Scene 4
虚惊一场

       For here's a paper written in his hand[1],
       A halting sonnet[2] of his own pure brain,
       Fashioned to[3] Beatrice.
HERO   And here's another,
       Writ in my cousin's hand, stol'n from her pocket,
       Containing her affection unto Benedick.

BENEDICK A miracle, here's our own hands against our hearts: come, I will have thee, but by this light[4] I take thee for pity.

BEATRICE I would not deny you, but by this good day, I yield upon great persuasion, and partly to save your life, for I was told, you were in a consumption[5].

BENEDICK Peace I will stop your mouth.

DON PEDRO How dost thou, Benedick the married man?

BENEDICK I'll tell thee what, prince: a college of witcrackers[6] cannot flout me out of my humour: dost thou think I care for[7] a satire or an epigram[8]? No, if a man will be beaten with brains, a shall wear[9] nothing handsome about him: in brief, since I do purpose to marry, I will think nothing to any purpose that the world can say against it, and therefore never flout at me, for what I have said against it: for man is a giddy[10] thing, and this is my conclusion: for thy part, Claudio, I did think to have beaten thee, but in that thou art like to be my kinsman[11], live unbruised, and love my cousin.

CLAUDIO I had well hoped thou wouldst have denied Beatrice, that I might have cudgelled[12] thee out of thy single life, to make thee a double dealer[13], which out of question thou wilt be, if my cousin do not look exceeding narrowly to thee[14].

BENEDICK Come, come, we are friends, let's have a dance ere we are married, that we may lighten our own hearts, and our wives' heels.

LEONATO We'll have dancing afterward.

BENEDICK First, of my word, therefore play music. Prince, thou art sad, get thee a wife, get thee a wife, there is no staff more reverend than one tipped with horn[15].

         Enter MESSENGER

MESSENGER My lord, your brother John is ta'en[16] in flight[17],
       And brought with armed men back to Messina.

BENEDICK Think not on him till tomorrow, I'll devise thee brave punishments for him: strike up, pipers.

         Dance [*and exeunt*]

Much Ado About Nothing
虚惊一场

Looking back at the play 本剧回顾
Activities for groups or individuals

1 The wedding video

The play leaves us with several unanswered questions and some doubt about how successful the marriages will prove. Explore your thoughts about the characters and the play's ending by creating the wedding video. Plan, prepare and film some or all of the following:

- Benedick's best man speech for Claudio
- Hero's maid of honour speech for Beatrice
- interviews with the guests – what message or advice would the different characters want to offer the happy couples?
- bridal preparations – an interview with both Beatrice and Hero as they get ready for the wedding, in which they reveal their true feelings about their imminent marriages.

2 *Much Ado* in the future

It is five years later, and the two couples are visitors at Leonato's house. Which of the two couples is more secure and happy? Are Benedick and Claudio fully reconciled?

a In groups of five or more, improvise this reunion scene in your group. Evaluate what worked well in the scene, and use this to write a script and director's notes. Perform this scripted scene in front of the class.

b Explore the development of these relationships further by improvising another scene, in which the two couples go to see a marriage guidance counsellor. Think about how to effectively stage the two couples' sessions simultaneously – overlapping/alternating speech, freeze-frames and so on.

3 Gathering evidence

By now, you will have developed your own ideas and opinions about the play's characters, events and themes. You will probably be asked to write about some or all of these aspects in one form or another. Whatever you are writing, your opinions and ideas will always require evidence to support them. Look back at key moments and collect as many important quotations, favourite lines or powerful images/techniques as you can to reflect the following areas:

- love
- appearance/reality (tricks/deceptions)
- male power and the role of women
- Elizabethan society and modern values
- moments of theatrical power or impact.

4 Writing to analyse the play

Below are some typical essay or analysis questions covering the areas listed in the activity above. You might be asked to take one of these and develop an answer, or you might wish to do so independently to further your understanding of the play.

- How does Shakespeare present love and falling in love in *Much Ado About Nothing*?
- Explore the ways in which appearances and 'noting' are important in *Much Ado About Nothing*.
- How far do you agree that the women in *Much Ado About Nothing* are treated as second-class citizens?
- '*Much Ado About Nothing* is impossible for a twenty-first-century audience to take seriously.' Discuss.
- Describe the ways in which *Much Ado About Nothing* can be a theatrical and dramatic treat for an audience.

Refer to the following sections for ideas and commentary on these themes and discussion points. For more advice on planning and writing essays about the play, read the 'Writing about *Much Ado About Nothing*' section on page 200.

Much Ado About Nothing 虚惊一场

Perspectives and themes 视角与主题

Throughout this book, the 'Themes' boxes on the left-hand pages have drawn your attention to moments or sequences in the play in which certain key ideas are most powerfully present. Shakespeare would have been very conscious of some of these themes when writing the play, while other themes have taken on greater significance as audiences and attitudes have changed over the years.

- As a group or class, create a mind map or discuss the major themes identified in *Much Ado About Nothing*. For example, how many different types or aspects of love are explored?
- *Much Ado About Nothing* is now performed all around the world in hundreds of different languages and cultures. Conduct an Internet search on the play. List as many different current productions, or reviews of recent productions, as you can. Look at the variety of countries, settings and interpretive styles in which it appears. Write notes on how particular themes of the play could be explored in different productions.

Background and historical context

Much Ado About Nothing was written around 1598 and has remained a popular play for more than 400 years. A verse by Leonard Digges published in 1640 shows how it filled theatres at that time:

> Let but Beatrice
> And Benedick be seen, lo in a trice (眨眼间)
> The Cockpit (池座), galleries (廊座), boxes (包厢), all are full.

The comic and heart-warming appeal of the 'merry war' has a lot to do with this play's lasting popularity, but there are many other reasons. Its wider themes have universal appeal: deception, relationships between men and women, fashions and appearances, the ways in which we perceive one another and, of course, love. The moods of the play swing from light comedy to dark, life-threatening menace. There is always something happening: a fresh breakout of an old conflict, another plot, another misunderstanding, even songs and dancing!

▼ Beatrice and Benedick are wearing seventeenth-century dress in this English production from the 1980s.

It is important for a modern audience to understand the historical and cultural background of the play, as it differs greatly to our own contemporary situation.

The **treatment of women**, notably Hero and Beatrice, by men is an important theme in the play. Beatrice is strong, wilful and resilient (有适应力), but Hero is presented as a much more submissive and passive character, especially in the company of men.

- Write a list of adjectives that you think describe Hero's character, and contrast this with a list to describe Beatrice. Rank the adjectives in order of which you think are the most admirable. Do you think the Elizabethans would agree with you? Why?

PERSPECTIVES AND THEMES

Fashions, clothing and appearances were very important in Elizabethan theatres, and this is one of the main themes in the play. The outfits worn by fashionable people in Shakespeare's time were rich, colourful and expensive.

◆ Use the information on pages 171–3 and the Internet to find out the types of clothes men and women of different social standing would have worn in Shakespeare's time. Choose two characters in the play and use this research to help you make sketches of appropriate Elizabethan-era costumes for them.

A love story with Italian roots

The Beatrice–Benedick story seems to be Shakespeare's own invention, but the Hero–Claudio narrative has a long history. The tale of a lover who is deceived into believing that his beloved has been unfaithful to him, because he has seen a man at her bedroom window, goes back many centuries. Shakespeare probably based his Hero–Claudio story on Italian versions popular in Elizabethan England.

A reflection of Elizabethan society and everyday life

Despite the foreign names, Messina is presented as a very English community, much like the household of a wealthy Elizabethan lord. Many Elizabethan sports and pastimes are mentioned in the play: angling (垂钓), archery (射箭), falconry (驯鹰), eating and drinking, gambling, brothel-visiting (狎妓) and fighting.

Many prosperous Elizabethan merchants and landowners sought to climb up into the ranks of the aristocracy, rather as Leonato's family does. This tension between the old aristocratic order and the newly wealthy commercial class is very much reflected in the play. Leonato at first shows suitable respect for his noble guests. He is clearly delighted to have Count Claudio as a future son-in-law and heir, and he believes the accusations against Hero simply because they are made by his superiors (Act 4 Scene 1, line 145).

Just as Shakespeare was originally inspired by Italian love stories and poems, modern writers and directors around the world use his plays as the starting point for (sometimes radical) new creations in film, television, theatre, dance and other forms of media.

◆ The picture above shows a scene from a 2011 American production called *Funk It Up About Nothin'*, which used freestyle rap (即兴说唱) to re-imagine the verbal sparring (斗嘴) of Beatrice (MC Lady B) and Benedick. Some people argue that Shakespeare should not be performed in modern dress or 'messed around with', as in *Funk It Up About Nothin'*. Discuss this view with a partner, and decide what you think. How might Shakespeare have felt about it?

◆ Can you think of any modern movies or TV shows that contain similarities to the Claudio–Hero love story, or to the romantic conflict between Beatrice and Benedick? Are there any themes in the play that do not seem relevant to a twenty-first-century audience?

Much Ado About Nothing
虚惊一场

Women in a patriarchal world

Men (particularly fathers) dominated Elizabethan society. Traditional assumptions of male superiority were widespread. It was largely accepted that a wife should submit to her husband. She was his legal property and was rarely expected to think for herself.

However, women in London enjoyed a greater degree of freedom than in other parts of the country. Queen Elizabeth I showed that a woman could match any man. She was highly educated, fluent in several languages and a skilful politician.

Elizabethan men drew on a variety of stereotyped views about women as they attempted to explain, justify and control the subordinate place of woman in society.

- **Woman as whore or wife** Women had just two functions. They were either prostitutes to be bought or wives to be owned.
- **Woman as goddess** The courtly lover placed women on a pedestal (崇高地位). But is worshipping a woman as a goddess a way of silencing her as a human being?
- **Woman as adulterer** Virginity was a virtue and female adultery an unforgivable sin. An heiress proved unchaste was deprived of her inheritance.
- **Woman as shrew and scapegoat** Women were often blamed by men for all the faults of the world. A woman who spoke up for herself was a 'curst' shrew who needed 'taming'.

◆ *Much Ado About Nothing* explores (and challenges) a wide range of men's attitudes to the place of women in society. Make a list of comments made by men in the play that echo the attitudes described above. Also note down quotations where women express similar sentiments.

In a world of men, the women of Messina have two main options: to submit or to resist. Hero submits. Wooed first by the prince, then given to Claudio and promptly rejected, she is handed over a second time to the very man who had so cruelly spurned (拒绝) her.

◆ Write a script, or perform a roleplay, in which a director and the actor playing Hero discuss how to give credibility to Hero's silence and compliance (顺从).

◆ Beatrice clearly resists her stereotypical 'feminine' role. Starting with her interruption of the Messenger in Act 1 Scene 1, list the occasions when she shows her independence and defiance. Use your findings to write a character study of Beatrice (pp. 174–6 may help you).

Men in a world of honour and reputation

Men and male values dominated Elizabethan society. Every Elizabethan male was expected to train to fight for his country if needed. Sunday practice with the longbow at the archery butts (射箭场) was obligatory (Act 2 Scene 1, lines 186–7). Close bonds of male friendship, especially ones forged in war, were very much valued – but a man prized his honour and reputation above all else.

Status: 'thou/thee/thine' and 'you/your'

Use of these **pronouns** and **adjectives** sent very clear social signals in Shakespeare's time. When addressing one person, the use of 'you' implied distance, suggesting respect for a superior or courtesy to a social equal. 'Thou' could imply either closeness or superiority. It could signal friendship towards an equal or superiority over a servant. Used to address one of higher rank, it was aggressive and insulting.

◆ Rank, respect, allegiance and friendship are put to the test when Claudio denounces Hero. Identify how Benedick and Leonato use the 'thou/you' forms in Act 5 to address Claudio. Explain why Dogberry uses both 'thou' and 'you' to address Borachio and Conrade in Act 4 Scene 2.

Perspectives and themes

▲ Some critics argue that Beatrice represents a strong female role model in her determined refusal to submit to Benedick. To what extent do you think Beatrice's actions are that of a twenty-first-century female heroine?

▶ The treatment of Hero was intended to be shocking and unjust. Modern feminist critics have argued that the way in which both Hero and Beatrice accept marriage so simply and quietly at the end of the play is difficult to reconcile with modern values of greater equality between the sexes. What do you think? Is this a sexist play?

Much Ado About Nothing
虚惊一场

Tangled webs: plot, sub-plots and confusions

The play has three major dramatic plots or stories. The main plot is the Hero–Claudio love story. The 'gulling' (欺骗) of Beatrice and Benedick and Don John's ruining of Hero's reputation are the two sub-plots. The close-knit nature of Messina society, where everybody wants to know everybody else's business, is reflected in the way in which these three plots are so closely interwoven.

- Discuss these questions in pairs or small groups:
  - Which characters are most entangled in the events of all three plots?
  - Which characters are the catalysts (诱因) or the initiators (发起人) of events?

- The Hero–Claudio story is technically the main plot because it sparks off all other events in the play. Write a paragraph showing how Claudio's love for Hero leads to the Beatrice–Benedick and Don John sub-plots.

Deception: tricks and hoaxes (骗局)

The play contains many tricks and deceptions, both deliberate and accidental. There are malevolent (wicked/evil) and benevolent (kind/generous) tricks, as well as both deliberate and accidental deceptions.

- Find examples of each type of trick/deception, and discuss any overlap or ambiguity in your classification of them.

- One writer said that the play 'is composed of three hoaxes, four withheld secrets and three metamorphoses' (a metamorphosis is a profound change). Identify and write about what each of these might be. This could form the basis of an extended piece of writing.

Nothing and noting: Truth and illusion

The punning on 'nothing' and 'noting' in the title (see pp. 10 and 50) suggests from the start that the play will be concerned with how people perceive one another. Characters are continually faced with the question 'Can I be certain that what I see, or hear or know, is true?' Their difficulties are often caused by the deliberate deceptions of others, but just as often they stem from self-deception or their own human fallibility (难免犯错).

- Rank the fallibility of the major characters in the play. Add a short justification next to each one. Remember, fallibility is about the *capacity* to make a mistake rather than any deliberate wrongdoing (such as the cruel plots of Don John).

- Identify some of the more difficult behaviours to excuse or explain in the play. For example, is Leonato simply an innocent victim of Don John's deception, or should we condemn his own self-importance and self-interest? Write a short case study for each of these more challenging examples, and come to a final 'judgement' on the characters' motivations and shortcomings.

Kenneth Branagh's 1993 film of *Much Ado About Nothing* begins with Beatrice ironically speaking the song (from Act 2 Scene 3) 'Sigh no more, ladies, sigh no more'. Turn to page 53 to remind yourself of the song. Discuss the extent to which you think it catches the spirit of the whole play.

◀▶ The Truth and Illusion Theatre Company has come to Messina to present a show that will reveal all the deceptions and self-deceptions that have taken place during the past few days. Be as inventive as you can in presenting a short drama that highlights the play's many comic and serious deceptions.

Much Ado About Nothing
虚惊一场

Love in the world of Messina

Claudio and Hero's story demonstrates the conventional rituals of aristocratic Elizabethan courtship and marriage:

- wooing by proxy (代理) (not in person – perhaps by letter, poem or through an intermediary)
- settlement of the dowry (the amount of money, land or status the woman brings to the marriage)
- formal betrothal (official promise to marry)
- wedding ceremony.

To these, Shakespeare adds a second, masked betrothal that resolves the story.

- ◆ Identify when you think these five stages occur in the play. For each stage, speculate on the nature of Claudio and Hero's feelings for each other at that point. Give evidence from the play where possible. Do you think that by the end of the play they have found true love? Write a paragraph explaining your judgement and listing your reasons for it.

- ◆ Although Beatrice and Benedick's journey from hostility to love is long and difficult, many people think that their story culminates (结束) in a 'marriage of true minds', a union of equals. However, some critics claim that the way Benedick promises Beatrice he will 'stop [her] mouth' (with a kiss) is sexist and controlling. Write what you think Beatrice may want to say next. Will she really be silenced, or will their marriage always be tempestuous (鸡飞狗跳)?

Fashion and appearance
时尚与外貌

The Elizabethan aristocrat was a rich and glittering sight. Costumes for both sexes were extremely ornate (华丽) and vastly expensive. The way someone dressed was an indication of their rank, and people were forbidden by law from wearing fabrics belonging to higher ranks. For example, cloth of gold, a material woven with pure gold threads (see Act 3 Scene 4, lines 14–18), could only be worn by royalty and nobility.

In the eyes of some more conservative people, men's fashions had become particularly effeminate (女人气) by the end of the 16th century. Some noblemen wore make-up, had their hair curled at the barber's, smothered themselves in perfume, and wore single earrings. These fashions angered the traditionalists of the day. We can only wonder what they might have made of an all-female version of the play, such as that staged at Shakespeare's Globe in 2004 (pictured right).

The fashionable English gallant also copied any foreign style that took his fancy. Such extremes in dress meant that the Englishman was often laughed at for his outrageous mixing of foreign fashions (see Act 3 Scene 2, lines 24–30). The stylish combination for 1598 was German or Dutch trunk hose (短紧腿裤), French doublet, Spanish hat and Italian neckwear. Foreigners often commented on how frequently the English changed their fashions, particularly their hats, which 'ever changes with the next block' (Act 1 Scene 1, line 56). A 'block' was the wooden mould used to help form a hat into the desired shape.

▲ This all-female production at Shakespeare's Globe in 2004 used elaborate Elizabethan costumes to great effect. Elaborate hats 'ever changed with the next block'.

◀ Benedick wore bright colours, very baggy breeches (短马裤) and sported the long hair so fashionable among noblemen of the late sixteenth century.

Much Ado About Nothing
虚惊一场

'what a deformed thief this fashion is'

Costumes for both sexes distorted the natural human shape. The fashionable male peascod (豌豆荚式) doublet was heavily padded in front to give the appearance of a large paunch (肚子). The male trunk hose (breeches) were also padded to accentuate this pear shape.

Women's costumes were even more extreme and uncomfortable. Corsets (紧身衣) formed tiny waists and stomachers flattened the breasts and abdomen (腹部). Clumsy metal farthingales (裙撑) ballooned the skirts into a huge bell shape (see right).

The fashionable aristocrat of 1598 (could this be Count Claudio?)

The Earl of Southampton (see left) was Shakespeare's patron (sponsor). Shakespeare dedicated two long poems to him: *Venus and Adonis* and *The Rape of Lucrece*. Some people believe that he may be the young man to whom Shakespeare addressed many of his sonnets.

This portrait, painted at about the time the play was written, shows him dressed in the latest style. His doublet has very little padding (the heavily padded peascod doublet was beginning to go out of fashion), but his trunk hose are still very heavily padded. Notice the expensive gloves, the ornate armour and the long lovelock – a piece of long hair curled with hot irons – trailing over his left shoulder.

- ◆ If you were to set a production of *Much Ado About Nothing* in the present day, how would you dress the actors to suggest a modern equivalent to these extremes of style and fashion? Sketch and label a couple of designs as examples.

FASHION AND APPEARANCE

Much ado about appearance?

- This play is filled with references to fashion and external appearance. List all the fashion/appearance words you can find in the opening scene.

- From the information on pages 84, 88 and 171–2, write several sentences giving your view on whether Borachio was right to comment so cynically on Elizabethan fashion in Act 3 Scene 3.

- Read Act 3 Scene 2, lines 1–54 and decide how much like a fashionable Elizabethan gallant Benedick has become. Suggest how the actor (and the others on stage) could highlight these changes.

- The Watch, being lower class, would wear very different clothes from the aristocrats. Design their costumes for an Elizabethan, Victorian or modern-day production (see examples in the photo gallery and on pp. 80 and 180–1).

- Choose a character and identify the fashion words/images they use during the course of the play. What does this tell the audience about them?

- Find lines or words about fashion that help to convey the difficulty of knowing the difference between outward show and inner truth.

- Where in the play do dress and costume take on a serious and symbolic significance?

Kenneth Branagh said about his 1993 film version (see both pictures on p. vi in the photo gallery and pp. 169–70):

> We consciously avoided setting this version in a specific time, but instead went for a look and an atmosphere that worked within itself, where clothes, props, architecture, language and customs all belong to the same timeless world. This imaginary world could exist anywhere along a continuum (连续统一体) from 1700 to 1900.

- Try your hand at designing a costume for either Beatrice or Benedick that has a 'timeless' quality.

▲ A portrait of an Elizabethan lady in all the splendour of the richest of contemporary costumes. Search the library and the Internet for other examples of dress in Shakespeare's time.

173

Much Ado About Nothing 虚惊一场

Characters 人物分析

You can build up your understanding of a character by examining their actions, what they say, and what other characters say about them. This is helpful not just for understanding the major characters, but the lesser characters too.

As you follow characters through the play:

- Select the lines or phrases that you think are typical of them at particular moments.
- Note down examples of what other characters say about them.
- List their actions – actions, as well as words, reveal what a character is like.
- Carefully examine what some characters tell the audience directly when they are alone (in their soliloquies). Although these speeches appear to reveal the innermost thoughts of the character speaking, they can be partial and represent a one-sided version of events, of which the audience needs to be sceptical.
- Pay particular attention to how characters change and develop, and how Shakespeare shows us the different sides of their personalities.

Then try one of the following activities:

◆ Make a visual display (e.g. a wall chart, or a folder of illustrations, quotations and your own comments) of the information that you have gathered about different characters.

◆ Use the evidence you have found in the script to write an essay about one character. You should explore how that character changes and develops through the play, and comment on the effect that this has on the audience.

◆ Devise essay questions on a chosen character or a pair of characters. Examples might include:

- Why does Shakespeare include the character of Dogberry in the play?
- How does Shakespeare contrast Don Pedro and Don John?
- In what ways might a director show the tragedy as well as the comedy of Benedick and Beatrice's attitudes to love?
- Why has Shakespeare set the play in and around Leonato's house?

◆ Choose at least one question and produce an essay plan. Create a short presentation based on this plan. Your speech should provide detail and analysis for the rest of the class. You can use slides with quotations and visual aids to support and illustrate your ideas.

Beatrice

Actors must 'find' their character as the play comes to life around them in rehearsal and performance. The actor Susan Fleetwood talks below about what she 'found' when she played Beatrice:

Beatrice is life-giving, energetic, witty, intelligent, fun-loving, but lonely. In playing her, I was conscious of her as the orphaned cousin, being on the outside of things in many ways. Yet her position in the household also allows her freedom to be outrageous in a way that Hero cannot be.

Beatrice has an absolute hatred of the hypocrisy of the age, of all the sham (虚假) nonsense and social hierarchy which aims to control. That's why I stood apart from the group, waiting, observing, flexing (晃着) the sword I'd just used in the mock fight with Leonato.

Beatrice doesn't only challenge the accepted opinion of war, she is critical of all masculine values. She is a mature woman who rages against the masculine solidarity (团结) which can so easily destroy a woman's reputation. She means it when she says 'Kill Claudio'.

At the end of the play, Beatrice is a liberated character who flings herself into the dance in celebration. The kiss is a real physical commitment, indicative of her love and passion.

Unless the audience really believes that Beatrice and Benedick want to be together, there is no real joy at the end.

'I do suffer love indeed, for I love thee against my will.' Falling in love, despite initially loathing each other, allows the actors playing Beatrice and Benedick to try out many interpretations of the way their love for each other develops. Some are comic, some disturbingly serious and others tinged with sadness. Compare this image to others of Beatrice and Benedick that are included in this book. Which actors do you think most closely resemble the characters described in the script?

Much Ado About Nothing
虚惊一场

Sinead Cusack (below right) played a young, self-confident, flirtatious (调情) Beatrice who really discomfited (使窘迫) Benedick, until Hero's public shaming reduced her to impotent (没有用的) tears.

Judi Dench (below) played a Beatrice heading towards middle age. Central to her role was the reference to a previous encounter when Benedick had won her heart 'with false dice' (Act 2 Scene 1, lines 211–16) – a past betrayal that clearly still hurt her.

◆ Actors often use rehearsal techniques to get into the mind and understand the past story of complicated characters such as Beatrice. With a partner, take turns in becoming Beatrice whilst the other person asks searching, personal questions. Try to analyse Beatrice's motivations, contradictions and complexities. You could start with these questions:

- Why does Benedick provoke such strong feelings in her? (both positive and negative)
- How did she react to growing up and becoming a woman, and facing expectations of submission and docility (温顺)?
- What feelings does she have for Hero? Love, pity, concern, envy?
- Would she say that she changes her attitude at the end of the play? If so, why?

Characters

Benedick

Some of Benedick's lines could give the appearance of an eternal bachelor-soldier, a 'professed tyrant' to women (Act 1 Scene 1, lines 122–4). Is this just a pose, though? Some Benedicks have swaggered (大摇大摆地走) initially, as if they were 'the life and soul of the party'; others have used their wit almost like a mask, to hide a secret fear of women.

In many productions, Benedick finds himself bested (斗败) in the word battles with Beatrice. He also suffers numerous comic indignities during the 'gulling' scene (Act 2 Scene 3) and is cruelly mocked for his lovesick appearance (Act 3 Scene 2). One Benedick tottered (踉跄) on stage in fashionable high-heeled shoes; another Benedick had to endure his friends snatching his new hat, handkerchief, scarf – even his underpants – and throwing them about.

But does Benedick become more than just a figure of fun? His character develops to show maturity, and he rejects his former comfortable male comradeship. Tricked by his friends into believing Beatrice loves him, it seems that he responds wholeheartedly to her desperate unhappiness at Hero's disgrace. His response to her command to 'Kill Claudio' is brave and admirable, and his resignation from the prince's service is spoken with great dignity.

In this production, Benedick was a jaunty (活泼) and dashing bachelor who knew exactly how to annoy Beatrice. In his soliloquies, he seemed to be surprised by his own thoughts and feelings.

It seems that Benedick is self-aware, for he is almost always able to laugh at himself. Some have suggested that his final admission of his earlier foolishness could almost sum up the whole play: 'for man is a giddy thing, and this is my conclusion'.

- ♦ How do you feel about the development of a 'serious' Benedick? List reasons why you think that this is or is not an effective change in the character. Pair up and share your ideas, or debate in a larger group.

- ♦ In spite of his dishevelled (衣衫不整) and comic manner, Benedick appears to be a successful soldier and has influential friends. Step into role as a biographer and use clues from the script to piece together Benedick's life story up to the time of the opening scene. Include details that the other characters 'reveal' in the script.

- ♦ At what points in the play does Benedick does show a sense of humour about himself? List examples and explain what effect this might have on the audience.

◀ This Benedick returned from the war with his head covered in a blood-stained bandage – which he removed, when all the civilians had gone, to reveal no trace of a wound. How do you think this would affect the audience's overall impression of Benedick?

Much Ado About Nothing
虚惊一场

Hero and Claudio

Beatrice and Benedick may dominate the play, but the main plot concerns Hero and Claudio, whose love story begins the action and drives the subsequent events. They seem to be a conventional aristocratic young couple, who happily conform to the accepted rituals of Elizabethan courtship and marriage: wooing by proxy, settlement of the dowry, formal betrothal and marriage.

Hero appears to be a dutiful and obedient young woman, largely silent and passive in the presence of men. Her name symbolises faithful love (see p. 104). Many modern actresses have found it hard to stomach Hero's passivity, saying they would have stood up to Claudio's accusations.

- Why might Hero not say more? Does it reveal her to be shallow, or just young and unconfident? Consider whether Shakespeare gives some depth to her character in the two intimate, all-female scenes (Act 3 Scenes 1 and 4).

- Hero is betrothed a second time to a penitent (忏悔的) Claudio (pictured below). Write notes for the actor playing Hero, describing how she should speak and behave in Act 5 Scene 4. Is she fully forgiving or is there some remaining bitterness towards Claudio?

Claudio appears again to be the model Elizabethan lord, courageous in battle and a close friend of the prince. But he is young and inexperienced, which leaves him vulnerable to Don John's plotting.

- Although Elizabethan audiences may have seen nothing mercenary (唯利是图) in his enquiring after Hero's inheritance and would have understood his anger at being foisted (强迫接受) with an unchaste bride, how might a modern audience respond to his interests? In the context of the times, Hero's suggested infidelity brings dishonour on Claudio, as the wives of Elizabethan noblemen had to be morally virtuous. Even so, do you think that his treatment of her is justified? How does it reflect on Claudio?

- In groups, perform an improvised scene in which Claudio is interviewed on a TV talk show. One person takes the role of Claudio, and another person that of the show's host. The rest of the group makes up the audience, and raises their hands to address questions to Claudio. Decide whether the audience members are interested in Claudio's 'celebrity' wedding, or whether they will hold him to account for his attitude towards Hero and women in general.

Characters

Don John

Struggles for power within a royal family were not unusual in Shakespeare's time. Although the play was written towards the end of Elizabeth I's reign (in around 1598), the audience would be familiar with the problems of royal succession that resulted from her father Henry VIII's multiple marriages. Elizabeth herself was even accused of being a 'bastard', a child that was illegitimate (unlawful) because its parents were not married. Her own father passed a law – the Second Succession Act – after her mother was put to death, to make Elizabeth illegitimate.

A 'bastard' offspring like Don John was a particular threat, because he could challenge the legitimate claims of his brother. During the reign of her sister Mary I, Elizabeth I was sometimes imprisoned in the Tower of London or put under a form of house arrest because she was suspected of being involved in plots against her sister.

Upper-class illegitimate children were more common than might be thought in these times, but they were usually kept away from sight. Some were not allowed to appear at formal occasions and struggled to find a place in society. The status of a 'bastard' also challenged family property inheritance rules, an all-important matter to wealthy Elizabethans. Some parents understandably wanted to support all their children regardless of their legal status and of society's disapproval. Henry FitzRoy (meaning 'Son of the King'), 1st Duke of Richmond and Somerset, was the illegitimate child of Henry VIII; he was given a title, land, wealth and considerable power, and some suggested that he may have succeeded his father if he had not died young. Don John seems to enjoy a title and some royal status, but harbours a great deal of bitterness about his position.

Playing upon the connections of the words 'base', meaning low and socially inferior, 'bastards' were often portrayed as evil and malicious. They were frequently portayed as villains on stage. Shakespeare uses the villainous 'bastard' in other plays, such as *King John*, so audiences may have been wary (提防，謹慎) of Don John from the outset.

◆ In what way is the virtually silent Don John an unsettling presence from the start of the play? To what extent do you think that his prose dialogue throughout is a sign of his baseness?

◆ Consider how Don John manipulates Don Pedro, Claudio and Leonato by playing on their fear of the unfaithful wife and the bastard offspring. Is Don John really a threat to Messina society? What other functions might he serve in the play? He is, for example, quite slow to catch on to Borachio's plan (Act 2 Scene 2) and Shakespeare allows him to fade from the scene once the wedding has been ruined.

◆ In a group, improvise a scene that puts Don John in the 'hot-seat'. One person takes the role of Don John, and the other group members ask him questions to try and find out why he acts the way he does in the play.

▲ Leonato (left) greets Don Pedro (centre) and a smiling Don John (right). How has this production tried to show the contrast between the royal brothers? Think of other ways in which you might do this.

Much Ado About Nothing
虚惊一场

Don Pedro

Don John's half-brother is a Spanish prince and ruler of Sicily, who seems assured and confident at the start of the play. During the recent military campaign, he has apparently taken Claudio under his wing. He continues this upon their return from battle, but now tutors him in the art of courtship rather than war.

Don Pedro appears to share with his half-brother a liking for trickery and plotting, although his deceptions have no malicious intent. Yet, despite his apparently jovial (快乐) nature, many productions have him end the play as a rather sad and lonely figure; he is envious of 'Benedick the married man', who advises him 'get thee a wife'.

◆ Is Don Pedro essentially a good man, or does he lack compassion? Do you find him cold, heartless or arrogant at any point? Consider his denouncement of Hero as a 'common stale' (a prostitute) at the wedding, and his dismissiveness towards Leonato's grief in Act 5 Scene 1. At the same time, remember that he seems to be quickly chastened when Borachio confesses, and begs to make amends.

Leonato

Signor Leonato is the governor of Messina in Sicily. He seems to enjoy a carefree existence as the highest official in a colonial outpost (前哨) where soldiers come to recuperate (康复) after battle.

He is at the heart of the story due to his connections to many of the characters. He is the father of Hero, who becomes romantically involved with Claudio until her disgrace. He is the uncle of Beatrice, who seems to have been orphaned many years ago and taken in by Leonato. Whilst he wants to see his niece married well, as if she were his own daughter, it is clear from Act 1 Scene 1 that Leonato is amused by both his niece and her 'merry war' with Benedick.

Leonato plays host to most of the action, which mainly takes place in his house. Some productions have sought to demonstrate Leonato's wealth through the setting. Several have had characters hanging around and talking on the terraces, patios (露台) and rooms of the house, and the English National Theatre production of 2007 even had the actors sitting around and sometimes falling into a swimming pool!

◆ Consider where in the world you would set Leonato's house and how you would show this on the stage. What sort of decoration and furnishings would you include in the house? How would you emphasise the central role Leonato holds as host? Draw a plan of the set, and annotate it with detailed notes, or build a model and present it to the class with an explanatory talk.

Leonato is able to play many parts. We see his mischievous side when he is involved in the 'gulling' of Benedick in Act 2 Scene 3. When he discovers Hero's dishonour, he wishes that he never had a daughter or that she were dead. However, when he is won around to believing Hero, he quickly proves able to play tragedy – mourning her loss of reputation and convincing Claudio and Don Pedro of his grief after her 'death'. He plays a part in tricking Claudio into marrying Hero's 'cousin' to make amends for Hero's 'death'. He appears to be delighted at their ultimate reconciliation and wedding.

Dogberry, Verges and the Watch

Dogberry and Verges are a comic double act. One of their functions in the play is to discover the plot against Hero, yet be so incompetent that the news

CHARACTERS

is almost never reported to Leonato. The comedy they bring also helps to balance the near-tragic events that surround them.

Dogberry is not merely a comic mangler of words as he attempts to ape the elegant language of the aristocrats. He has a range of moods: grovellingly (卑躬屈膝) respectful to Leonato, condescending (居高临下) towards his partner Verges, outraged that he should be called an ass. The naïve dignity of his response to this insult is laughable, yet rather touching. However, his pride and his wit suggest that some of his actions and expressions may be intentionally ambiguous and provocative.

▼ Some productions cast professional comedians in the role of Dogberry, just as Shakespeare's company did. Who would you cast in the role? What would their popularity and reputation add to the performance of the character and the impact of the play's comedy on the audience?

Verges, Dogberry's constant companion and deputy, may be considered to be the 'straight man' (捧哏，滑稽配角). He has often been played as a small, ancient man, in contrast to the more robust Dogberry.

In some productions, Verges is eager to assist and agree with his superior, who promptly puts him down whenever he shows the slightest hint of initiative (Act 3 Scene 5, lines 23–31).

The Town Watch (nightwatchmen) have always been a rich source of comedy. When one Dogberry instructed them to 'call at all the alehouses' (Act 3 Scene 3, line 36), they immediately rushed off stage to do just that and had to be recalled by a blast from his whistle.

In Shakespeare's company of players, comic parts were often taken by Will Kemp, who played similar parts in other plays, such as Bottom in *A Midsummer Night's Dream*. Kemp's popularity, **ad libs** (即兴台词) (additions to the script) and performance skills may have been as much a draw as Shakespeare's writing. Actors and comedians may still ad lib topical references, talk with the audience and add slapstick to make their performances even funnier.

Much Ado About Nothing
虚惊一场

The language of *Much Ado About Nothing*
《虚惊一场》的语言

Shakespeare uses language in *Much Ado About Nothing* to convey a wide range of thoughts and feelings. He quickly moves the audience from light, confident, friendly and volatile (灵活多变) conversations to dark, hurtful and angry accusations. He achieves this through a varied use of vocabulary and different prose and verse styles, and through the multiple layers of meaning that words and phrases suggest to the audience.

Nothing/noting

In Shakespeare's time, words were often pronounced differently from the way they are today. 'Nothing' and 'noting' were **homophones** – words that sound identical, but have different meanings. These words and related words, such as 'note', occur frequently throughout the play and point to some of its major concerns. 'Noting' has the literal meaning of noticing, to observe, but might also refer to the men 'noting' the appearance of women. This word might also highlight the idea of a contrast between how things appear and how they are in reality (see p. 168).

The 'noting' that is often achieved through eavesdropping (as with Benedick and Beatrice), or only seeing a partial picture (as with Claudio) can lead to miscommunication or mistaken conclusions. Shakespeare uses this in the play to both comic and tragic ends.

The 'much ado' of the title carries the idea of making a great fuss. This might point to the disgrace of Hero based on 'nothing', as she is innocent; it could also be based on 'noting' – the rumour, gossip and hearsay of the other characters. Similarly, 'nothing' in Shakespeare's time was a slang word for the female genitalia (外生殖器) ('a no thing') and so the play might be said to be a lot of fuss about romance and sex. **Double entendre** (words with a double, usually sexually suggestive, meaning) are used in the play for comedy, particularly in Beatrice and Benedick's wordplay (see p. 185).

It is significant that the play leads us from 'noting', focusing on the outward appearance, to knowing and discovering the reality and truth about characters such as Don John and Hero – and, of course, Benedick and Beatrice.

Language in Shakespeare's world

Shakespeare's writing reflects the changing attitudes of his time. As Shakespeare's society moved away from the Catholic Church's influence, it also rejected its image-based storytelling methods – statues, paintings, and grand enactments of Bible stories (such as the medieval mystery plays). Instead, the newly Protestant society was focused more on the 'word of God', the word of the Bible, and the power of the word in general. In this context, we can see how crucial the language itself is in Shakespeare's plays.

The search for the right word to express exactly the right detail is also important to the way that Shakespeare writes. His quest for this led him to mix the language of society's elite with the language that he heard in the inns where some of his plays were performed. Compare Don Pedro's eloquent speech in Act 1 Scene 1 with Beatrice's foul language and **innuendo** (an indirect reference or insinuation, usually toward a sexual meaning) in Act 2 Scene 1, to see how Shakespeare draws language from many sources.

It is because of this ability to mix and manipulate language that the first recorded uses of many words and phrases are attributed to Shakespeare. Some of these words, such as 'employer', 'mortifying', 'reclusive' and 'schoolboy', which apparently appear for the first time in *Much Ado About Nothing*, may have already existed in part in the language. Some of them may have been another part of speech (a noun, an adjective, and so on) that was transformed, with the addition of a suffix or prefix, into another useful addition to the language. Through this inventive use of language, Shakespeare was able to immediately conjure up (使联想起) for the audience exactly what he had in his mind.

The language of Much Ado About Nothing

Imagery

Imagination (note the linguistic connection with imagery) was very important to the audience at the Globe Theatre, or at the inns and great houses where *Much Ado About Nothing* might have been performed. It is important to remember that in Shakespeare's time, there were few special effects available to the playwright. There was no electric lighting, for a start, as this had not yet been invented! Rather than using scenery that was difficult and expensive to produce, actors would mainly rely on the physical characteristics of the performance space.

The language often simply marks where and when the action takes place, and without an elaborate set and lighting/sound scheme the audience must imagine the rest. For example, the audience knows that Dogberry and Verges are assembling the Watch at night (Act 3 Scene 3) because they say 'good night', rather than because the lighting is darker. This sometimes makes simpler, more authentic productions difficult for modern audiences, who are used to the visual storytelling of television and movies. But *Much Ado About Nothing* is rich in imagery: vivid words and phrases that help the audience conjure up emotionally charged mental pictures or associations. Imagery stirs the imagination, deepens dramatic impact and gives insight into character.

Certain images recur, most notably images of outward appearance, as when Claudio likens Hero to a 'rotten orange' (Act 4 Scene 1, line 27), evoking a sense of outer beauty and inner corruption. A related image theme that runs through the play is fashion and clothes ('apparel'). In the opening scene, Beatrice declares that Benedick 'wears' his loyalty 'but as the fashion of his hat, it ever changes with the next block (hat shape)'.

Shakespeare's imagery uses metaphor, simile (明喻) and personification (拟人). All are ways of making effective comparisons and helping to create mental pictures for the audience.

A **simile** compares one thing to another, using 'like' or 'as'. Don Pedro, on hearing Borachio confirm Hero's innocence, asks Claudio, 'Runs not this speech like iron through your blood?' Benedick thinks Beatrice would exceed Hero 'as much in beauty as the first of May doth the last of December' – if only she didn't have such a terrible temper!

A **metaphor** is also a comparison, suggesting that two apparently dissimilar things are actually the same. Benedick says of the disappointed Claudio, 'Alas poor hurt fowl, now will he creep into sedges (thick grass)'.

Personification turns things into people, giving them human feelings or attributes. Beatrice, for example, talks of 'Repentance ... with his bad legs' and how a 'star danced' when she was born.

Classical allusions (典故) also contribute to the richness of the play's imagery. Educated Elizabethans loved to display their learning and command of language, and would certainly have enjoyed the references to Classical mythology as they watched a performance of *Much Ado About Nothing*:

- **Jove** In Roman mythology, Jove was king of the gods. When he travelled the Earth in human disguise, Philemon, a poor peasant, gave him hospitality in his humble cottage (see Act 2 Scene 1, lines 69–70). Jove was a habitual adulterer. To keep his sexual liaisons secret from his wife, he adopted many disguises (e.g. bull, satyr [萨堤尔; 羊身男], swan), and was thus able to seduce many young women like Europa (see Act 5 Scene 4, lines 43–51) and make them pregnant.

- **Troilus and Cressida** Troilus loved Cressida faithfully. She swore to be true to him, but proved faithless (see Act 5 Scene 2, line 24).

- **Hercules** Hercules was the ancient Greek strong-man. He performed many mighty physical tasks (the 'Hercules labours', see Act 2 Scene 1, line 275) and numerous sexual ones too, such as impregnating all fifty daughters of the king of Thespis in one night! Cupid later punished him by making him the love-slave of Omphale, queen of Lydia, who beat and ridiculed

Much Ado About Nothing
虚惊一场

him, dressing herself in his armour while he was set to do the cooking, spinning and other female tasks (see Act 2 Scene 1, line 191).

◆ Find out which characters make the allusions above. Write down the quotations and alongside each write why they use them (e.g. to impress, amuse, express fear or anger). Afterwards, write an explanation of how the references to Jove, Hercules and Troilus and Cressida echo particular themes in the play.

◆ Simile, metaphor, personification and Classical allusion are all used one after another during Benedick's account of his traumatic masked dance with Beatrice, 'Oh she misused me … perturbation follows her' (Act 2 Scene 1, lines 181–97). Write down the relevant quotations and label them.

Opposing images
Antithesis (对偶) is the opposition of ideas, words or phrases against each other, as when Beatrice exclaims 'I had rather hear my dog bark at a crow than a man swear he loves me' (Act 1 Scene 1, lines 97–8). Antithesis expresses conflict (e.g. 'dog bark' stands in contrast to 'man swear') and is especially powerful in *Much Ado About Nothing*, with its oppositions between men and women, brother and brother, father and daughter, marriage and independence, truth and lies. Shakespeare makes the language match this conflict, reinforcing the impression of the onstage action in the audience's imagination.

In a play full of deceptions and disguises, appearance is constantly in conflict with reality. Claudio, for example, is convinced he has been an eye-witness to Hero committing an act of infidelity. Turn to Act 4 Scene 1, lines 28–37, 50–55 and 96–101. Write down all the antitheses he uses to express what he believes is Hero's outward purity but inner corruption.

Many images
Shakespeare seems to have enjoyed 'piling up' words and phrases rather like a list, as in Don Pedro's description of Benedick's multinational fashion sense: like 'a Dutchman today, a Frenchman tomorrow … a German from the waist downward … and a Spaniard from the hip upward' (Act 3 Scene 2, lines 25–8). A more sombre list is Don John's brooding self-analysis: 'I cannot hide what I am …' (Act 1 Scene 3, lines 10–13).

Sometimes the repetition of a word or phrase – known as **anaphora** (首语叠用) – adds a sense of reality or excitement to the words that the character is speaking. For an example of this, look at the number of times 'and', 'I', 'thou' and 'will' are used by Don Pedro in Act 1 Scene 1, lines 232–54. Think about what he is talking about, and why Shakespeare would use such a technique at this point in the play.

Repeated words, phrases, rhythms and sounds add intensity to the moment or episode. **Repetitions** are at first used elegantly and playfully, as when Benedick jokes with his friends about 'troths and faiths':

> DON PEDRO   *By my troth, I speak my thought.*
> CLAUDIO   *And in faith, my lord, I spoke mine.*
> BENEDICK   *And by my two faiths and troths, my lord,*
> *I spoke mine.*
>   Act 1 Scene 1, lines 166–8

This contrasts sharply with, for example, Leonato's outburst of shame and disappointment at the wedding, where he repeatedly asks questions and repeats 'I', 'thou', 'one', 'she', 'mine'.

Racist images?
Benedick, Margaret and Claudio refer unflatteringly in the play to Turks, Ethiops (i.e. black-skinned people) and Jews (a grudgingly tolerated minority in Shakespeare's England, often subject to verbal abuse).

Read their words and the context in which they say them (Act 2 Scene 3, line 212, Act 3 Scene 4, line 42, and Act 5 Scene 4, line 38). Is Shakespeare racist, or would you argue that these are the characters' words that signal their attitudes, rather than Shakespeare's own thoughts?

Confusing images
Dogberry's particular talent is for **malapropisms** (mistakenly using one word for another that sounds similar – this name is drawn from Mrs Malaprop,

The language of Much Ado About Nothing

a character in Richard Brinsley Sheridan's 1775 play *The Rivals*). Where others in the play deliberately use language to distort and deceive, Dogberry baffles people without realising he is doing so. For the audience member who listens carefully, there is great comedy to be had in the images that Dogberry unintentionally conjures. Dogberry's attitude to law enforcement (Act 3 Scene 3, lines 21–60) is the exact opposite to what it should be: go to sleep on duty, keep away from criminals and so on. Look at the malapropisms he uses (see pp. 78, 94 and 120).

Wordplay

If Shakespeare's history plays are full of sword-fighting, his comedies are full of wordplay. Plenty of characters in the play employ puns to deliver killer lines that can surprise, amuse or even hurt. When a word has two or more different meanings, playing on that ambiguity is called **punning**. Nearly everyone in Leonato's household enjoys playing with words, particularly if they have a possible sexual meaning.

Beatrice (Act 2 Scene 1, line 223) says the jealous and resentful Claudio is as 'civil as an orange', punning on the similarities of the two words 'civil' and 'Seville'

(a bitter-tasting orange). 'Dies' was a euphemism for orgasm, so when Claudio says that Beatrice 'dies' for love of Benedick (Act 3 Scene 2, lines 50–1) Don Pedro can't resist replying that she will have to be 'buried with her face upwards'.

Sometimes the wordplay bounces back and forth between characters (termed **repartee** [反唇相讥]). Shakespeare uses this very early on in the play, first between Beatrice and the Messenger to show her sharply barbed wit and then between her and Benedick to set up their bristlingly witty relationship (Act 1 Scene 1, lines 23–70 and 86–107).

◆ Speak together the following examples of repartee: Act 1 Scene 1, lines 151–215, Act 3 Scene 2, lines 1–54 and Act 5 Scene 4, lines 40–51. Decide how and why the men's repartee changes in tone.

◆ Read Beatrice and Leonato's conversation (Act 2 Scene 1, lines 1–60) and Margaret and Benedick's (Act 5 Scene 2, lines 1–16). Decide why each woman uses such 'foul language'.

◆ Read Act 4 Scene 1, lines 265–316 and Act 5 Scene 2, lines 32–79. Can you detect anything more than comedy in Beatrice and Benedick's wordplay?

▼ Actors often use gestures to highlight the wordplay in their speeches. Think up a witty line that Beatrice's gesture here could illustrate.

Much Ado About Nothing
虚惊一场

Verse and prose: why does it switch?

Shakespeare is known as a playwright who wrote in verse, and much of his drama work is written in **blank verse** (素体诗) (see 'Verse', p. 188).

An Elizabethan audience would have expected high-status characters to speak verse, particularly in scenes of high drama or emotional intensity. **Prose** was the traditional mode of expression for low-status characters in more relaxed comic scenes. Dogberry, for example, always speaks in prose. Shakespeare, however, bends the rules in subtly dramatic ways.

The intelligent and worldly-wise Beatrice and Benedick prefer prose. High-status characters like Leonato, Claudio and Don Pedro will speak an elegant and witty prose when relaxed, but at more intense moments readily switch to verse. Claudio, for example, leads Don Pedro into verse to talk of his love for Hero (Act 1 Scene 1, line 216).

- Find the moments when even Beatrice and Benedick speak in verse. Decide what has prompted them to do so.

- The men speak largely in prose when tricking Benedick (Act 2 Scene 3). The women speak entirely in verse when tricking Beatrice (Act 3 Scene 1). Suggest three possible reasons for the difference.

- Look at the transitions between verse and prose in Act 4 Scene 1 and Act 5 Scene 1. At each transition, write down the particular change of mood that is being signalled. For example, Don Pedro and Claudio switch from joking prose to serious verse when they learn to their horror that Hero was innocent of any misconduct (Act 5 Scene 1, lines 214–21).

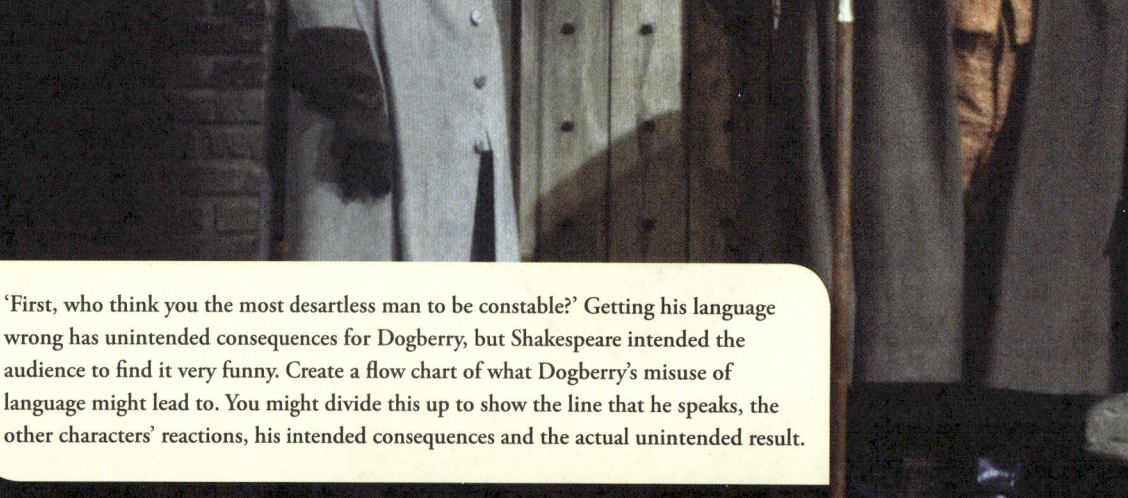

'First, who think you the most desartless man to be constable?' Getting his language wrong has unintended consequences for Dogberry, but Shakespeare intended the audience to find it very funny. Create a flow chart of what Dogberry's misuse of language might lead to. You might divide this up to show the line that he speaks, the other characters' reactions, his intended consequences and the actual unintended result.

The language of Much Ado About Nothing

Prose

The majority of *Much Ado About Nothing* is written in a flexible prose style that changes its qualities with each new character and situation. But while it may be fluid, Shakespeare's prose is nonetheless carefully structured in its imagery, rhythms, repetitions, antitheses, lists and wordplay. The result is prose dialogue where the sentences, phrases and words constantly balance, reflect and oppose each other. The following are examples of the variety of effects that Shakespeare creates.

Elegant politeness Leonato, Don Pedro and the Messenger set the tone in the opening scene (see Activity 1, p. 4). Each strives to outdo the other in elegantly balanced compliments and observations (e.g. 'figure of a lamb … feats of a lion', Act 1 Scene 1, line 12). Beatrice, of course, refuses to play this game!

Good-natured wit and repartee Don Pedro, Claudio and Benedick love to demonstrate their friendship in banter (斗嘴) and teasing (see Act 1 Scene 1, lines 151–215). When, for example, Don Pedro asks to know what 'secret' his friends were discussing, Benedick playfully gives his 'short' answer: Claudio is in love with 'Leonato's short daughter'.

Rambling incoherence Dogberry's wandering sentences match his rambling brain. He studiously explains why the Watch must have nothing to do with criminals (Act 3 Scene 3, lines 21–50) and fails at great length to tell Leonato vital information that might have averted (避免) Hero's public humiliation (Act 3 Scene 5). When he is not botching the cross-examination, he is smarting at being called an ass (Act 4 Scene 2).

Much Ado About Nothing
虚惊一场

Attack and counter-attack The sharpest encounters in the play are between Beatrice and Benedick. What begins apparently playfully (Act 1 Scene 1, lines 86–107) becomes at the masked dance increasingly acrimonious (唇枪舌剑), leaving Benedick wishing he could be anywhere else 'rather than hold three words conference with this Harpy' (Act 2 Scene 1, line 204).

Rigid single-mindedness Don John's speech is like a mask. His first words (Act 1 Scene 1, line 116) show an outward politeness, but his inner malice and resentment are revealed in the stiff and heavy sentence patterns of his remarks in Act 1 Scene 3, lines 8–13 and 20–27. Later, his hatred is concealed behind the apparently concerned manner of his warning to Don Pedro and Claudio (Act 3 Scene 2, lines 59–100).

Complex and intense dialogue Much of the prose Beatrice and Benedick speak generates a sense of two very intelligent minds at work. The way they speak to each other in their initial encounters is aggressive and searching, as each probes the other's defences:

BEATRICE	I wonder that you will still be talking, Signor Benedick, nobody marks you.
BENEDICK	What, my dear Lady Disdain! Are you yet living?

Act 1 Scene 1, lines 86–8

However, beneath the mockery lies a more complex relationship. As the play unfolds, both show a certain insecurity, a fear of either losing the other's respect ('she told me, not thinking I had been myself, that I was the prince's jester', Act 2 Scene 1, lines 183–4) or admitting their own vulnerability ('marry once before he won [my heart] of me, with false dice', Act 2 Scene 1, lines 212–13).

Hero's dishonouring, however, forces them to shed their defensive posture. The prose they speak to each other takes on the complexity and intensity of verse, a subtle and fluctuating meeting of minds. See Activity 1 on page 116 for a way to explore the complex dialogue leading up to and after Beatrice's famous challenge to 'Kill Claudio'.

Verse

Although only one third of the play is written in blank (unrhymed) verse, it is spoken at significant moments and with powerful effect, as explained above. There is nothing difficult about Shakespeare's blank verse. Many believe it is based very closely on the natural rhythms of English speech. Each line is an iambic pentameter (抑扬五音步). In Greek, penta means five and an iamb is a 'foot' (音步) of two syllables, the first unstressed (×) and the second stressed (/). So an iambic pentameter is five sets of unstressed + stressed syllables (often expressed as 'de-DUM, de-DUM, de-DUM, de-DUM, de-DUM'). The first verse line of the play is a good example:

× / × / × / × / × /
My liege, your highness now may do me good.

Act 1 Scene 1, line 216

This rhythmic pattern and energy is frequently varied (but never completely lost), so that many different effects are created. Sometimes a line is shaped into two halves with a mid-line pause (**caesura** [音顿]) and an end-of-line pause (**end-stopping**). Very often, one line will 'flow' into the next (**enjambement** [跨行连续] or **run-on line**).

◆ Read the following examples aloud to hear some of these differences:
  - Claudio's farewell to Hero (Act 4 Scene 1, lines 93–101)
  - Leonato's grief (Act 4 Scene 1, lines 129–36)
  - Friar Francis's plan (Act 4 Scene 1, lines 203–36).

The language of Much Ado About Nothing

Couplets, quatrains and sonnets

Shakespeare occasionally uses rhymed verse in *Much Ado About Nothing* to heighten theatrical effect, to deepen the emotional and imaginative power of a scene, or to create a sense of closure.

- The sad exit of Hero and her family (Act 4 Scene 1, lines 244–7) is marked by four rhyming lines (ABAB) called a quatrain. Practise speaking the Friar's lines as solemnly as you can.

- Don Pedro and Claudio speak quatrains at the conclusion of the memorial tribute to Hero (Act 5 Scene 3, lines 24–7 and 30–3). What effect do these lines create?

- Why does Shakespeare have Hero speak a couplet (two rhyming lines) as she exits at Act 3 Scene 1, lines 105–6?

Everyone laughs when Beatrice and Benedick's sonnets (poems of fourteen lines, written in iambic pentameter) are produced at the end of the play. Many Elizabethans loved sonnets and they were collected as we might now have a music collection. Sonneteers (poets who write **sonnets** – like Shakespeare himself) would write sequences (collections of many sonnets) that people would buy and discuss. In fact, Shakespeare's sonnets were published and sold during his lifetime, whereas his plays, though often performed, were only published after his death.

Shakespeare's sonnets had a rhyme scheme of three quatrains (ABAB/CDCD/EFEF) and a final couplet (GG). There are variations in sonnet rhyme schemes, but this one is still widely known as a **Shakespearean sonnet**.

Sonnets are poems of love or remembrance. They are often written by the poet to impress a **muse** (object of affection or inspiration for the poetry). Sometimes the muse is imaginary and sometimes it is based on real people that the poet knows or genuinely wants to impress. However, they often reveal more to the reader about the writer than they do about the subject.

- What might we interpret from the fact that Beatrice and Benedick have written sonnets about each other? Why do you think that their poems' contents are not revealed to the audience?

Songs

Shakespeare was well aware of the power of music and song to enhance dramatic effect. Balthasar's song 'Sigh no more, ladies' (Act 2 Scene 3, lines 53–68), for example, is placed at one of the turning points in the Beatrice–Benedick plot to sound a mocking echo to the play's theme of deception and 'The fraud of men'. Despite Don Pedro's and Benedick's comments, this song has often been movingly sung.

Benedick's song, 'The God of love' (Act 5 Scene 2, lines 18–22) is undoubtedly badly sung, as even Benedick has to admit. The song was very popular in Shakespeare's time and much imitated, so the comedy of Benedick as melancholy lover would have been immediately apparent.

Few people have been impressed with the words of the funeral song, 'Pardon, goddess of the night' (Act 5 Scene 3, lines 12–21). The **doggerel** (打油诗) rhymes (trivial, poor or simple verse) seem to suggest an amateur composed the lines, and it does not quite bring the reverence to the occasion that one might expect at a funeral.

- Step into role as a director. Would you include the funeral song in your production? Is it meant to be comic? Could it be played tragically? What effect does it have on the audience and the way that it views the scene? Debate your decision with a partner, who should take the opposite view to you.

- Rewrite the song in a popular music style (e.g. rap, pop, country) to help you better understand the impact of the song in Shakespeare's time.

MUCH ADO ABOUT NOTHING
虚惊一场

Much Ado About Nothing in performance
《虚惊一场》的演出

Performances at the Globe

In Elizabethan times, attending the theatre was a very popular and lively pursuit. Today we often associate visiting the theatre with darkened auditoriums, comfortable padded seats and technically impressive sets, lights and sound. The Globe Theatre (where it is likely *Much Ado About Nothing* was performed) was a very different sort of theatrical experience. Most of the audience would have stood throughout the play in the open air. When it rained, the audience got wet. When it was hot, the audience had little shade. As a consequence, the actors needed to work hard to hold the attention and patience of a lively and sometimes uncomfortable audience!

◆ There are many opportunities for interaction with the audience in *Much Ado About Nothing*. Identify a number of sequences or 'moments' when you can imagine an actor drawing the audience into the performance for comic effect.

It is likely that there were no elaborate sets on the bare stage of the Globe. Only a few props were used (swords, chairs and so on), but the actors did wear attractive and expensive costumes, usually the fashionable dress of the times.

The reconstructed Shakespeare's Globe is on London's Bankside, close to the site of the original Globe. Many of the productions here are staged just as Shakespeare's audiences probably saw them. Because women were banned from acting in public in Shakespeare's day, Beatrice, Hero, Margaret and other female parts would originally have been played by boys. In an intriguing reversal of this Elizabethan practice, the 2004 production of *Much Ado About Nothing* (pictured opposite) was performed with an all-female cast.

◆ Make a list of the benefits and drawbacks of single-sex casts. Do you think the comedy or romance of the play is enhanced or limited by such an approach? Why do you think this?

▼ The reconstructed Shakespeare's Globe in London. In this image, you can see the audience standing around the stage as well as sitting in the galleries opposite. Just as in Shakespeare's time, every production at the Globe ends with a lively dance, whether the play is a comedy or a tragedy! Why do you think this was a feature of Shakespeare's plays in Elizabethan times? Do you think it adds something to the performance, or detracts from it? Or does it depend on the play? Write a list of 'pros' and 'cons' for this dancing.

MUCH ADO ABOUT NOTHING IN PERFORMANCE

◀ The stage of the modern, reconstructed Shakespeare's Globe. You can see the upper gallery above the stage, where some scenes are performed and where musicians usually sit. Can you think of any scenes in *Much Ado About Nothing* in which the balcony could be used for effect? How would you suggest to actors that they use it? Write director's notes to guide and instruct them.

▲ A swaggering (大摇大摆) (female!) Benedick, dressed in the baggiest of breeches (Globe, 2004). There are many images of Beatrice and Benedick in this book. Based on any of these images, which production would you like to see most?

◀ An angry and formidable (令人生畏) Beatrice from the same production. Can you suggest during which scene or line this image might be taken?

191

▲ A drawing of the church scene (Act 4 Scene 1) from Henry Irving's 1882 production. It was particularly praised for its 'splendour of spectacle' and 'minute (细致入微) attention to detail'.

Eighteenth- and nineteenth-century stagings of *Much Ado About Nothing*

In the eighteenth century, *Much Ado About Nothing* was extremely popular in Britain. The famous and flamboyant (派头十足) actor-manager of the period, David Garrick, put on swift, lively, entertaining productions of the play in which the interplay and romance between Beatrice and Benedick was the dominant interest. By now, women were allowed to perform on stage on much more equal terms with men. Costumed in the fashionable dress of the day, Garrick and his leading ladies played the 'merry war' as an aggressively vigorous battle for supremacy.

Nineteenth-century productions paid more attention to visual effects and 'realism', with rich Elizabethan-style costumes, elaborate scene changes and large casts, all of which slowed the pace of performances considerably. Some productions even featured live horses! The dominant mood, as championed by the famous actor-director Henry Irving, was of romantic happiness with little emphasis on the darker elements of the play. The most admired Beatrices of this period were those who softened her aggressive energy and conformed more to the Victorian stereotype of ideal womanhood: sweet, gentle and delicate.

◆ Find out more about David Garrick and Henry Irving. Suggest what they would think about the modern reconstruction of the Globe Theatre. Try writing an imagined dialogue between the two men, in which they argue or debate the 'best' way of staging the play.

▶ The theatre impresario (剧团经理) of the 18th century, David Garrick, in rich costume as Benedick.

MUCH ADO ABOUT NOTHING IN PERFORMANCE

Much Ado About Nothing around the world

Shakespeare is the most performed playwright in the world. Productions of *Much Ado About Nothing* can be found in most countries, and have resonance or meaning in every culture imaginable. Not only is the play performed internationally, but, over the years, directors have chosen to set the play in a number of different cultural contexts. Elements of the story are sometimes altered, and contemporary language is sometimes added. Over the years, academics and playwrights have translated the play into hundreds of different languages.

◆ Looking at the image below, how many of the characters can you identify? Do their costumes and poses suggest which scene the image might show?

The picture on this page shows a scene in an experimental Austrian production from 2006. The director decided to set the play in a highly artificial world of confusing appearances and superficial illusion. As you can see, the stage resembles a desert island or beach. The exact time and place were left deliberately unclear, allowing the confusing appearances the play explores to extend to the stage itself!

◆ Write a brief letter or email to this director, asking him about his choices and decisions in staging the play. Look in detail at the picture below and focus your questions on the more unexpected or striking elements that you notice.

The unusual stage setting of the Burgtheater's 2006 production. The production used few props or scene changes, and featured actors falling off the stage and performing from the aisles. What do you think this approach might have brought to the play? Can you suggest why so many directors choose to set Shakespeare's plays in new settings or contexts?

Much Ado About Nothing
虚惊一场

This Royal Shakespeare Company production from 2006 was set on the island of Cuba in 1953. One reviewer said that the setting provided a 'plausibly military' context with 'raffish (艳俗) glamour' and was full of 'endless opportunities'. The music in this production was of particular note, including lots of rumba (伦巴舞) and samba (桑巴舞).

MUCH ADO ABOUT NOTHING IN PERFORMANCE

▲ This production from 2009 was staged in Regent's Park Open Air Theatre. Beatrice hid behind fruit trees when trying not to be spotted by the other characters.

▶ This 2011 production was set in the 1980s on the Anglo-Spanish peninsula of Gibraltar (直布罗陀). It featured lots of drinking, wild partying and colourful costumes. At one point, Benedick entered the stage on a golf buggy (高尔夫球)! One innovation of this production was to change the character of Antonio to Leonato's wife, rather than his brother. What are the implications and benefits (or limitations) of this change?

Much Ado About Nothing
虚惊一场

Directing *Much Ado About Nothing*

This book is packed with images from a range of productions and interpretations of *Much Ado About Nothing*. Any script by Shakespeare should be read as a plan for a live performance, so it is essential that you think about how it can or should be staged.

◆ Talk together about the period and place in which you would like to set your version of the play. It is likely to be in a place and time where wealth and social class, fashion and costume, and male and female codes of honour and duty are important. You have a huge amount of freedom in your decisions, as long as you can justify the choices you have made. Then choose one or more, possibly all, of the following activities. Your finished assignment could be a file of drawings, notes and suggestions, a live presentation of your ideas (for example, a talk) or perhaps even an actual performance.

- **Design the set** (布景) How can it be used for particular scenes? Will it change much through the play? How will it reflect your chosen setting? Will you attempt to reflect a period or physical place, or will your design be more abstract or unusual?
- **Design the costumes** (a significant element in this play!) Look at past examples, but invent your own. In particular, consider the importance of hats and uniforms in most productions.
- **Design the props** Furnishings, hand props (masks, swords and so on) and larger props. Would you include any period or 'unusual' props?
- **Plan a lighting and sound programme** (this could be for the whole play or just for selected scenes). Will you use colours to symbolise a mood or feeling? How will music be used to enhance the production?
- **Design the publicity poster** What elements of your production will you emphasise? Will you include a quotation as a 'slogan'? Which character(s) or scene(s) will you give the most prominence in the publicity image(s)?
- **Write the programme introduction** Aim for around 500–1000 words. Justify your vision of the production to an audience who are about to watch your masterpiece!
- **Write character notes for actors' guidance** Write around 100 words for each actor, outlining how you think they should approach the part they are going to play.
- **Prepare director's rehearsal notes** Annotate a scene or a couple of pages of script with director's notes. Include the movements you want the actors to make, the emphasis you'd like the actors to place on certain words, and any stage 'action' you'd like to be taking place.

The 2012 Royal Shakespeare Company production used an Indian setting and cast to explore the play.

Much Ado About Nothing in performance

Watching *Much Ado About Nothing*

It isn't always possible to see a live production of the play while you are studying it – but if there is a production on near you, make sure you go and see it! If you do see a production, or if you watch a movie or television version, try to do the following things beforehand:

- Choose a character that you will watch especially closely. Afterwards, note down at least five actions, ways of speaking or facial expressions that the actor used to bring the character to life. Analysing a performance in detail like this should help you to appreciate the skill and craft of acting in Shakespeare plays.

- Get hold of a couple of reviews of the production, but don't read them until after you've seen the play. Critics will have their opinion, and you may or may not agree, but you shouldn't let their ideas overshadow your own. Afterwards, use the reviews and your own opinions to talk about, write about or debate your feelings about the production.

Be a good critic!

Reviews can be harsh or full of praise, but they usually try to give a considered and well-rounded (全面) response. They often comment on the following areas:

- the director's central vision for the setting, design, music and lights
- the success of the central performances
- notable or interesting aspects of the way minor characters are presented
- particularly impactful (or unsuccessful) moments
- their lasting or overall impression.

◆ Write a review of a production (it can be a screen adaptation) that you have seen. If you haven't seen any productions or adaptations, write an imagined review of one that you have planned. Be creative, critical and engaging!

Shakespeare's Globe, 2004

Opinions were mixed about this performance (pictured above). One critic called the production a 'howling disappointment' that was 'rough, raw and unready'. However, some reviewers praised the all-female cast – particularly the central characters. Yolanda Vasquez gave a 'ferocious' and 'determined' performance as Beatrice, while Josie Lawrence gave a 'winning' performance as Benedick.

Wyndham's Theatre, 2011

Reviews of this production were almost all very positive, agreeing that Josie Rourke's 'supremely well-cast' production was a 'notable success'. Catherine Tate gave an 'excellent account' as Beatrice, and David Tennant was 'especially good' as Benedick with 'great comic moments'. The production used 'colourful circumstantial detail' to provide an evening of great 'gaiety' (欢乐).

MUCH ADO ABOUT NOTHING
虚惊一场

Writing about Shakespeare 笔论莎士比亚

The play as text

Shakespeare's plays have always been studied as literary works – as words on a page that need clarification, appreciation and discussion. When you write about the plays, you will be asked to compose short pieces and also longer, more reflective pieces like controlled assessments, examination scripts and coursework – often in the form of essays on themes and/or imagery, character studies, analyses of the structure of the play and on stagecraft. Imagery, stagecraft and character are dealt with elsewhere in this edition. Here, we concentrate on themes and structure. You might find it helpful to look at the 'Write about it' boxes on the left-hand pages throughout the play.

Themes

It is often tempting to say that the theme of a play is a single idea, like 'death' in *Hamlet*, or 'the supernatural' in *Macbeth*, or 'love' in *Romeo and Juliet*. The problem with such a simple approach is that you will miss the complexity of the plays. In *Romeo and Juliet*, for example, the play is about the relationship between love, family loyalty and constraint; it is also about the relationship of youth to age and experience; and the relationship between Romeo and Juliet is also played out against a background of enmity between two families. Between each of these ideas or concepts there are tensions. The tensions are the main focus of attention for Shakespeare and the audience, and they also happen to be how drama operates – by the presentation of and resolution of tension.

Look back at the 'Themes' boxes throughout the play to see if any of the activities there have given rise to information that you could use as a starting-point for further writing about the themes of the specific play you are studying.

Structure

Most Shakespeare plays are in five acts, divided into scenes. These acts were not in the original scripts, but have been included in later editions to make the action more manageable, clearer and more like 'classical' structures. One way to get a sense of the structure of the whole play is to take a printed version of the play (not this one!) and cut it up into scenes and acts. Then display each scene and act, in sequence, on a wall, like this:

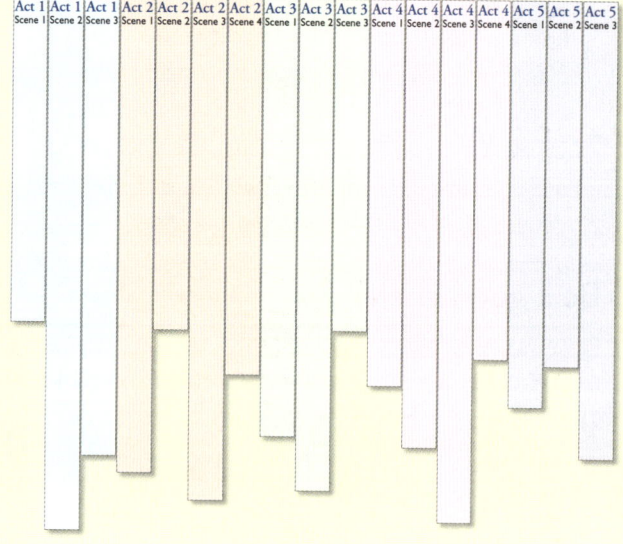

As you set out the whole play, you will be able to see the 'shape' of each act, the relative length of the scenes, and how the acts relate to each other (such as whether one of the acts is shorter, and why that might be). You can annotate the text with comments, observations and questions. You can use a highlighter pen to mark the recurrence of certain words, images or metaphors to see at a glance where and how frequently they appear. You can also follow a particular character's progress through the play.

Such an overview of the play gives you critical perspective: you will be able to see how the parts fit together, to stand back from the play and assess its shape, and to focus on particular parts within the context of the whole. Your writing will reflect a greater awareness of the overall context as a result.

The play as script

There are different, but related, categories when we think of the play as a script for performance. These include *stagecraft* (discussed elsewhere in this edition and throughout the left-hand pages), *lighting*, *focus* (who are we looking at? Where is the attention of the audience?), *music and sound*, *props and costumes*, *casting*, *make-up*, *pace and rhythm*, and other *spatial relationships* (e.g. how actors move across stage in relation to each other). If you are writing about stagecraft or performance, use the notes you have made as a result of the 'Stagecraft' boxes throughout this edition of the play, as well as any material you can gather about the plays in performance.

What are the key points of dispute?

Shakespeare is brilliant at capturing a number of key points of dispute in each of his plays. These are the dramatic moments where he concentrates the focus of the audience on difficult (sometimes universal) problems that the characters are facing or embodying.

First, identify these key points in the play you are studying. You can do this as a class by brainstorming what you think the key points are in small groups, then debating the long-list as a whole class, and then coming up with a short-list of what the class thinks are the most significant. (This is a good opportunity for speaking and listening work.) They are likely to be places in the play where the action or reflection is at its most intense, and which capture the complexity of themes, character, structure and performance.

Second, drill down at one of the points of contention and tension. In other words, investigate the complexity of the problem that Shakespeare is exploring. What is at stake? Why is it important? Is it a problem that can be resolved, or is it an insoluble one?

Key skills in writing about Shakespeare

Here are some suggestions to help you organise your notes and develop advanced writing skills when working on Shakespeare:

- Compose the title of your writing carefully to maximise your opportunities to be creative and critical about the play; or explore the key words in your title carefully. Decide which aspect of the play – or which combination of aspects – you are focusing on.
- Create a mind map of your ideas, making connections between them.
- If appropriate, arrange your ideas into a hierarchy that shows how some themes or features of the play are 'higher' than others and can incorporate other ideas.
- Sequence your ideas so that you have a plan for writing an essay, review, story – whichever genre you are using. You might like to think about whether to put your strongest points first, in the middle, or later.
- Collect key quotations (it might help to compile this list with a partner), which you can use as evidence to support your argument.
- Compose your first draft, embedding quotations in your text as you go along.
- Revise your draft in the light of your own critical reflections and/or those of others.

The following pages focus on writing about *Much Ado About Nothing* in particular.

Much Ado About Nothing
虚惊一场

Writing about *Much Ado About Nothing*
笔论《虚惊一场》

1 Organising thinking for essay writing

Many writing tasks on the play will ask you to simultaneously consider a variety of ideas and concepts. In the preceding pages, you will have seen that *Much Ado About Nothing* has many themes and plot points. It can be difficult to recall and organise these when you are asked to write something about them or to form an argument. As a preparation for your writing, it is useful to structure your thoughts and create a memory aid by producing a visual web of events and key quotations or topics.

An effective way to do this is by creating a mind map. Begin by writing your task in the centre of a large piece of paper. Write your main Points (P) along branches. Add sub-branches to these branches. On these, add pieces of Evidence (E), such as quotations from the script to support your points. Also include points of Analysis (A), in which you examine and explain possible audience reactions, Shakespeare's intentions and your personal response to the topics.

You will often be asked to write specifically about an aspect of the play and its impact – for example, on certain characters or on the audience. A mind map will help you with this by forcing you to separate and organise your thoughts about wider subject areas. It will also later provide you with a visual reminder of how the larger concepts are sub-divided. For example, a mind map about the comic effect of wordplay might have sections on intended humour (puns, irony) and unintended humour (including malapropisms).

Mind maps can be created as a simplified, concise summary of revision notes. Return to your mind map over time to see if you can develop your ideas and add in more detail. Experiment with drawing links between ideas or even between different themed mind maps.

You can even use the structure and labels (P, E and A) of your mind map to organise the contents of paragraphs in your writing task. The PEA system of putting forward a Point (P), supporting it with Evidence (E) and then applying your own Analysis (A) is an effective structure for an essay or other piece of in-depth writing. Try using a mind map to write an essay outline, with bullet points for the evidence and analysis that support each point you make.

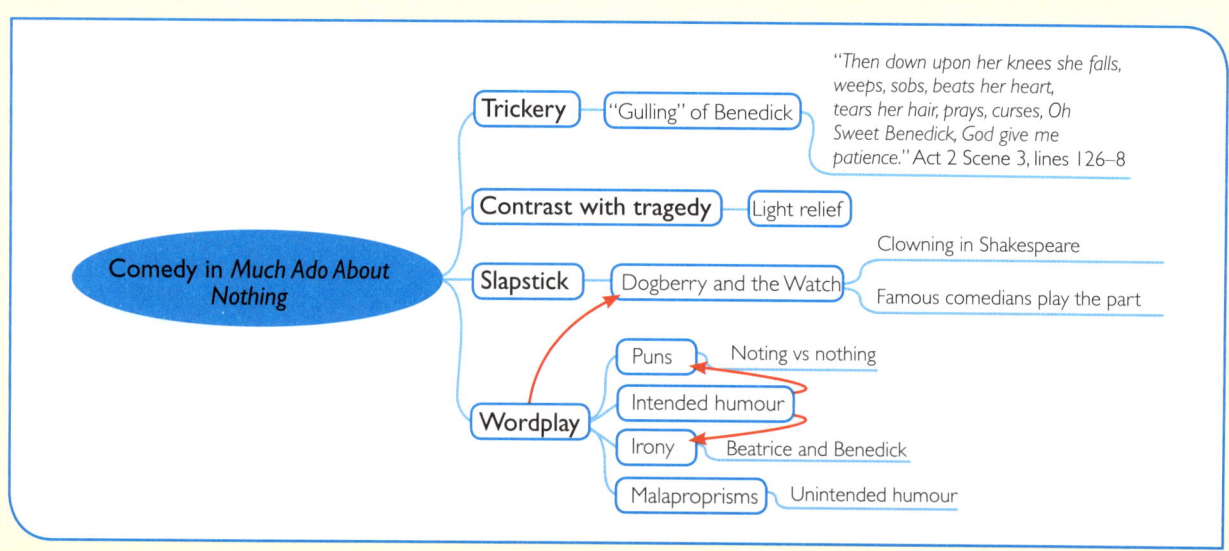

2 Generating your own titles for writing

If your revision is based upon answering questions on general themes, and/or planning answers only for actual past assessment questions, it can mean that you are not making new links and having original thoughts about the play. Sometimes, exam questions can appear similar to previous ones that you have practised, but a different focus on a certain character or theme can make it very difficult to answer the question if you are narrowly prepared. Thinking of possible questions and planning answers is key to not getting caught out.

- In pairs, collect as many past assessment questions as you can. You may wish to look on the Internet for examination-board papers or questions aimed at different age groups.

- Look carefully at the wording of the questions, then create your own versions of the questions by swapping the names of characters and ideas or themes.

- Practise with the question below by substituting the underlined words with the words in the table:
    How important is <u>Don John</u> to the <u>story</u> in *Much Ado About Nothing*?

Character	Aspect
Dogberry	comedy
Hero	tragedy
Benedick	wordplay
Beatrice	battle of the sexes

Can you think of any other characters (or events) and aspects (or themes) that could be used to substitute the underlined words? List them.

- Swap your list of possible question elements with another pair, and use a mind map to produce a plan that shows how you would answer a question that you have not encountered before.

3 Alternative forms of writing

If you are performing the play, producing a piece of creative writing based on *Much Ado About Nothing*, or answering an exam question that asks you to write in the role of someone in the play, it can be helpful to use writing tasks to get under the skin of the characters. Use the following activities to imagine what it is like to be one of the Messinians encountered in the play.

- Write a eulogy (speech that praises somebody's accomplishments, particularly after their death) that Beatrice or another character might deliver at Hero's funeral. What might the speaker want to hide or make very clear?

- Write the sonnet(s) of Benedick and/or Beatrice that we do not get to hear in Act 5 Scene 4. What will they reveal about their feelings for the other?

- Don John disappears from the play without much explanation. Write a dialogue between Don John and Don Pedro in which the former justifies his actions. How would Don Pedro respond to this?

4 The essay – an alternative view

In order to produce the best answer possible to a question about the play, it is vital that you consider alternative views and ways of seeing. *Much Ado About Nothing* is a comedy with tragic elements, so it creates varied interpretations and responses from audiences.

- Use an imagined exam question to produce a plan for a mind map. Add in sub-branches that give alternative audience responses, perhaps those that are opposite to your own reaction. Imagine the different responses that might come from people in Shakespeare's time and now, older and younger people, or men and women. Can you think of other groups of people that may have alternative ways of seeing the performance?

Much Ado About Nothing
虚惊一场

William Shakespeare 莎翁年表
1564–1616

1564	Born Stratford-upon-Avon, eldest son of John and Mary Shakespeare.
1582	Marries Anne Hathaway of Shottery, near Stratford.
1583	Daughter Susanna born.
1585	Twins, son and daughter Hamnet and Judith, born.
1592	First mention of Shakespeare in London. Robert Greene, another playwright, described Shakespeare as 'an upstart crow beautified with our feathers'. Greene seems to have been jealous of Shakespeare. He mocked Shakespeare's name, calling him 'the only Shake-scene in a country' (presumably because Shakespeare was writing successful plays).
1595	Becomes a shareholder in The Lord Chamberlain's Men, an acting company that became extremely popular.
1596	Son, Hamnet, dies, aged eleven. Father, John, granted arms (acknowledged as a gentleman).
1597	Buys New Place, the grandest house in Stratford.
1598	Acts in Ben Jonson's *Every Man in His Humour*.
1599	Globe Theatre opens on Bankside. Performances in the open air.
1601	Father, John, dies.
1603	James I grants Shakespeare's company a royal patent: The Lord Chamberlain's Men become The King's Men and play about twelve performances each year at court.
1607	Daughter Susanna marries Dr John Hall.
1608	Mother, Mary, dies.
1609	The King's Men begin performing indoors at Blackfriars Theatre.
1610	Probably returns from London to live in Stratford.
1616	Daughter Judith marries Thomas Quiney. Dies. Buried in Holy Trinity Church, Stratford-upon-Avon.

The plays and poems

(no one knows exactly when he wrote each play)

1589–95	*The Two Gentlemen of Verona*, *The Taming of the Shrew*, *First*, *Second* and *Third Parts* of *King Henry VI*, *Titus Andronicus*, *King Richard III*, *The Comedy of Errors*, *Love's Labour's Lost*, *A Midsummer Night's Dream*, *Romeo and Juliet*, *King Richard II* (and the long poems *Venus and Adonis* and *The Rape of Lucrece*).
1596–99	*King John*, *The Merchant of Venice*, *First* and *Second Parts* of *King Henry IV*, *The Merry Wives of Windsor*, **Much Ado About Nothing**, *King Henry V*, *Julius Caesar* (and probably the Sonnets).
1600–05	*As You Like It*, *Hamlet*, *Twelfth Night*, *Troilus and Cressida*, *Measure for Measure*, *Othello*, *All's Well That Ends Well*, *Timon of Athens*, *King Lear*.
1606–11	*Macbeth*, *Antony and Cleopatra*, *Pericles*, *Coriolanus*, *The Winter's Tale*, *Cymbeline*, *The Tempest*.
1613	*King Henry VIII*, *The Two Noble Kinsmen* (both probably with John Fletcher).
1623	Shakespeare's plays published as a collection (now called the First Folio).

Acknowledgements 鸣谢

Cambridge University Press would like to acknowledge the contributions made to this work by Rex Gibson, Mary Berry and Michael Clamp.

Picture Credits

p. iii: 1993 *Much Ado About Nothing* movie, © Sam Goldwyn/Renaissance Films/BBC/The Kobal Collection/Clive Coote; p. v top: Royal Shakespeare Theatre 1996, © Donald Cooper/Photostage; p. v bottom: Royal Shakespeare Theatre 1996, © Donald Cooper/Photostage; p. vi top: 1993 *Much Ado About Nothing* movie, © Sam Goldwyn/Renaissance Films/BBC/The Kobal Collection/Clive Coote; p. vi bottom: 1993 *Much Ado About Nothing* movie, © Sam Goldwyn/Renaissance Films/BBC/The Kobal Collection/Clive Coote; p. vii: Theatre Royal Bath 2005, © Donald Cooper/Photostage; p. viii top: Barbican Theatre 1991, © Donald Cooper/Photostage; p. viii bottom: National Theatre 1981, © Donald Cooper/Photostage; p. ix top: Royal Shakespeare Theatre 2002, © Donald Cooper/Photostage; p. ix bottom: Royal Shakespeare Theatre 1996, © Donald Cooper/Photostage; p. x top: Open Air Theatre London 2000, © Donald Cooper/Photostage; p. x bottom: Royal Shakespeare Theatre 1996, © Donald Cooper/Photostage; p. xi top: Wyndham's Theatre 2011, © Johan Persson/ArenaPAL; p. xi bottom: Royal Shakespeare Theatre 1990, © Donald Cooper/Photostage; p. xii top: Theatre Royal Bath 2005, © Donald Cooper/Photostage; p. xii bottom: National Theatre 1965, © Zoë Dominic; p. 2: Royal Shakespeare Theatre 2002, © Donald Cooper/Photostage; p. 4: Royal Shakespeare Theatre 1990, © Ivan Kyncl; p. 6: Royal Shakespeare Theatre 1996, © Donald Cooper/Photostage; p. 10: Theatre Royal Bath 2005, © Geraint Lewis; p. 12: Theatre Royal Stratford East, © Donald Cooper/Photostage; p. 16: Shakespeare's Globe 2011, © Geraint Lewis; p. 20: 1993 *Much Ado About Nothing* movie, © Everett Collection/Rex Features; p. 22: Royal Shakespeare Theatre 1996, © Donald Cooper/Photostage; p. 25: Royal Shakespeare Theatre 2002, © Donald Cooper/Photostage; p. 26: National Theatre 2007, © Donald Cooper/Photostage; p. 28: Wyndham's Theatre 2011, © Johan Persson/ArenaPAL; p. 32: Theatre Royal Bath 2005, © Donald Cooper/Photostage; p. 36: Royal Shakespeare Theatre 1988, © Donald Cooper/Photostage; p. 38: Royal Shakespeare Theatre 2002, © Donald Cooper/Photostage; p. 40: Royal Shakespeare Theatre 1996, © Donald Cooper/Photostage;; p. 42: Royal Shakespeare Theatre 1996, © Donald Cooper/Photostage; p. 46: Salzburg Festival 2006, © AFP/Getty Images; p. 48: National Theatre 2007, © Donald Cooper/Photostage; p. 50: Royal Shakespeare Theatre 1996, © Donald Cooper/Photostage; p. 54: Royal Shakespeare Theatre 2002, © Donald Cooper/Photostage; p. 56: Royal Shakespeare Theatre 1996, © Donald Cooper/Photostage; p. 58: Theatre Royal Bath 2005, © Geraint Lewis; p. 60: Shakespeare's Globe 2011, © Geraint Lewis; p. 63: Courtyard Theatre, © Donald Cooper/Photostage; p. 72: costume drawings for Benedick from 1950, © Mander and Mitchenson University of Bristol/ArenaPAL; p. 74: Royal Shakespeare Theatre 1996, © Donald Cooper/Photostage; p. 80: Crucible Theatre 2008, © Donald Cooper/Photostage; p. 82: wooden model of the Globe Theatre, © Adam Woolfitt/Corbis; p. 88: portrait of Queen Elizabeth II, © Mary Evans/Everett Collection; p. 92: Playhouse Theatre 1988, © Donald Cooper/Photostage; p. 96: Shakespeare's Globe 2011, © Pete Jones/ArenaPAL; p. 99: Swan Theatre 2006, © Donald Cooper/Photostage; p. 102: painting of Claudio's accusation of Hero, © Marcus Stone; p. 108: Crucible Theatre 2005, © Donald Cooper/Photostage; p. 110: Courtyard Theatre 2012, © Donald Cooper/Photostage; p. 118: Royal Shakespeare Theatre 1990, © Ivan Kyncl; p. 120: Royal Shakespeare Theatre 1996, © Donald Cooper/Photostage; p. 124: Swan Theatre 2006, © Donald Cooper/Photostage; p. 127: Shakespeare's Globe 2011, © Geraint Lewis; p. 128: Royal Shakespeare Theatre 1990, © Donald Cooper/Photostage; p. 132: Royal Shakespeare Theatre 1996, © Donald Cooper/Photostage; p. 138: Theatre Royal Bath 2005, © Donald Cooper/Photostage; p. 142: Royal Shakespeare Theatre 1996, © Donald Cooper/Photostage; p. 148: Swan Theatre 2006, © Donald Cooper/Photostage; p. 150: Queen's Theatre 1993, © Donald Cooper/Photostage; p. 154: Royal Shakespeare Theatre 1996, © Donald Cooper/Photostage;

Much Ado About Nothing
虚惊一场

p.160: Royal Shakespeare Theatre 1990, © Donald Cooper/Photostage; p. 163: Wyndham's Theatre 2011, © Geraint Lewis; p. 164: Royal Shakespeare Theatre 1984, © Donald Cooper/Photostage; p. 165: Theatre Royal Stratford East, © Donald Cooper/Photostage; p. 167 top: Royal Shakespeare Theatre 1996, © Donald Cooper/Photostage; p. 167 bottom: Swan Theatre 2006, © Nigel Norrington/ArenaPAL; p. 168: Swan Theatre 2006, © Nigel Norrington/ArenaPAL; p. 169 top: 1993 *Much Ado About Nothing* movie, © Sam Goldwyn/Renaissance Films/BBC/The Kobal Collection/Clive Coote; p. 169 bottom: Regent's Park Open Air Theatre 2009, © Nigel Norrington/ArenaPAL; p. 170: 1993 *Much Ado About Nothing* movie, © Sam Goldwyn /Renaissance Films/BBC/The Kobal Collection/Clive Coote; p. 171 top: Shakespeare's Globe 2004, © Donald Cooper/Photostage; p. 171 bottom: Shakespeare's Globe 2004, © Donald Cooper/Photostage; p. 172: c. 1600 portrait of the 3rd Earl of Southampton, © The Granger Collection/Topfoto; p. 173: Portrait of Arabella Stuart by Marcus Gheeraerts the Younger, © The Granger Collection/Topfoto; p. 175: National Theatre 2007, © Donald Cooper/Photostage; p. 176 top: Royal Shakespeare Theatre 1984, © Chris Davies; p. 176 bottom: Royal Shakespeare Theatre 1976, © Donald Cooper/Photostage; p. 177 top: Barbican Theatre 1991, © Donald Cooper/Photostage; p. 177 bottom: Queen's Theatre 1993, © Donald Cooper/Photostage; p. 178: Royal Shakespeare Theatre 1990, © Donald Cooper/Photostage; p. 179: Royal Shakespeare Theatre 1996, © Donald Cooper/Photostage; pp. 180–81: Open Air Shakespeare Festival 2002, © Donald Cooper/Photostage; p. 185: Shakespeare's Globe 2004, © Donald Cooper/Photostage; pp. 186–87: National Theatre 1981, © Donald Cooper/Photostage; p. 190: performance of *Richard III* at Shakespeare's Globe in 2012, © Franz-Marc Frei/Corbis; p. 191 top: stage of Shakespeare's Globe, © Tohma; p. 191 bottom left: Shakespeare's Globe 2004, © Donald Cooper/Photostage; p. 191 bottom right: Shakespeare's Globe 2004, © Elliott Franks/ArenaPAL; p. 192 top: Sketch by John Forbes Robertson illustrating a scene from *Much Ado About Nothing* at The Lyceum Theatre, London in 1882, © V&A Images; p. 192 bottom: Watercolour of David Garrick as Benedick in *Much Ado About Nothing*, © V&A Images; p. 193: Burgtheater 2006, © George Koulek/Burgtheater; p. 194: Swan Theatre 2006, © Geraint Lewis; p. 195 top: Regent's Park Open Air Theatre 2009, © Robbie Jack/Corbis; p. 195 bottom: Wyndham's Theatre 2011, © Donald Cooper/Photostage; p. 196: Courtyard Theatre 2012, © Donald Cooper/Photostage; p. 197 top: Shakespeare's Globe 2004, © Donald Cooper/Photostage; p. 197 bottom: Wyndham's Theatre 2011, © Geraint Lewis.

Produced for Cambridge University Press by White-Thomson Publishing
+44 (0)843 208 7460
www.wtpub.co.uk

Project editor: Alice Harman
Designer: Clare Nicholas
Concept design: Jackie Hill